BANKS AND BANKING DEVELOPMENTS

U.S. FINANCIAL REGULATORY STRUCTURE: OVERVIEW, COMPLEXITIES, AND THE EFFECTS OF FRAGMENTATION AND OVERLAP

BANKS AND BANKING DEVELOPMENTS

Additional books in this series can be found on Nova's website under the Series tab.

Additional e-books in this series can be found on Nova's website under the e-book tab.

BANKS AND BANKING DEVELOPMENTS

U.S. FINANCIAL REGULATORY STRUCTURE: OVERVIEW, COMPLEXITIES, AND THE EFFECTS OF FRAGMENTATION AND OVERLAP

LAURENCE WATSON
EDITOR

nova publishers
New York

Library of Congress Cataloging-in-Publication Data

ISBN: 978-1-63485-636-2

Published by Nova Science Publishers, Inc. † New York

CONTENTS

PREFACE

Financial regulatory policies are of interest to Congress because firms, consumers, and governments fund many of their activities through banks and securities markets. Furthermore, financial instability can damage the broader economy. Financial regulation is intended to protect borrowers and investors that participate in financial markets and mitigate financial instability. This book provides an overview of the regulatory policies of the agencies that oversee banking and securities markets and explains which agencies are responsible for which institutions, activities, and markets. Some agencies regulate particular types of institutions for risky behavior or conflicts of interest, some agencies promulgate rules for certain financial transactions no matter what kind of institution engages in them, and other agencies enforce existing rules for some institutions, but not for others. These regulatory activities are not necessarily mutually exclusive.

In: U.S. Financial Regulatory Structure
Editor: Laurence Watson
ISBN: 978-1-63485-636-2

Chapter 1

WHO REGULATES WHOM AND HOW? AN OVERVIEW OF U.S. FINANCIAL REGULATORY POLICY FOR BANKING AND SECURITIES MARKETS*

Edward V. Murphy

SUMMARY

Financial regulatory policies are of interest to Congress because firms, consumers, and governments fund many of their activities through banks and securities markets. Furthermore, financial instability can damage the broader economy. Financial regulation is intended to protect borrowers and investors that participate in financial markets and mitigate financial instability. This report provides an overview of the regulatory policies of the agencies that oversee banking and securities markets and explains which agencies are responsible for which institutions, activities, and markets. Some agencies regulate particular types of institutions for risky behavior or conflicts of interest, some agencies promulgate rules for certain financial transactions no matter what kind of institution engages in them, and other agencies enforce existing rules for some institutions, but not for others. These regulatory activities are not necessarily mutually exclusive.

* This is an edited, reformatted and augmented version of a Congressional Research Service, Publication No. R43087, dated January 30, 2015.

Banking

U.S. banking regulation traditionally focuses on prudence. Banks' business decisions are regulated for safety and soundness and adequate capital. In addition, banks are given access to a lender of last resort, and some bank creditors are provided guarantees (deposit insurance). Regulating the risks that banks take is believed to help smooth the credit cycle. The credit cycle refers to periodic booms and busts in lending. Prudential safety and soundness regulation and capital requirements date back to the 1860s when bank credit formed the money supply. The Federal Reserve (Fed) as lender of last resort was created following the Panic of 1907. Deposit insurance was established in the 1930s to reduce the incentive of depositors to withdraw funds from banks during a financial panic.

Securities, Derivatives, and Similar Contract Markets

Federal securities regulation has traditionally focused on disclosure and mitigating conflicts of interest, fraud, and attempted market manipulation, rather than on prudence. Securities regulation is typically designed to ensure that market participants have access to enough information to make informed decisions, rather than to limit the riskiness of the business models of publicly traded firms. Firms that sell securities to the public must register with the Securities and Exchange Commission (SEC). SEC registration in no way implies that an investment is safe, only that material risks have been disclosed. The SEC also registers several classes of securities market participants and firms. It has enforcement powers for certain types of industry misstatements or omissions and for certain types of conflicts of interest. Derivatives trading is supervised by the Commodity Futures Trading Commission (CFTC), which oversees trading on the futures exchanges, which have self-regulatory responsibilities as well. The Wall Street Reform and Consumer Protection Act (Dodd-Frank Act, P.L. 111-203) required more disclosures in the over-the-counter (off-exchange) derivatives market than prior to the financial crisis and has granted the CFTC and SEC authority over large derivatives traders.

Government Sponsored Enterprises

The Federal Housing Finance Agency (FHFA) oversees a group of government-sponsored enterprises (GSEs). Two of the GSEs, Fannie Mae and Freddie Mac, securitize residential mortgages, and they were placed in conservatorship following mortgage losses in 2008. In the conservatorship, the Treasury provides financial support to the GSEs and FHFA and Treasury have managerial control over the enterprises. FHFA also regulates the Federal Home Loan Bank (FHLB) system, a GSE composed of regional banks to bankers owned by the 8,000 financial institutions that they serve.

Changes Following the 2008 Financial Crisis

The Dodd-Frank Act created the interagency Financial Stability Oversight Council (FSOC) and authorized a permanent staff to monitor systemic risk and consolidated bank regulation from five agencies to four. The DFA granted the Federal Reserve oversight authority and the Federal Deposit Insurance Corporation (FDIC) resolution authority over the largest financial firms. The Dodd-Frank Act consolidated consumer protection rulemaking, which had been dispersed among several federal agencies, in the new Consumer Financial Protection Bureau.

Special Topics

The appendices in this report include additional information on topics, such as the regulatory structure prior to the Dodd-Frank Act (DFA), organizational differences among financial firms, and the rating system that regulators use to evaluate the health of banks. A list of common acronyms and a glossary of common financial terms are also included as appendices.

INTRODUCTION

Most people in the United States (and other developed nations) have rejected the Shakespearean maxim, "neither a borrower nor a lender be." Many people use loans to finance at least part of their education and job training during their youth, use mortgages to finance at least part of their home while starting a family, invest in stocks and bonds during middle age, and rely on the returns to the value of their stocks, bonds, and homes to at least partially pay for retirement during old age. Business firms, municipalities, and sovereign governments also rely on the financial system to help build the productive capital necessary for a well-functioning society and to foster economic growth. Financial regulatory policies are of interest to Congress because of the repercussions for individual constituents, the financing of firms and governments, and long-run economic growth.

This report provides a framework to help answer the question, "who regulates whom in U.S. financial markets, and how?" At the federal level, the answer often depends on first identifying both the policy problem and the proposed solution. For example, there are federal regulatory overlaps in which one agency can oversee a firm because of the firm's charter, a second agency regulates some of the activities that the firm is engaging in, but a third agency controls a government initiative to resolve or alleviate a problem related to the firm or its activities. On the other hand, there are regulatory gaps in which some of the firms participating in a financial activity do not have regulated charters, and the activity believed to be causing a problem does not have a regulator. Thus, answering "who regulates whom" requires first identifying the problem to be regulated, and how.

This report provides an analysis of financial regulatory policy. It is not intended as a roadmap of legal jurisdiction; rather, it helps to match financial regulatory agencies to financial regulatory policies based on the kinds of financial difficulties that they generally address. Many of these difficulties are related to what economists call *market failures*, which can be loosely described as instances in which market prices and participants do not fully take into account all of the costs and benefits of their actions.

Table 1 presents a list of financial regulators. In the United States, it may be useful to distinguish between regulators that generally focus on *prudence* (i.e., monitoring and regulating the risks that a specific firm engages in) and regulators that generally focus on *disclosure* (i.e., monitoring and regulating the information that firms and exchanges provide to potential market participants). Four federal agencies have prudential authority to examine banks, thrifts, and credit unions.[1] Two agencies oversee markets for financial contracts (securities and derivatives). The agencies listed in the "other" category regulate housing government-sponsored enterprises (GSEs) and consumer financial products, respectively. The entities listed in the coordinating forum category are made up of the other financial regulators with related duties or functions and facilitate communication and coordination among member agencies. Two agencies either regulate an activity regardless of the type of institution that engages in it or provide prudential regulation to nonbanks.[2] The agencies are discussed in more detail below.

Table 1. Federal Financial Regulators and Organizations (acronyms and area of authority)

Prudential Bank Regulators	Securities and Derivatives Regulators	Other Regulators of Financial Activities	Coordinating Forum
Office of the Comptroller of the Currency (OCC)	Securities and Exchange Commission (SEC)	Federal Housing Finance Agency (FHFA)	Financial Stability Oversight Council (FSOC)
Federal Deposit Insurance Corporation (FDIC)	Commodities Futures Trading Commission (CFTC)	Consumer Financial Protection Bureau (CFPB)	Federal Financial Institutions Examinations Council (FFIEC)
National Credit Union Administration (NCUA)			President's Working Group on Capital Markets (PWG)
Federal Reserve Board (FRB, or the Fed)			

Source: The Congressional Research Service (CRS).

The policy problems and regulatory approaches of the agencies listed in **Table 1** vary considerably. Before providing a detailed analysis of each agency, it may be useful to consider how the agencies are related to each other and briefly sketch the types of policies they generally pursue. The prudential bank regulators and the Federal Housing Finance Agency (FHFA) examine firms with specific charters and monitor and limit the risks that their chartered firms engage in. Securities and derivatives regulators monitor exchanges that host the trading of financial contracts, oversee the disclosures that market participants provide, and enforce rules against deceptive or manipulative trading practices. Unlike prudential bank regulators, securities regulators generally do not monitor the composition of assets and liabilities of the firms participating in their markets (although they may require collateral or margin to be posted for some activities, and they may monitor the financial condition of exchanges).[3] These and other general differences may exist because of the various missions and risks to financial stability that the agencies address.

A specific event in the financial industry is often regulated by multiple agencies because firms subject to institution-based regulation often conduct financial transactions that that are subject to activity-based regulation. JPMorgan's losses in derivatives markets in 2012 may provide a helpful illustration. JPMorgan's depository bank subsidiary had a risk management unit called CIO. This unit had significant losses on trades related to complex derivatives (called the London Whale trades at the time), which JPMorgan asserted were designed to guard against systemic risk. When revelations of the losses became public, and people wanted to know who JPMorgan's regulator was, the answer was that there were many regulators related to JPMorgan's London Whale trades, depending upon which aspect of the event a person was interested in.

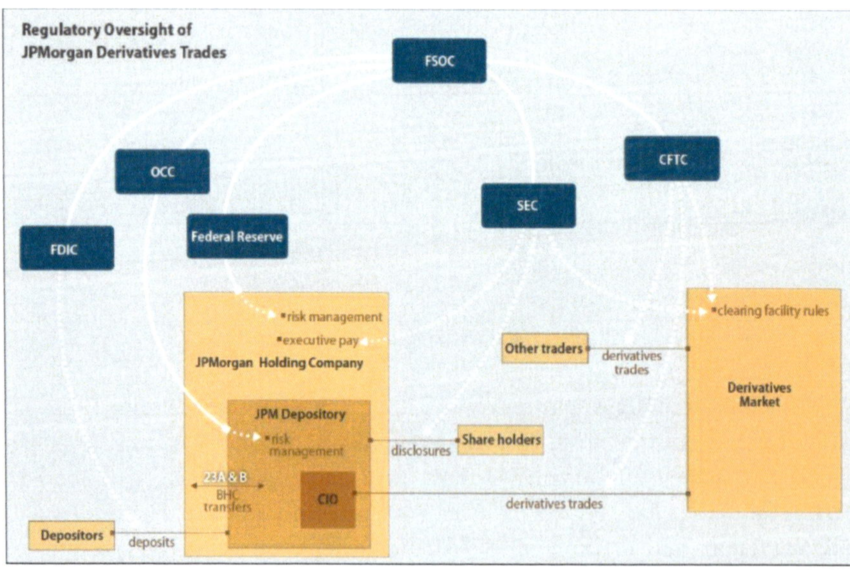

Source: CRS.

Figure 1. An Example of Regulation of JPMorgan Derivatives Trades.

The regulatory policy areas of agencies related to JPMorgan's derivatives trades are presented in **Figure 1**. As a bank, JPMorgan's risk management was subject to prudential regulation by the OCC at the depository level, and by the Federal Reserve on a consolidated basis at the holding company level. As a public company, JPMorgan's disclosures of the trades to its stockholders were regulated by the SEC. As a participant in derivatives markets, JPMorgan's transactions were subject to CFTC regulation. As an insured depository institution, JPMorgan's safety and soundness was also subject to the FDIC.

Table 2 compares the general policy options and approaches of the banking regulators to the securities market regulators, which is drawn from *Banking Regulation versus Securities Regulation*, by Franklin Allen and Richard Herring. The table lists many of the categories of regulations that are often considered for banks and securities markets. It does not mean that each category is in place at all times; for example, there have been times during which the United States has restricted interest payments on bank deposits, and times when the United States has not. Many of these categories of policy options are discussed in more detail in later sections of this report.

Table 2. Policies for Banking Regulation and Securities Regulation

Types of Banking Regulatory Policies	Types of Securities Regulatory Policies
Asset Restrictions	Disclosure Standards
Capital Adequacy	Registration Requirements
Conduct of Business Rules	Manipulation Prohibition
Competition Policy (Anti-Trust)	Insider Trading Prohibition
Conflict of Interest Rules	Takeover Rules
Investment Requirements	Protection of Minority Shareholders
Customer Suitability Rules	Investment Management Rules
Deposit Insurance	
Fit and Proper Entry Tests	
Limits on Interest on Deposits	
Limits on Interest on Loans	
Liquidity Requirements	
Reporting Large Transactions	
Reserve Requirements	
Restrictions on Geographic Reach	
Restrictions on Services and Product Lines	

Source: *Banking Regulation versus Securities Regulation*, Franklin Allen and Richard Herring, Wharton Financial Institutions Center, 2001.

In Allen's and Herring's view, banking regulatory policies and securities regulatory policies are directed at fundamentally different problems. They view bank regulation as being directed at *systemic risk*, which may be loosely defined as risk faced by the financial system as a whole, distinct from the costs and benefits faced by the failure or losses of a single firm or a price movement in a single market. In contrast, they attribute many of the securities market regulator's policies to *investor protection* and *efficiency enhancement* (including aligning corporate management with stockholder interests). Therefore, it may be useful to compare the general policy problems of banking and securities markets.

This report is organized as follows. The first section briefly discusses several policy problems associated with financial intermediation. The second section describes various modes of financial regulation to address these concerns and includes a table identifying the major federal regulators and the types of institutions and markets they supervise. The table also identifies certain emergency authorities available to the regulators, including those that relate to systemic financial disturbances. The third section focuses on the regulation of firms with bank charters. The fourth section focuses on the regulation of financial trading markets, especially securities and derivatives. The fifth section focuses on certain other financial regulators and markets that either do not easily fit into banking or securities or markets that do not have a dedicated regulator. The appendices topics include organizational differences among financial firms, the rating system that regulators use to evaluate the health of banks, the regulatory structure prior to the Dodd-Frank Act, a list of common acronyms, and a glossary of common financial terms.

POLICY PROBLEMS IN BANKING AND SECURITIES MARKETS

Ultimately, the function of the financial system is to coordinate the flow of resources from savers to borrowers, and back again. Two common methods to provide this financial intermediation include (1) firms that directly gather funds from savers to directly lend to borrowers (banks, for example) and (2) markets that facilitate the trading of financial obligations (securities and derivatives exchanges, for example). The range of financial obligations includes, but is not limited to,

- debts—repayment of principal and interest,
- equities—share in ownership and returns,
- hybrids—mixture of debt and equity features,
- insurance—payment contingent on occurrence of a future event,
- swaps—promises to exchange one type of stream of payment for another, and
- forwards—promises for future delivery at a particular place and time.

Although there are many ways to organize a firm that offers bank-like services, and there are many types of contracts that combine elements of bank-like loans with securities contracts, the regulation of the financial system in the United States has historically focused on distinguishing banks, securities markets, and insurance.

The analytical tradition in the United States has been to distinguish commercial banking from investment banking. Commercial banks accept customer deposits and offer commercial loans. Investment banks underwrite and register new securities and market them to individual or institutional investors. Investment banks also provide brokerage services, advice on corporate financing and proprietary trading, and assistance to merger and acquisition proposals.

Although insurance issues are beyond the scope of this report, banking and securities markets are discussed briefly below.

Banks

Banks are intermediaries between savers and borrowers. In its simplest form, the business model of commercial banks is to accept deposits from savers in order to make loans to borrowers—in other words, banks borrow from depositors and offer loans to individuals, business firms, nonprofits, and governments. Although savers could offer loans directly to potential borrowers, there are several advantages of relying on specialized lenders. For example, savers essentially pay banks to act on their behalf (an agency relationship[4]), identifying credit-worthy borrowers, writing and administering loan contracts, and enforcing the loan terms if the borrower defaults. Another potential source of profit centers on timing. Since long-term interest rates are generally higher than short-term interest rates, banks can earn profits by borrowing short-term in order to offer longer-term loans (often referred to as a maturity transformation or maturity mismatch).

This is not an exhaustive list of commercial bank services or earnings, but it is a useful list to illustrate several recurring economic issues.

The business model of banks also creates a number of economic policy problems. Like any other agency relationship, bank managers do not necessarily always act in the best interests of bank investors or depositors. The maturity mismatch makes banks vulnerable to interest rate volatility and to "runs" if depositors withdraw their funds simultaneously in a panic. The effort to identify credit-worthy borrowers and projects can cause bankers to affect pools of borrowers in ways that create credit shortages, or base lending decisions on criteria that do not further social goals of the community (e.g., discrimination).

These policy problems may be addressed by regulations for individual banks. Some of these regulations include restrictions on conflicts of interest of bank managers, the use of deposits, and the ability of depositors to withdraw their funds; limitations on the proportion of bank resources that can be devoted to or drawn from particular markets or counterparties; rules on the loan application process; and laws to prevent lending discrimination.

Banking is also subject to systemic problems beyond the activities of any one institution. Another potential source of profit (related to the agency relationship) is for the bank to take excessive risk. That is, compared with other banks, an individual bank can keep fewer resources available against the possibility of depositor withdrawal, or offer more loans in the heightened-risk categories (that typically pay higher interest), and depend on its ability to borrow from other banks if it suffers excessive withdrawals or higher defaults. Although a single bank that follows a higher-risk strategy might be able to borrow from other banks if it suffers higher than expected losses or greater than expected depositor withdrawals, all banks cannot successfully follow this strategy simultaneously because there would be too few healthy banks to borrow from should loan defaults be higher than expected or should depositors withdraw funds in greater amounts than expected.

This systemic banking problem involves a fallacy of composition, and it can be illustrated using the example of a stadium. If a single person stands at the stadium, it is likely that the person will be able to see the event better, but if everyone stands in the stadium, most people will not have a better view of the event and will be less comfortable. Similarly, if a single bank expands its lending for a given amount of capital, that bank is likely to make higher profits without endangering financial stability, but if many banks follow a similar strategy, none gains a competitive advantage over the others, and all are less able to obtain interbank loans during a crisis.

Excessive risk taking by banks can have systemic consequences. One systemic problem may be that a large number of banks will attempt to borrow from each other at the same time, causing a spike in interest rates or the absence of new bank credit altogether. If many banks follow this strategy, then all banks may be unable to find an institution willing and able to lend to them in the event of depositor withdrawals, and the banking system as a whole may temporarily cease to be a source of credit for the wider economy.

Banks might contribute to a boom-bust cycle for debt-sensitive assets. During booms, banks that intend to rely on emergency lending from other banks may offer too much credit, and on terms that do not adequately account for the risk that the bank's own access to credit may decline if market conditions change. The resulting cheap credit may help fuel a price bubble in the asset or trading activity financed with the debt. During busts, more banks are likely to fail than would have occurred if banks had reserved the appropriate amount of resources for the amount of risk that they incurred. Thus, the higher bank failure rate (compared to if more banks had been cautious during the boom) could cause the total amount of credit available to the wider economy to shrink more than would have occurred if financial risks had been adequately accounted for.

There are a number of possible policy responses to these systemic concerns in banking. Bank regulators can be empowered to restrict bank balance sheets. Some of these restrictions, discussed in more detail below, include safety and soundness regulation and requirements to hold adequate capital. Even though these regulations may be applied at the institution level, they have systemic effects because in the aggregate the lending activity of the banking system as a whole has an important impact on credit booms and busts. Bank depositors could be offered insurance to reduce their incentive to withdraw funds. Banks that cannot borrow from other banks during emergencies can be provided a lender of last resort.

Markets to Trade Securities, Futures, and Other Contracts

In contrast to a commercial banking institution that originates and holds loans, a securities market is just a venue to exchange financial contracts. Markets can facilitate the trading of debts, equities, futures, or a variety of other financial instruments. Financial institutions that help facilitate the marketing of debts, equities and other financial instruments are sometimes called investment banks.

Although these financial markets are being presented as an alternative to commercial banking, there is no reason that a commercial bank would be unable to participate in securities markets as either a buyer or a seller (although in some cases it may be unlawful to do so). Loans to the government of the United States may be a useful illustration. While it is possible for a single bank to originate and hold an individual loan to the U.S. government, the borrowing of the government is overwhelmingly conducted by issuing debts (Treasury securities) that are traded. Banks are just one group among the many buyers of U.S. Treasury securities. Private firms have also issued tradable debt securities for centuries. Like lending institutions, tradable contracts have a long history and are subject to a number of well-known potential market failures.

Several enduring economic inefficiencies related to securities markets are caused by the limited availability of information and potential conflicts of interest. Some market participants may have an information advantage—such as providers of confidential services to financial firms. A related issue is the "lemons problem," named for the used-car market in which potential buyers of used cars might discount all used cars because of the fear that used-car salesmen may withhold negative information about the quality of a specific car being offered. Potential securities buyers may fall prey to securities dealers and brokers if the latter have an incentive to help place securities that the seller knows may have some undisclosed flaw (lemons). Furthermore, like any agent[5] relationship, securities professionals may not always act in the best interests of their clients.

Other potential economic inefficiencies can arise that are related to specific types of contracts that are traded. For example, some financial contracts are for future delivery of a physical commodity, such as wheat of a certain quality and quantity, at a particular place and time (forward or futures contract). This means that at any time, for example, there will be both a spot market for wheat (its price to be obtained currently) and the forward price (the current price for delivery on the specified future date). If there is no formal organization of trading rules, it might be possible for someone to use forward contracts to lock up most of the deliverable supply on a specific future date, leaving only a "corner" of the spot market for sale on that date. But even if such attempts to corner commodity markets are rarely successful, the attempts themselves might introduce additional price distortions that could contribute to financial instability.

Potential economic inefficiencies are also related to formal trading organizations and platforms, if they are used. Having experienced many of the policy problems described above, financial traders have from time to time organized formal market exchanges, adopted rules of trading, and limited membership. However, the exchange itself can then become a potential source of financial instability if it does not have enough resources to withstand the failure of one of its members to honor its obligations to the exchange, or if its rules exacerbate the problems described above. For example, nonmembers of the exchange could lose confidence (and willingness to participate) if they feel that members have important trading advantages, such as if the trades of members are executed first even if they are not submitted first.

There are a number of policy responses to concerns related to trading financial contracts. Some are listed in **Table 2**, including requiring that securities and traders be registered and investors be provided adequate disclosures regarding the characteristics of the securities. Given that formal exchanges are organized in part to address some of the known inefficiencies, policymakers might require that certain types of contracts be traded on formal exchanges. The organization and membership of the formal exchanges could be regulated. Providers of securities-related services may be regulated for minimum professional qualifications and potential conflicts of interest. Issuers of new securities may be required to meet certain financial thresholds and disclose specific information in a format and venue that is readily accessible to the investing public. Some potential buyers of securities may be excluded for lack of sufficient financial literacy or sophistication or have to exceed a minimum financial wherewithal (as a proxy or substitute for sophistication).

Securities markets may also create systemic concerns. Like bank lending, if securities markets fail to adequately address the risks of the activities being funded (thus overstating potential rewards compared with risks), then "too much" savings may be channeled into a particular asset class. As a result, prices in that asset class will tend to be bid up until the true risks manifest themselves, at which time the market collapses. Leveraged and collateralized funding can also cause securities markets to contribute to a boom-bust cycle. That is, if securities buyers are able to increase their purchasing power with debt, especially if the purchased securities form the collateral of the loan, then a decline in the price of the security can lead to "fire sales" as the loans taken out by the buyers default, and then the securities purchased with the loans are liquidated in an already falling market. Some are concerned that algorithmic or program trading can also contribute to systemic events if unanticipated events or technical shortcomings cause trading algorithms, which may be on autopilot, to pursue extreme strategies.

A number of possible policies can address systemic concerns in securities markets. One approach is to temporarily halt trading if market prices vary by more than some pre-specified amount during a set time. Another approach is to limit the amount, and collateral, of debt that can be used to fund securities purchases under some circumstances. Yet another approach is to require firms that facilitate securities issuance to retain some of the risk of the securities issued, sometimes referred to as *skin in the game*.

The Shadow Banking System

As discussed above, banking and securities markets are not mutually exclusive, nor are all financial obligations easily categorized. The term *shadow banking* is sometimes used to refer to the funding of loans through securities markets instead of banks—or to the funding of banks through securities markets instead of deposits. Other times, shadow banking is used to refer to financial activity that is ineligible for a government backstop. One type of government backstop is a financial guarantee, such as deposit insurance. Another type is access to emergency loans from the government, such as the ability to borrow from the Federal Reserve's discount window. What the definitions have in common is they describe alternatives to the simplistic banking model, that is, alternatives to banks that are funded with insured deposits and that only offer commercial loans.

Parts of the shadow banking system are regulated. For example, a lender could borrow money through securities markets rather than from traditional retail depositors. One way to do that is through a repurchase agreement (repo), in which the lender sells a security (such as a U.S. Treasury) today and promises to repurchase it in the near future at a higher price. The price differential represents a form of interest payment similar to a collateralized loan. Thus, rather than a bank borrowing money from traditional depositors, a bank can borrow from other financial institutions through repos. If a chartered bank signs a repo with a chartered bank, both firms are banks and both are regulated; nevertheless, under some definitions the transaction would be considered shadow banking. However, chartered banks are not the only firms that can use repurchase agreements—non-banks can raise funds through repurchase agreements in order to fund other investments, including loans. If a non-bank signs a repo with a non-bank, and uses the proceeds to fund other investments, neither non-bank may be subject to prudential regulation, have access to the Federal Reserve's discount window, have creditors with deposit insurance.

The repos described above are only one of many alternatives to deposits that can be used to fund loans. Other examples include relatively short-term commercial debt that is backed by pools of loans (asset-backed commercial paper, or ABCP). A bank could sponsor a facility that issues ABCP in order to buy loans. If so, the bank's participation (usually promising to provide liquidity if the market is unexpectedly disrupted) is subject to prudential regulation. As with repos, banks are not the only firms that can sponsor ABCP; thus, it is possible for the market to be funded by firms without access to the Fed's discount window and without insured deposits. However, activities being called shadow banking are often still subject to securities regulation.

Many of the general policy problems of banks and securities markets also apply to shadow banking. For example, if a class of loans (such as mortgages or sovereign debt) is funded through securities markets, potential flaws in securities issuance and pricing can contribute to a boom-bust cycle in assets purchased with those loans. If nonbanks (such as money market mutual funds and hedge funds) invest a fraction of the funds they gather, and promise to allow their own investors to withdraw funds at will, these nonbanks can suffer runs if many investors attempt to withdraw simultaneously. The reach of financial regulators to address policy problems in shadow banking varies from activity to activity and from class of firm to class of firm.

WHAT FINANCIAL REGULATORS DO

The regulatory missions of individual agencies vary, sometimes as a result of historical accident. Some agencies have powers over particular firms, but not over all of the other participants in the market that the firm might participate in. Other regulators have authority over markets or activities, and this authority applies to a variety of the firms that participate. As a result, a single firm might have to answer to both the regulator of its charter and to the regulator of a particular activity (i.e., regulatory overlap). However, there may also be instances in which a corner of the financial system has neither a regulator of the specific firms, nor a regulator of the particular activities (i.e., regulatory gap). This section of the report summarizes several categories of regulation, provides a table of specific financial regulators in the United States and their policy spheres, and describes the basic regulatory approach for banks (prudence) and securities markets (disclosure).

Regulatory Architecture and Categories of Regulation

The term *regulatory architecture* describes the organization of the agencies that regulate a particular policy sphere. A possible architecture is to have a single regulatory agency with examination powers over all industry firms, rulemaking authority for all industry-related activities, and power to enforce its rules and resolve controversies that arise in the industry. An alternative architecture is to have specialized regulators that focus on a subset of industry-related policy problems.

The United States has historically provided one or more regulator for each category of financial regulation, rather than a single agency with authority for all financial markets, activities, and institutions. From time to time, the perceived drawbacks to the multiplicity of federal regulators bring forth calls for regulatory consolidation. Even prior to the financial panic in September 2008, the Department of the Treasury had issued a framework for financial reform.[6] After the crisis, the legislative debate over the Dodd-Frank Act included different views on the topic: early versions of the Senate bill would have replaced all the existing bank regulators with a single Financial Institution Regulatory Authority. Dodd-Frank created two new agencies (and numerous regulatory offices) and merged the Office of Thrift Supervision (OTS) with the Office of the Comptroller of the Currency (OCC).

Choosing a regulatory architecture may involve trade-offs. As one economist explained,

> On the one hand, one might conclude that the need to compete with other agencies would motivate a regulator to perform its tasks as effectively and efficiently as possible. On the other hand, one might argue that the desire to attract more clients could drive a regulatory agency to be loose.[7]

In addition, it is not clear that countries with single regulators fare better during crises or are more successful at preventing them. For example, the 2008 financial crisis damaged the financial systems of countries with significantly different regulatory approaches. While the U.S. response was to create a single council to coordinate its varied regulators, the United Kingdom (UK) in May

2010 broke up its Financial Services Authority, which had jurisdiction over securities, banking, derivatives, and insurance.

Here is a description of different ways to regulate financial firms and services:

- **Regulate Certain Types of Financial Institutions.** Some firms become subject to federal regulation when they obtain a particular business charter, and several federal agencies regulate only a single class of institution. Depository institutions are a good example: a depository may be subject to the regulations of multiple prudential regulators, but typically only one agency is granted primary oversight authority based on the bank's charter—national bank, state bank, credit union, etc.—and the choice of charter may not greatly affect the institution's permissible business mix. Government-sponsored enterprises (GSEs) also have a primary prudential regulator.
  Regulation keyed to particular institutions has at least two perceived disadvantages. First, regulator shopping, or *regulatory arbitrage*, may occur if regulated entities can choose their regulator. Second, unchartered firms engaging in the identical business activity as regulated firms may escape institutional regulation altogether.
- **Regulate a Particular Market.** Some markets become subject to federal financial regulation when they host the trading of covered financial products. The New York Stock Exchange (NYSE) and the Chicago Mercantile Exchange (CME) are two examples. The Securities and Exchange Commission (SEC) regulates the trading of stocks and bonds and the Commodity Futures Trading Commission (CFTC) regulates the trading of commodity futures. The SEC and CFTC generally do not regulate the prices of stocks or futures traded on the exchanges; rather, they regulate the organization and membership of the exchanges, rules for trading, and attempt to prevent fraud, conflicts of interest, or manipulation by market participants.
  Regulation keyed to markets has at least two perceived disadvantages. First, market evolution can create jurisdictional ambiguities among the regulators. Second, innovation in financial products may create regulatory gaps.
- **Regulate a Particular Financial Activity.** Some financial activities are subject to federal regulation no matter which institutions engage in them and no matter who hosts the trades in them. For example, the

Consumer Financial Protection Bureau (CFPB) regulates certain classes of loans to consumers no matter who extends the loan (bank or nonbank). If the lender is a bank, the lender has to comply with both the regulations of the CFPB and the rules of its bank regulator.

Regulation keyed to activities can be problematic. As discussed above, there are often multiple methods to achieve similar financial objectives (combining different contracts). Therefore, if one type of transaction is regulated, it may be possible for people to use another type of contract, one that is not currently regulated or through institutions that are not regulated.

- **Regulate for Systemic Risk.** One definition of systemic risk is that it occurs when each firm manages risk rationally from its own perspective, but the sum total of those decisions produces systemic instability under certain conditions. Similarly, regulators charged with overseeing individual parts of the financial system may satisfy themselves that no threats to stability exist in their respective sectors, but fail to detect risks arising from the interaction of firms and markets. Yet, regulation of institutions, markets, and activities may also have a component of systemic risk regulation. For example, regulation of bank capital may affect the potential for booms and busts in asset markets. The Dodd-Frank Act created the Financial Stability Oversight Council (FSOC) to assume a coordinating role among the heads of financial regulatory agencies; the FSOC has a permanent staff to monitor financial-sector risks as a whole.

What does it mean to be regulated?

It is common to refer to a firm or a market as being regulated or unregulated. However, this simplification can mask important distinctions for any given policy discussion because regulators can have limited scope of operation. That is, agencies may have rulemaking authority or enforcement powers to address one set of policy concerns but not for other policy issues. Firms may be subject to different regulators for different aspects of their business.

The point can be illustrated with a more familiar industry. Are restaurants regulated? There is no federal Department of Restaurants; however, the Occupational Safety and Health Administration (OSHA) can make rules for worker safety (including food service employees), and the Department of Justice can enforce employment discrimination laws (including in restaurants). Furthermore, restaurants are typically subject to state and local health inspectors and related laws. If the policy topic is health and safety, it would be inaccurate to characterize restaurants as unregulated. On the other hand, many potential policy issues related to restaurants are typically unregulated. For example, the restaurant menu and prices are not typically regulated. A food service is typically free to pair nonstandard items (white wine with red meat) and charge very high prices.

Are financial institutions, markets, and activities regulated? Like the restaurant example above, the answer depends on the policy issue being discussed. Take the example of stocks. Firms with outstanding common stock must register with the SEC, file a prospectus, and make regular public disclosures. Marketplaces that facilitate stock market trading must register and comply with SEC regulations. However, the price of an individual stock is not typically regulated, and the amount of stock that an individual firm wishes to offer for sale is not typically regulated. However, even stock prices and trading volume may be subject to circuit breakers to temporarily limit trading during periods of exceptional volatility.

The information in **Table 3** sets out the general federal financial regulatory architecture for banks and securities markets. **Appendix D** contains a pre-Dodd-Frank version of the same table. Supplemental material—charts that illustrate the differences between banks, bank holding companies, and financial holding companies—appears in **Appendix B**.

Table 3. Federal Financial Regulators and Who They Supervise

Regulatory Agency	Institutions Regulated	Emergency/Systemic Risk Powers	Other Notable Authority
Federal Reserve	Bank holding companies and certain subsidiaries, financial holding companies, securities holding companies, savings and loan holding companies, and any firm designated as systemically significant by the FSOC.	Lender of last resort to member banks (through discount window lending) In "unusual and exigent circumstances," the Fed may extend credit beyond member banks, to provide liquidity to the financial system,	Numerous market-level regulatory authorities, such as checking services, lending markets, and other banking-related activities.

Table 3. (Continued)

Regulatory Agency	Institutions Regulated	Emergency/Systemic Risk Powers	Other Notable Authority
	State banks that are members of the Federal Reserve System, U.S. branches of foreign banks, and foreign branches of U.S. banks. Payment, clearing, and settlement systems designated as systemically significant by the FSOC, unless regulated by SEC or CFTC.	but not to aid failing financial firms. May initiate resolution process to shut down firms that pose a grave threat to financial stability (requires concurrence of two-thirds of the FSOC). The FDIC and the Treasury Secretary have similar powers.	
Office of the Comptroller of the Currency (OCC)	National banks, federally chartered thrift institutions		
Federal Deposit Insurance Corporation (FDIC)	Federally insured depository institutions, including state banks and thrifts that are not members of the Federal Reserve System.	After making a determination of systemic risk, the FDIC may invoke broad authority to use the deposit insurance funds to provide an array of assistance to depository institutions, including debt guarantees.	Operates a deposit insurance fund for federally and state chartered banks and thrifts.

Regulatory Agency	Institutions Regulated	Emergency/Systemic Risk Powers	Other Notable Authority
National Credit Union Administration (NCUA)	Federally chartered or insured credit unions	Serves as a liquidity lender to credit unions experiencing liquidity shortfalls through the Central Liquidity Facility.	Operates a deposit insurance fund for credit unions, known as the National Credit Union Share Insurance Fund (NCUSIF).
Securities and Exchange Commission (SEC)	Securities exchanges, brokers, and dealers; clearing agencies; mutual funds; investment advisers (including hedge funds with assets over $150 million) Nationally recognized statistical rating organizations Security-based swap (SBS) dealers, major SBS participants, and SBS execution facilities Corporations selling securities to the public must register and make financial disclosures.	May unilaterally close markets or suspend trading strategies for limited periods.	Authorized to set financial accounting standards in which all publicly traded firms must use.
Commodity Futures Trading Commission (CFTC)	Futures exchanges, brokers, commodity pool operators, and commodity trading advisors Swap dealers, major swap participants, and swap execution facilities	May suspend trading, order liquidation of positions during market emergencies.	

Table 3. (Continued)

Regulatory Agency	Institutions Regulated	Emergency/Systemic Risk Powers	Other Notable Authority
Federal Housing Finance Agency (FHFA)	Fannie Mae, Freddie Mac, and the Federal Home Loan Banks	Acting as conservator (since Sept. 2008) for Fannie Mae and Freddie Mac	
Bureau of Consumer Financial Protection	Nonbank mortgage-related firms, private student lenders, payday lenders, and larger "consumer financial entities" to be determined by the Bureau Consumer businesses of banks with over $10 billion in assets Does not supervise insurers, SEC and CFTC registrants, auto dealers, sellers of nonfinancial goods, real estate brokers and agents, and banks with assets less than $10 billion		Writes rules to carry out the federal consumer financial protection laws

Source: The Congressional Research Service (CRS), with information drawn from agency websites, and financial regulatory legislation.

a. See Appendix B.

REGULATING BANKS, THRIFTS, AND CREDIT UNIONS

In general, the term *bank* will be used in this section to refer to firms (or subsidiaries) with bank, thrift, or credit union charters.[8] Banking regulators in the United States attempt to address many of the general policy problems described in the introduction by focusing on the health of chartered banks. Bank charters limit the range of permissible activities and affiliations of banks.

Bank regulators employ examiners to monitor and evaluate the financial health of the banks they regulate. Furthermore, deposit insurance and a system to coordinate bank reserves and provide emergency lending is available to participating banks. The primary prudential regulator of a given bank depends on its charter; however, other policies (such as lending to a troubled bank or resolving a failed bank) are applied by a single agency regardless of the charter. Activity-based regulation applies to chartered banks—thus the SEC retains its authority for communications between publicly traded banks and their stockholders, and the CFPB regulates many classes of loans that banks make to consumers.

Is this a bank?

Functionally, the simplest form of bank accepts deposits in order to offer loans.[9] Although this is not a legal definition of a bank, it does capture the basic intermediary function of banking. In practice, it is often difficult to precisely distinguish banking from other services. It is tempting to ascribe this difficulty to financial innovation, but in reality many modern "innovations" are really just minor variations on old practices. Because in discussions of financial regulation, the term *bank* is often reserved for firms with specific charters, it may be useful to distinguish chartered-depository banks from other institutions and people who offer similar services.

Many institutions and organizations have offered bank-like services throughout history. For example, ancient Chinese records describe lenders that required borrowers to offer small goods as collateral for loans (similar to a modern pawn shop). People in Medieval Europe sometimes deposited precious metals with silversmiths (who had their own reasons for extra security) for safekeeping, and some silversmiths then offered loans to third parties, counting on the depositors to not withdraw simultaneously.

One controversial example is Whalebone Cafe Bank (WCB), an ice cream shop in Pittsburgh, Pennsylvania. Reportedly, customers can make a deposit at the ice cream shop and receive the equivalent of 5.5% interest in gift cards for ice cream and other goods sold at the store.[10] It has also been reported that WCB offered loans, including a $510-cash loan to a man who will pay it back in $60 installments, which includes a $25 fee. The Pennsylvania Department of Banking, according to reports, is investigating, but there are questions as to whether the agency can shut down an ice cream shop or ban stores from rewarding customers with gift cards.[11]

> Several major banking laws limit their application to firms with federally insured deposits, specific banking charters, or affiliations with depository banks. As a result, some investment firms that are sometimes referred to as Wall Street banks are not banks for certain regulatory purposes, nor are some pawn shops and ice cream stores, even if they offer bank-like services.

As listed in **Table 1**, four prudential regulators coordinate the examinations policies of depositories through the Federal Financial Institution Examinations Council (FFIEC) in order to prevent inconsistencies in the stringency of regulatory oversight. A bank or thrift may organize itself with a depository subsidiary owned by a larger holding company, in which case the holding company may have a different primary regulator than the depository subsidiary. The OCC regulates depository banks and thrifts that have a federal charter (subsidiaries if in a holding company structure). The FDIC regulates banks with a state charter that are not members of the Federal Reserve System (subsidiaries if in a holding company structure). The NCUA regulates credit unions that have a federal charter. In addition to these federal regulators, state governments have their own agencies to administer state banking laws. The Federal Reserve regulates state-chartered member banks (subsidiaries) and holding companies of banks and thrifts. The Conference of State Bank Supervisors (CSBS) serves as a forum for state banking agencies, but is not itself a regulator. State banking supervisors choose a nonvoting representative to serve the FSOC in an advisory capacity.

Many prudential regulations are of degree, not of kind. That is, there are many categories of activities that banks may participate in, but they must either limit their concentration or offset related risks in another manner. For example, banks may offer 30-year fixed-rate mortgages; but, an individual bank may have to manage its resulting interest rate risk by offering other loans with shorter maturities or by acquiring derivatives that hedge interest rate risk. As a result, prudential regulation is not always about catching lawbreakers or policing legal violations, but is often about monitoring the risks that banks engage in or the procedures bank managers have in place to control risk. Even banks that have not violated any statute may be required to adjust their lending or other business practices in response to the regulator's evaluation of risks in current conditions.

This section describes five prominent elements of bank regulation that each primary prudential regulator supervises for its chartered firms: (1) safety and soundness, (2) capital requirements, (3) asset management, (4) consumer compliance, and (5) community reinvestment. In many cases the primary prudential regulator will not be the sole policymaker or regulatory authority for these issues. For example, rules for capital requirements and safety and soundness may be coordinated with other bank regulators, and banks may have to comply with consumer regulations issued by the CFPB in addition to satisfying their own primary prudential regulator. There may not be a clear delineation between each regulatory element; for example, adequate procedures for asset management might be important to maintain safety and soundness. **Appendix C** includes a discussion of the official ratings system that regulators apply to covered firms.

Safety and Soundness

Safety and soundness refers to a broad range of issues that relate to the health of a financial institution. Safety and soundness encompasses risk management, capital requirements, the diversification of a bank's portfolio, provisions for liquidity, allowances for loan and lease losses, concentrations of transactions with a single counterparty or in a single region, exposure to potentially expensive litigation, adequate training and expertise of management and staff, adequate procedures for internal controls, and many other issues. This section will not attempt to address all of the categories of safety and soundness regulation listed in **Table 2** above. Safety and soundness regulation is conducted prospectively—that is, banks can be examined prior to any indication of excess risk or any evidence of wrongdoing.

Safety and soundness regulation relates to economic policy issues because it can affect the credit cycle and conflicts of interest. The rapid decline in the price of one product (and thus a rapid rise in loan defaults by related firms, employees, etc.) is less likely to cause a wave of bank failures if banks are not permitted to concentrate their loan exposure to one industry or one line of business. Owners and counterparties of banks are more likely to effectively monitor bank managers if banks maintain clear and transparent systems of control.

Each loan has a variety of risk characteristics of concern to lenders and their regulators. Some of these risks can be estimated at the time the loan is issued. Credit risk, for example, is the risk that the borrower will fail to repay the principal of the loan as promised. Rising interest rates create another risk because the shorter-term interest rates that the lender often pays for its funds (e.g., deposit or CD rates) rise while the longer-term interest rates that the lender will receive from fixed-rate borrowers remain unchanged. Falling interest rates are not riskless either: fixed-rate borrowers may choose to repay loans early, reducing the lender's expected future cash flow. Federal financial regulators take into account expected default rates, prepayment rates, interest-rate exposure, and other risks when examining the loans issued by covered lenders.

The risk of a portfolio of bank assets is not just the sum of the risks of the individual loans and securities that make it up. Lenders can adjust the composition of their balance sheets to reduce or enhance the risks of the individual loans that make it up. A lender with many loans exposed to prepayment risk when interest rates fall, for example, could compensate by acquiring some assets that rise in value when interest rates fall. One example of a compensating asset would be an interest-rate derivative contract. Lenders are required to keep capital in reserve against the possibility of a drop in value of loan portfolios or other risky assets. Federal financial regulators take into account compensating assets, risk-based capital requirements, and other prudential standards when examining the balance sheets of covered lenders.

When regulators determine that a bank is taking excessive risks, or engaging in unsafe and unsound practices, they have a number of tools at their disposal to reduce risk to the institution (and ultimately to the federal deposit insurance fund). They can require banks to reduce specified lending or financing practices, dispose of certain assets, and order banks to take steps to restore sound balance sheets. In enforcement, regulators have "life-or-death" options, such as withdrawing deposit insurance, revoking the charter, or taking over a failing bank. In practice, bank regulators rarely use draconian tactics, and banks are given an opportunity to address concerns raised during an examination if the failure of the bank is not imminent.

Capital Requirements

As a general accounting concept, capital refers to the equity of a business—the amount by which its assets exceed its liabilities.[12] The more capital a firm has, the greater its capacity to absorb losses and remain solvent. Capital is related to leverage (various measures of the firm's reliance on debt and derivatives to fund its activities); firms that fund themselves with more equity capital (instead of debt) tend to have lower leverage ratios.

Capital regulation relates to economic policy problems because it can affect the credit cycle. One way higher bank capital affects the credit cycle is its potential to make the banking system more resilient during downturns. Unexpected loan losses are less likely to cause a bank to fail if it holds more capital. In the aggregate, higher capital requirements will tend to make the banking system more resilient because distressed banks may drain other banks of their liquid reserves while general liquidity is declining. On the other hand, banks are part of a broader financial system, therefore it may be possible that higher capital requirements for banks might not make the system as a whole safer if the cost of capital causes more financial activity to migrate to securities markets or shadow banking.

Capital regulation can also affect the credit cycle by affecting the amount of bank credit made available. Higher bank capital requirements tend to lower the leverage that banks can achieve, which reduces the potential lending that the banking system can offer to the broader economy. Whether higher capital requirements for banks lower total lending in the economy is more difficult to determine because it depends in part on how securities markets and shadow banking react.

Financial regulators require the institutions they supervise to maintain specified minimum levels of capital—defined in various ways—to increase the resilience of firms to shocks and to minimize losses to investors, customers, and taxpayers when failures occur. The riskiness of a bank's business model affects its capital requirements; for example, a bank that specializes in relatively risky credit card lending may have higher effective capital requirements than a bank that has a relatively safer and more diversified portfolio of commercial lending. Capital requirements, if they are set above what a firm would choose on its own, represent a cost to businesses because they reduce the amount of funds that may be loaned or invested in the market. Thus, there is a perpetual tension: individual banks adjust their own capital ratio to maximize profits, whereas regulators continually modify capital standards to either prevent excessive risk-taking or to promote the availability of credit to the wider economy.

The actual capital held by banks should not be confused with statutory minimums. Banks may choose to hold excess capital if bank management believes that economic conditions may deteriorate. For example, in 2007 and 2008, JPMorgan executives referred to their portfolio as a "fortress balance sheet" in part because it was believed to be prepared for a worsening economic environment. Bank regulators may encourage regulated banks to hold additional capital to make the banking system more resilient. Following the financial turmoil of September 2008, banking regulators oversaw an increase in bank capital without the need for new legislation, new notice and comment rulemaking, or new international negotiations because bank regulators can require changes by insured depositories under existing authority (whether due to encouragement of regulators or changed preferences for prudence by bank managers).

U.S. banking regulators cooperate with banking regulators in other countries. The general approach to capital standards are based on the Basel Accords, an international framework developed under the auspices of the Bank for International Settlements.[13] Although the Basel Accords use the term *requirement*, Basel capital standards are not enforceable if a member country does not implement them (unlike the WTO dispute resolution process, for example). In other words, each participating country sets its own capital standards, but member countries use the Basel framework to establish best practices and harmonize banking regulation. The Basel committee describes its function thusly:

> The Basel Committee on Banking Supervision provides a forum for regular cooperation on banking supervisory matters. Its objective is to enhance understanding of key supervisory issues and improve the quality of banking supervision worldwide. It seeks to do so by exchanging information on national supervisory issues, approaches and techniques, with a view to promoting common understanding. At times, the Committee uses this common understanding to develop guidelines and supervisory standards in areas where they are considered desirable. In this regard, the Committee is best known for its international standards on capital adequacy; the Core Principles for Effective Banking Supervision; and the Concordat on cross-border banking supervision.[14]

A guiding principle of the Basel standards is that capital requirements should be risk-based. The riskier an asset, the more capital a bank should hold against possible losses. Risk-based regulations can be more prudent than simple leverage ratios because two firms with identical amounts of debt may have very different probabilities of failure if their assets are different. For example, one might lend primarily to households (credit cards, mortgages, student loans, and auto loans), whereas the other lends primarily to manufacturing businesses or agricultural service providers.

One possible drawback of a risk-based capital adequacy approach is that the regulation may become procyclical. That is, the capital standards themselves may reinforce the tendency for the banking system to expand credit during economic booms and contract credit during economic busts as views of risk evolve. If so, then risk-based capital requirements will make it more difficult for macro-prudential regulators to mitigate asset bubbles when they form, and will make it more difficult to promote additional credit expansion during economic downturns.

Procyclicality could occur if economic forecasters and financial analysts are overconfident that stable economic environments will continue or are over-pessimistic during unstable economic environments. To the extent that evaluating the risk of a long-term asset involves evaluating the probability of future economic instability, over-confidence will lead to lower than optimal capital requirements and over-pessimism will lead to higher than optimal capital requirements. If regulators and market participants are using the same financial models with similar historical data, it is unlikely that the regulators would provide much of a check on some sources of procyclicality in a risk-based system because the regulators and the banks could have similar measures of risk. On the other hand, regulators could require additional stress tests for the system as a whole, which an individual firm would not have the incentive or ability to conduct.

Asset Management

Asset management refers to providing financial products or services to a third party for a fee or commission. Examples of asset management include personal fiduciary services, such as wealth management for private clients. Other examples include acting as a custodian, providing security holder services, and offering investment advice.

Regulation of asset management activities relates to economic policy issues because the asset management services of banks can have broader effects. An example of the relation of asset management to the policy issues is the custodian role of banks for some complex financial transactions. For example, some forms of interbank lending include collateral, but who will hold the collateral for the duration of the contract? If custodian banks mismanage the assets, then disruptions in interbank lending markets can be magnified during periods of financial turmoil. During financial instability, banks may be turning to collateralized lending precisely because they have greater desire for safety, certainty, and speed. Disruptions to asset management services, through either the failure of central custodian banks or slow processing of existing custodian banks, may reinforce other banks' fears of uncertainty and slow processing.

Banks are not the only firms that offer asset management services. Thus, as discussed above, bank regulators do not make rules for the entire asset management industry; rather, they issue guidance to the firms with particular charters, and they provide examinations to insure that chartered banks have procedures in place that are consistent with sound asset management principles.

Consumer Protection Compliance

Lenders must comply with a variety of statutes and regulations when offering financial products to consumers. Prior to the financial crisis, authority to oversee consumer financial protection had been spread among a number of banking regulators, HUD, and the FTC. The Dodd-Frank Act gathered much of this authority and personnel into a new Consumer Financial Protection Bureau (CFPB), but bank regulators still supervise many consumer activities of their chartered firms. One reason is that poor customer relations can be a threat to the safety and soundness of the institution, in part because it is usually bad for business. The banking agencies examine banks for compliance with consumer laws and assist in resolving consumer complaints.

Bank regulators can facilitate consumer compliance by offering an ombudsman to assist in resolving complaints. Ombudsman offices are usually separate from those of the safety and soundness examiners. Such offices may help insure that consumers receive a fair and expeditious resolution of their concerns with a firm that is regulated by that agency. This may help reduce the time and expense of more formal complaint resolution options where consumers might otherwise seek redress (such as courts).

Some rulemaking activity for consumer compliance is shared between the CFPB and the bank regulators. For example, the CFPB has issued rules for appraisals of residential properties and mortgages. However, banks also rely on appraisals to establish collateral for their mortgage loans; thus, both the CFPB and bank regulators are involved in rulemaking for residential real estate appraisals.

Regulators of Firms with Bank Charters

In many cases, depository banks are owned within a larger holding company structure, and the primary prudential regulator of the holding company may not be the same as the primary prudential regulator of the bank subsidiary. There is a dual banking system, in which each depository institution is subject to regulation by its chartering authority: state or federal. In addition, because virtually all depository institutions are covered by federal deposit insurance, they are subject to at least one federal primary regulator (i.e., the federal authority responsible for examining the institution for safety and soundness and ensuring its compliance with federal banking laws).

The federal banking agencies are briefly discussed below, along with certain powers that these agencies have that are not limited to the firms of which each is the primary prudential regulator.

Office of the Comptroller of the Currency

The Office of the Comptroller (OCC) was created in 1863 as part of the Department of the Treasury to supervise federally chartered banks (i.e., "national" banks) and to replace the circulation of state-bank notes with a single national currency (Chapter 106, 13 Stat. 99). The OCC is the primary prudential regulator for federally chartered banks and thrifts. The head of the OCC, the Comptroller of the Currency, is also a member of the board of the FDIC and a voting member of FSOC. Like the other prudential regulators described below, the OCC has examination powers to enforce its responsibilities for the safety and soundness of nationally chartered banks, and strong enforcement powers, including the ability to issue cease and desist orders and revoke the charter of covered firms.

In addition to institution-level examinations, the OCC oversees systemic risk among nationally chartered banks and thrifts. One example of OCC systemic surveillance is the regular survey of credit underwriting practices. This survey compares underwriting standards over time and assesses whether OCC examiners believe the credit risk of nationally chartered bank portfolios is rising or falling. In addition, the OCC publishes regular reports on the derivatives activities of U.S. commercial banks.

Federal Deposit Insurance Corporation

The FDIC was created in 1933 to provide assurance to small depositors that they would not lose their savings if their bank failed (P.L. 74-305, 49 Stat. 684). The FDIC is the primary federal prudential regulator of state-chartered banks that are not members of the Federal Reserve System. It has, to some extent, similar examination and enforcement powers for the firms it regulates, as the OCC has for federally chartered banks. In addition to its role as a prudential bank regulator, the FDIC administers a deposit insurance fund and resolves failing depositories and certain systemic non-banks.

Deposit insurance relates to economic policy issues because it may help to stabilize an important source of bank funding during times of financial turmoil. Prior to the 1930s, American financial crises were often accompanied by rapid withdrawal of deposits from banks rumored to be in trouble (or actually in trouble). Even prudent, well-managed banks could have difficulty surviving these runs by depositors. Federal deposit insurance assures depositors that the full-faith and credit of the federal government guarantees their deposits up to a preset level. Despite occasional periods of bank failures, banks with insured deposits have suffered almost no depositor runs since the establishment of deposit insurance. Banks are assessed premiums by the FDIC for the deposit coverage.

The agency provides deposit insurance to all federally insured banks and thrifts (but not credit unions). In 2008, as the financial crisis worsened, Congress passed a temporary increase in the deposit insurance ceiling from $100,000 to $250,000 for most accounts.[15] The increase was made permanent by the Dodd-Frank Act.

The deposit insurance system has been revised a number of times. For example, legislative reform (P.L. 109-173, 119 Stat. 3601) in the mid-2000s raised the coverage limit for retirement accounts to $250,000 and indexed both its limit and the general deposit insurance coverage ceiling to inflation. The reform act made changes to the risk-based assessment system to determine the payments of individual institutions. Within a range set by the reform act, the FDIC uses notice and comment rulemaking to set the designated reserve ratio (DRR) that supports the Deposit Insurance Fund (DIF). The FDIC uses its power to examine individual institutions and issue regulations for all insured-depository institutions to monitor and enforce safety and soundness.[16]

Using emergency authority it received under the Federal Deposit Insurance Corporation Improvement Act of 1991 (FDICIA; P.L. 102-242),[17] the FDIC made a determination of systemic risk in October 2008 and announced that it would temporarily guarantee (1) newly issued senior unsecured debt of banks, thrifts, and certain holding companies and (2) non-interest bearing deposit transaction accounts (e.g., business checking accounts), regardless of dollar amount.[18] Under Dodd-Frank, the FDIC's authority to guarantee bank debt is made explicit. Although the 2008 emergency measures have expired, the FDIC has the authority to create some programs during a possible future crisis.

The financial crisis of 2008 revealed a number of lessons related to bank runs and deposit insurance. Several non-banks suffered the equivalent of depositor runs, including money market mutual funds and the interbank repo market. Because the equivalent of depositor runs can occur in other financial activities, Dodd-Frank expanded the assessment base for FDIC premiums to include a bank's entire balance sheet, not just its insured deposits. Furthermore, creditors of failing financial institutions may, under extreme circumstances, be provided with additional guarantees if the failure is determined to be a threat to the financial stability of the United States.

When banks fail, the FDIC disposes the assets and liabilities. The FDIC manages the DIF, which is derived from risk-based assessments levied on depository institutions. The fund is used for various purposes, primarily for resolving failed or failing institutions. The FDIC has broad jurisdiction because nearly all banks and thrifts, whether federally or state-chartered, carry FDIC insurance.

The Dodd-Frank Act also expanded the FDIC's role in liquidating troubled financial institutions. Under the act, the Financial Stability Oversight Council (FSOC) will designate certain financial institutions—banks and nonbanks—as systemically important. In addition to more stringent capital regulation, those firms are required to draw up "living wills," or plans for orderly liquidation. The Federal Reserve, with the concurrence of two-thirds of the FSOC, may determine that a firm represents a "severe threat" to financial stability and may order it closed. The FDIC will administer the resolution process for nonbanks as well as banks.[19]

The Federal Reserve

The Federal Reserve System was established in 1913 to provide stability to banks and trusts through the regulation of reserves (P.L. 63-43, 38 STAT. 251). The Federal Reserve System has three components: the Federal Reserve Board (FRB), the regional Federal Reserve Banks (FRBNY, FRBSF, etc.), and the Open Market Committee. The Fed is the primary prudential regulator for a variety of lending institutions, including bank holding companies, certain U.S. branches of foreign banks, and state-chartered banks that are members of the Federal Reserve System. Under the Gramm-Leach-Bliley Act (GLBA; P.L. 106-102), the Fed serves as the umbrella regulator for financial holding companies, which are defined as conglomerates that are permitted to engage in a broad array of financially related activities. As a primary prudential regulator, the Federal Reserve has similar authority as the OCC.

In addition to the charter class that the Federal Reserve regulates, the Dodd-Frank Act made the Fed the primary regulator of all financial firms (bank or nonbank) that are designated as systemically significant by the FSOC (of which the Fed is a member). Capital requirements for such firms may be stricter than for other firms. In addition, Dodd-Frank made the Fed the principal regulator for systemically important financial-market utilities. The Fed also regulates savings and loan holding companies and securities holding companies, formerly defined in securities law as an investment bank holding company.

In addition to its powers as a primary prudential regulator, the Federal Reserve conducts monetary policy, monitors the financial system, acts as the fiscal agent of the United States, and regulates the payment system and a number of financial activities. Examples of additional activities regulated by the Fed (sometimes only as a monitor and sometimes jointly with other agencies) include equal credit opportunity (Reg-B), Community Reinvestment Act (CRA) related agreements (Reg-G), and extensions of credit by brokers and dealers (Reg-T). The list of regulatory topics now extends from Reg-A to Reg-YY.

National Credit Union Administration

The National Credit Union Administration (NCUA), originally part of the Farm Credit Administration, became an independent agency in 1970 (P.L. 91-206, 84 STAT. 49). The NCUA regulates all federal credit unions and those state credit unions that elect to be federally insured. It administers a Central Liquidity Facility, which is the credit union lender of last resort, and the National Credit Union Share Insurance Fund, which insures credit union deposits. Credit unions are member-owned financial cooperatives and must be not-for-profit institutions. As cooperatives, they are exempt from corporate income tax. Many credit unions offer similar services as community banks, and this differential tax treatment is often the subject of legislative proposals in each congressional session.

Regulating Securities, Derivatives, and Other Contract Markets

Regulators of financial trading attempt to address many economic policy problems. As discussed in the introductory sections, financial markets may not be level playing fields—some people with access to confidential information may have a trading advantage. Furthermore, the people who issue and market new securities (or derivatives) may have the incentive to withhold or mischaracterize some of the information they have about the securities or derivatives being offered. Even if these market facilitators provide full information, the outcome might still be less than optimal if other market participants simply believe that material information is not being disclosed or that insiders are behaving strategically. As a result, much of the regulation of securities and derivatives markets has focused on resolving conflicts of interest and requiring full disclosure of material information, unlike bank regulation that tends to focus on prudence. In addition, much securities market regulation has been applied through enforcement against after-the-fact violations, rather than as prospective examinations of covered firms.

Non-Bank Financial Regulators

Securities and Exchange Commission

The SEC was created as an independent agency in 1934 to enforce newly written federal securities laws (P.L. 73-291, 48 Stat. 881). Although the SEC is concerned with ensuring the safety and soundness of the firms it regulates, its primary concern is maintaining fair and orderly markets and protecting investors from fraud. The SEC generally[20] does not have the authority to limit risks taken by non-bank financial institutions or the ability to prop up a failing firm, with some exceptions. Two types of firms come under the SEC's jurisdiction: (1) all corporations that sell securities to the public and (2) securities broker/dealers and other securities markets intermediaries.

Firms that sell securities—stocks and bonds—to the public are required to register with the SEC. Registration entails the publication of detailed information about the firm, its management, the intended uses for the funds raised through the sale of securities, and the risks to investors. The initial registration disclosures must be kept current through the filing of periodic financial statements: annual and quarterly reports (as well as special reports when there is a material change in the firm's financial condition or prospects).

Beyond these disclosure requirements, and certain other rules that apply to corporate governance, the SEC does not have any direct regulatory control over publicly traded firms. Bank regulators are expected to identify unsafe and unsound banking practices in the institutions they supervise and have the power to intervene and prevent banks from taking excessive risks. The SEC has no comparable authority; the securities laws simply require that risks be disclosed to investors. Registration with the SEC, in other words, is in no sense a government endorsement that a security is a good or safe investment.

To enable investors to make informed investment choices, the SEC has statutory authority over financial accounting standards. All publicly traded firms are required to use generally accepted accounting principles (GAAP), which are formulated by the Financial Accounting Standards Board (FASB), the American Institute of Certified Public Accountants (AICPA), and the SEC itself.

Besides publicly traded corporations, a number of securities market participants are also required to register with the SEC (or with one of the industry self-regulatory organizations that the SEC oversees). These include stock exchanges, securities brokerages (and numerous classes of their personnel), mutual funds, auditors, investment advisers, and others. To maintain their registered status, all these entities must comply with rules meant to protect investors' interests, prevent fraud, and promote fair and orderly markets. The area of SEC supervision most analogous to banking regulation is broker/dealer regulation. Several provisions of law and regulation protect brokerage customers from losses arising from brokerage firm failure. The Securities Investor Protection Corporation (SIPC), created by Congress in 1970, operates an insurance scheme funded by assessments on broker/dealers (and with a backup line of credit with the U.S. Treasury). SIPC guarantees customer accounts up to $500,000 for losses arising from brokerage failure or fraud (but not market losses). Unlike the FDIC, however, SIPC does not examine broker/dealers and has no regulatory powers.

Since 1975, the SEC has enforced a net capital rule applicable to all registered broker/dealers. The rule requires broker/dealers to maintain an excess of capital above mere solvency, to ensure that a failing firm stops trading while it still has assets to meet customer claims. Net capital levels are calculated in a manner similar to the risk-based capital requirements under the Basel Accords, but the SEC has its own set of risk weightings, which it calls "haircuts." The riskier the asset, the greater the haircut.

Although the net capital rule appears to be similar in its effects to the banking agencies' risk-based capital requirements, there are significant differences. The SEC has no authority to intervene in a broker/dealer's business if it takes excessive risks that might cause net capital to drop below the required level. Rather, the net capital rule is often described as a liquidation rule—not meant to prevent failures but to minimize the impact on customers. Moreover, the SEC has no authority comparable to the banking regulators' prompt corrective action powers: it cannot preemptively seize a troubled broker/dealer or compel it to merge with a sound firm.

The differences between bank and securities regulation with respect to safety and soundness came into sharp focus with the collapse of Bear Stearns, one of the five largest investment banks, in March 2008.[21] The SEC monitored Bear Stearns' financial condition until shortly before the collapse (which was precipitated by the refusal of other market participants to extend short-term credit to Bear Stearns), and it believed that the firm had sufficient levels of capital and liquidity. When bankruptcy suddenly loomed, it was the Federal Reserve that stepped in to broker the sale of Bear Stearns to JP Morgan Chase by agreeing to purchase $30 billion of "toxic" Bear Stearns assets.

The Bear Stearns situation highlighted several apparent anomalies in the U.S. regulatory structure. The SEC lacked safety and soundness powers over the institutions it supervised, and the Fed was forced to commit funds to an investment bank over which it had no regulatory jurisdiction. The anomaly became even more pronounced when the Fed subsequently established a lending facility to provide short-term credit to other investment banks.[22]

The Bear Stearns collapse showed the inability of the SEC to respond to a brokerage failure with systemic risk implications. There is more to the story, however, than the differences between bank regulation and the SEC's net capital rule. In 2004, the SEC devised a voluntary supervisory scheme for the largest investment banks, called the Consolidated Supervised Entities (CSE) program.[23] The CSE firms were all registered broker/dealers, but were also large holding companies with extensive operations carried on outside the broker/dealer unit. Thus, the SEC had no capital requirement that applied to the entire investment bank. Under CSE, this was to change: as a substitute for the net capital rule, the firms agreed to abide by the Basel risk-based standard and maintain that level of capital *at the holding company level*. On a voluntary basis, the firms agreed to grant the SEC the authority to examine and monitor their compliance, above and beyond the SEC's explicit statutory authority.[24]

Whatever the intent of the CSE program, it did not succeed in preventing excessive risk-taking by the participants.[25] By the end of September 2008, all five CSE investment banks had either failed (Lehman Brothers), merged to prevent failure (Merrill Lynch and Bear Stearns), or applied for bank holding company status (Morgan Stanley and Goldman Sachs).[26] On September 26, 2008, SEC Chairman Cox announced the end of the CSE program, declaring that "[t]he last six months have made it abundantly clear that voluntary regulation does not work. When Congress passed the Gramm-Leach-Bliley

Act, it created a significant regulatory gap by failing to give to the SEC or any agency the authority to regulate large investment bank holding companies."[27]

With the Dodd-Frank Act, Congress eliminated the investment bank holding company framework in Section 17 of the Securities Exchange Act of 1934. Section 618 of Dodd-Frank permits a securities holding company to be subject to consolidated supervision and submit to Federal Reserve regulation. Under Title I of Dodd-Frank, any securities firm that is deemed by the FSOC to be systemically significant will automatically come under the consolidated supervision of the Federal Reserve.

Other provisions of Dodd-Frank, however, gave the SEC new responsibilities that have aspects of safety and soundness regulation. Under Section 731, the SEC sets capital requirements for major security-based swap participants and security-based swap dealers. Section 956 gives the SEC new authority to prohibit compensation structures in broker/dealers and investment advisory firms that create inappropriate risks.

Commodity Futures Trading Commission

The CFTC was created in 1974 to regulate commodities futures and options markets, which at the time were poised to expand beyond their traditional base in agricultural commodities to encompass contracts based on financial variables, such as interest rates and stock indexes. The CFTC's mission is to prevent excessive speculation, manipulation of commodity prices, and fraud. Like the SEC, the CFTC oversees industry self-regulatory organizations (SROs)—the futures exchanges and the National Futures Association—and requires the registration of a range of industry firms and personnel, including futures commission merchants (brokers), floor traders, commodity pool operators, and commodity trading advisers.

The Dodd-Frank Act greatly expanded the CFTC's jurisdiction by eliminating exemptions for certain over-the-counter derivatives. As a result, swap dealers, major swap participants, swap clearing organizations, swap execution facilities, and swap data repositories are required to register with the CFTC. These entities are subject to business conduct standards contained in statute or promulgated as CFTC rules.

Like the SEC, the CFTC does not directly regulate the safety and soundness of individual firms, with the exception of newly regulated swap dealers and major swap participants, for whom it sets capital standards pursuant to Dodd-Frank.

Federal Housing Finance Agency

The FHFA was created in 2008 by the Housing and Economic Recovery Act of 2008 (P.L. 110- 289) to consolidate and strengthen regulation of a group of housing finance-related government-sponsored enterprises (GSEs): Fannie Mae, Freddie Mac, and the Federal Home Loan Banks.[28] The FHFA succeeded the Office of Federal Housing Enterprise Oversight (OFHEO) and the Federal Housing Finance Board (FHFB). FHFA authority includes both the safety and soundness authority of the former OFHEO and the housing mission goals for the GSEs that had been administered by HUD.

The impetus to create the FHFA came from concerns about risk—including systemic risk— arising from the rapid growth of the GSEs, particularly Fannie and Freddie. These two GSEs were profit-seeking, shareholder-owned corporations that took advantage of their government-sponsored status to accumulate undiversified investment portfolios of more than $1.5 trillion, consisting almost exclusively of home mortgages (and securities and derivatives based on those mortgages).

The FHFA was given enhanced safety and soundness powers resembling those of the federal bank regulators. These powers included the ability to set capital standards, order the enterprises to cease any activity or divest any asset that posed a threat to financial soundness, and replace management and assume control of the firms that became seriously undercapitalized.

One of the FHFA's first actions was to place both Fannie and Freddie in "voluntary" conservatorship.[29] Fannie and Freddie continue to operate, under an agreement with the U.S. Treasury. The Treasury provided capital to the two firms, by means of preferred stock purchases, to ensure that each remains solvent. In return, the government received warrants equivalent to a 79.9% equity ownership position in the firms. Treasury also sweeps the firms' retained earnings above a certain level of net worth.

Consumer Financial Protection Bureau

Title X of Dodd-Frank created the Consumer Financial Protection Bureau (CFPB) to bring the consumer protection regulation of depository and non-depository financial institutions into closer alignment.[30] The bureau is an independent entity within the Federal Reserve with authority over an array of consumer financial products and services (including deposit taking, mortgages, credit cards and other extensions of credit, loan servicing, check guaranteeing, collection of consumer report data, debt collection, real estate settlement, money transmitting, and financial data processing). CFPB serves as the primary federal consumer financial protection supervisor and enforcer of federal consumer protection laws over many of the institutions that offer these products and services.

However, the bureau's regulatory authority varies based on institution size and type. Regulatory authority differs for (1) depository institutions with more than $10 billion in assets, (2) depository institutions with $10 billion or less in assets, and (3) non-depositories. The Dodd-Frank Act also explicitly exempts a number of different entities and consumer financial activities from the bureau's supervisory and enforcement authority. Among the exempt entities are

- merchants, retailers, or sellers of nonfinancial goods or services, to the extent that they extend credit directly to consumers exclusively for the purpose of enabling consumers to purchase such nonfinancial goods or services;
- automobile dealers;
- real estate brokers and agents;
- financial intermediaries registered with the SEC or CFTC;
- insurance companies; and
- depository institutions with $10 billion or less in assets.

Regulatory Umbrella Groups

The need for coordination and data sharing among regulators has led to the formation of innumerable interagency task forces to study particular market episodes and make recommendations to Congress. Three interagency organizations have permanent status.

Financial Stability Oversight Council

Title I of the Dodd-Frank Act created the FSOC on the date of enactment.[31] The council is chaired by the Secretary of the Treasury, and the other voting members consist of the heads of the Federal Reserve, FDIC, OCC, NCUA, SEC, CFTC, FHFA, CFPB, and a member with insurance expertise appointed by the President. Nonvoting members, serving in an advisory capacity, include the director of the Office of Financial Research (created by Title I to support the FSOC), he head of the Federal Insurance Office (created by Title V of Dodd-Frank), a state banking supervisor, a state insurance commissioner, and a state securities commissioner. If an agency is headed by a board or a commission, only the chair serves in the FSOC, not the entire board or commission.

The FSOC is tasked with identifying risks to financial stability and responding to emerging systemic risks, while minimizing moral hazard arising from expectations that firms or their counterparties will be rescued from failure. The FSOC's duties include

- collecting information on financial firms from regulators and through the Office of Financial Research;
- monitoring the financial system to identify potential systemic risks;
- proposing regulatory changes to Congress to promote stability, competitiveness, and efficiency;
- facilitating information sharing and coordination among financial regulators;
- making regulatory recommendations to financial regulators, including "new or heightened standards and safeguards";
- identifying gaps in regulation that could pose systemic risk;
- reviewing and commenting on new or existing accounting standards issued by any standard-setting body; and
- providing a forum for the resolution of jurisdictional disputes among council members. The FSOC may not impose any resolution on disagreeing members, however.

The council is required to provide an annual report and testimony to Congress.

In contrast to some proposals to create a systemic risk regulator, the Dodd-Frank Act does not give the council authority (beyond the existing authority of its individual members) to eliminate emerging threats or close regulatory gaps it identifies. In most cases, the council can only make regulatory recommendations—it cannot impose change.

Although the FSOC does not have direct supervisory authority over any financial institution, it plays an important role in regulation, because firms that it designates as systemically important come under a consolidated supervisory regime that may be considerably more stringent than the standards that apply to non-systemic firms. The FSOC is also required to approve (by a two-thirds vote) decisions by the Federal Reserve to shut down systemically significant financial firms that pose a severe threat to financial stability.

Federal Financial Institution Examinations Council

The Federal Financial Institutions Examination Council (FFIEC) was created by legislation[32] in 1979 as a formal interagency body to coordinate federal regulation of lending institutions. Through the FFIEC, the federal banking regulators issue a single set of reporting forms for covered institutions. The FFIEC also attempts to harmonize auditing principles and supervisory decisions. The FFIEC is made up of the Federal Reserve, OCC, FDIC, NCUA, and CFPB. Except for the CFPB, the member agencies of the FFIEC are primary prudential regulators of depository institutions with specific charters as described above and employ examiners to enforce safety and soundness regulations for lending institutions. The examination powers of the CFPB for compliance with consumer protection rules varies across institutions, many of which may not have bank charters.

Federal financial institution examiners evaluate the risks of covered institutions. The specific safety and soundness concerns common to the FFIEC agencies can be found in the examiner's handbook to monitor lenders. Each subject area of the handbook can be updated separately. Examples of safety and soundness subject areas include important indicators of risk, such as capital adequacy, asset quality, liquidity, and sensitivity to market risk.

President's Working Group on Financial Markets

The President's Working Group on Financial Markets (PWG) was created by President Reagan through executive order in 1988.[33] The PWG includes the Secretary of the Treasury and the Chairmen of the Federal Reserve, the SEC, and the CFTC. It is not a formal agency subject to congressional oversight, although each member is subject to Senate confirmation at the time of appointment.

The impetus for the creation of the PWG was the stock market crash of October 1987, and specifically the role that the stock index futures markets (under CFTC jurisdiction) played in creating panic in the stock market (regulated by SEC). Studies conducted by the SEC, the CFTC, a blue-ribbon panel appointed by the President (the Presidential Task Force on Market Mechanisms, or Brady Commission), and the stock and futures exchanges reached strikingly different conclusions; the task of the PWG was to review the studies and issue a further report.

The PWG provides interagency coordination and information sharing and studies entities and products that raise intermarket regulatory issues, such as hedge funds and OTC derivatives. For example, in March 2008, the PWG issued a policy statement on the ongoing financial crisis.[34] Another example is the October 2010 PWG report called for changes to address systemic risk and reduce the susceptibility of money market mutual funds (MMFs) to runs.[35]

Non-Bank Capital Requirements

Federal Housing Finance Agency

The Federal Housing Finance Agency (FHFA) is authorized to set capital classification standards for the Federal Home Loan Banks, Fannie Mae, and Freddie Mac that reflect the differences in operations between the banks and the latter two GSEs.[36] The law defines several capital classifications and prescribes regulatory actions to be taken as a GSE's condition worsens. Limitations are placed on a GSE if it does not meet certain capital standards.

No growth in total assets is permitted for an *undercapitalized* GSE, unless (1) FHFA has accepted the GSE's capital restoration plan, (2) an increase in assets is consistent with the plan, and (3) the ratios of both total capital to assets and tangible equity to assets are increasing. An undercapitalized entity is subject to heightened scrutiny and supervision.

If a regulated entity is *significantly undercapitalized*, FHFA must take one or more of the following actions: elect new directors, dismiss directors or executives, and hire qualified executive officers, or other actions. Without prior written approval, executives of a significantly undercapitalized regulated entity may not receive bonuses or pay raises. In addition, FHFA may appoint a receiver or conservator for several specified causes related to financial difficulty or violations of law or regulation.

When a GSE becomes *critically undercapitalized*, receivership or conservatorship provisions apply. For example, FHFA must appoint itself as the receiver if a regulated entity's assets are (and have been for 60 days) less than its obligations to its creditors, or if the regulated entity has (for 60 days) not been generally paying its debts as they come due. Although both GSEs were technically adequately capitalized according to the March 2008 FHFA report, both firms were experiencing losses large enough to threaten continued solvency. In July 2008, Congress empowered Treasury to provide financial assistance to the GSEs, and the FHFA appointed itself conservator for both Fannie and Freddie in September 2008, before either GSE had failed to make timely payments on debt obligations.

FHFA may downgrade the capital classification of a regulated entity (1) whose conduct could rapidly deplete core or total capital, or (in the case of Fannie or Freddie) whose mortgage assets have declined significantly in value,

(2) that is determined (after notice and opportunity for a hearing) to be in an unsafe or unsound condition, or (3) that is engaging in an unsafe or unsound practice.

The SEC's Net Capital Rule

The SEC's net capital rule, set out in 17 CFR 240.15c3-1, imposes an "Aggregate Indebtedness Standard." No broker/dealer shall permit its aggregate indebtedness to all other persons to exceed 1500% of its net capital (or 800% of its net capital for 12 months after commencing business as a broker or dealer).[37] The 1500% (or 15-to-1) ratio of debt to liquid capital, is arithmetically equivalent to a 62/3% capital requirement.

To calculate liquid capital, SEC rules require that securities and other assets be given a "haircut" from their current market values (or face value, in the case of bonds), to cover the risk that the asset's value might decline before it could be sold. The haircut concept—the riskier the asset, the greater the haircut—is essentially the same as the standardized risk weights in the Basel Accords. For example, U.S. Treasury securities might have a lower haircut than municipal securities, which might have a lower haircut than corporate bonds, which in turn might have a lower haircut than common stock. Certain assets, such as unsecured receivables or securities for which no ready market exists, receive a haircut of 100%. The Dodd-Frank Act requires the SEC to set capital standards for major security-based swap dealers and major security-based swap participants.

CFTC Capital Requirements

Futures commission merchants (or FCMs, the futures equivalent of a securities broker/dealer) are subject to adjusted net capital requirements. Authority to enforce the capital rules is delegated by the CFTC to the National Futures Association (NFA), a self-regulatory organization created by Congress.

Each NFA member that is required to be registered with the CFTC as a futures commission merchant (member FCM) must maintain "Adjusted Net Capital" (as defined in CFTC Regulation 1.17) equal to or in excess of the greatest of

i) $500,000;
ii) For Member FCMs with less than $2,000,000 in Adjusted Net Capital, $6,000 for each remote location operated;

iii) For Member FCMs with less than $2,000,000 in Adjusted Net Capital, $3,000 for each associated person;
iv) For securities brokers and dealers, the amount of net capital specified by SEC regulations;
v) 8% of domestic and foreign domiciled customer and 4% of non-customer (excluding proprietary) risk maintenance margin/performance bond requirements for all domestic and foreign futures and options on futures contracts excluding the risk margin associated with naked long option positions;
vi) For Member FCMs with an affiliate that engages in foreign exchange (FX) transactions and that is authorized to engage in those transactions solely by virtue of its affiliation with a registered FCM, $7,500,000; or
vii) For Member FCMs that are counterparties to FX options, $5,000,000, except that FX Dealer Members must meet the higher requirement in Financial Requirements Section 11.[38]

The Dodd-Frank Act defines several categories of major derivatives participants and requires the CFTC to set capital standards for major security-based swap dealers and major security-based swap participants.

Foreign Exchange Markets

Buying and selling currencies is essential to foreign trade, and the exchange rate has major implications for a country's macroeconomic policy. Although the United States allows its currency to float, the foreign exchange market is not completely free because of the actions of central banks. For example, the central banks of other countries may seek to peg their currency to the dollar. The market is one of the largest in the world, with average daily foreign exchange turnover in excess of $4 trillion.[39] Federal Reserve monetary policies affect the value of the dollar (even if the Fed does not intentionally target the value of the dollar), but no agency is granted sole authority to regulate the mechanics of foreign exchange trading, except to the extent foreign exchange futures are offered on regulated exchanges.

Trading in currencies takes place between large global banks, central banks, hedge funds and other currency speculators, commercial firms involved in imports and exports, fund managers, and retail brokers. Currency trading is largely conducted in the over-the-counter market.

U.S. Treasury Securities

Like the foreign exchange market, there is no central exchange for the resale market for U.S. Treasuries, but there are a number of proprietary, computer-based transaction systems. Treasury securities were exempted from SEC regulation by the original securities laws of the 1930s and under the Volcker Rule in the Dodd-Frank Act. In 1993, following a successful corner of a Treasury bond auction by Salomon Brothers, Congress passed the Government Securities Act Amendments (P.L. 103-202), which required brokers and dealers in government securities that were not already registered with the SEC to register as government securities dealers. (Existing broker/dealer registrants were simply required to notify the SEC that they were in the government securities business.) Nevertheless, the government securities market remains much more lightly regulated than the corporate securities markets.

The primary market in Treasury securities, in which new debt instruments are sold to fund government operations, is monitored by the Federal Reserve Bank of New York (FRBNY). A principal channel for the distribution of new Treasuries is a group of firms called primary dealers, who purchase securities at auction for their own accounts and for their customers. The primary dealers are 19 commercial and investment banks, both foreign and domestic. The primary dealer list is maintained by the FRBNY, which also issues a list of practices that it expects primary dealers to comply with. FRBNY conducts auctions for the Treasury, but its relationship to the dealers is commercial, rather than providing prudential regulation.[40] The New York Fed does, however, collect certain data about primary dealers' transactions in government securities.

In March 2008, as part of its multifaceted attempt to supply liquidity to the financial system, the Federal Reserve established a Primary Dealer Credit Facility, to make short-term loans against a variety of collateral (including asset-backed and mortgage-backed securities) to the primary dealers.[41] This step attracted attention in part because the primary dealer group included investment banking firms of which the Fed had no regulatory authority.

Private Securities Markets

The securities laws mandate registration of, and extensive disclosures by, public securities issuers, but also provide for private sales of securities, which are not subject to disclosure requirements. Private placements of securities may only be offered to limited numbers of "accredited investors" who meet certain asset tests. (Most purchasers are life insurers and other institutional investors.) There are also restrictions on the resale of private securities.

The size of the private placement market is subject to considerable variation from year to year, but at times the value of securities sold privately exceeds what is sold into the public market. In recent decades, venture capitalists and private equity firms have come to play important roles in corporate finance. The former typically purchase interests in private firms, which may be sold later to the public, while the latter often purchase all the stock of publicly traded companies and take them private.

APPENDIX A. CAPITAL REQUIREMENTS: PROVISIONS IN DODD-FRANK

The Dodd-Frank Act includes numerous provisions that seek to strengthen capital requirements of banks and to extend capital regulatory approaches to certain non-bank financial firms and markets. The general thrust of these provisions is that systemically significant firms, derivatives trading platforms, and other financial market utilities should be required to hold extra capital to compensate for the risk that their failure might pose to the system at large. Title I requires banking regulators to establish minimum risk-based capital requirements and leverage requirements on a consolidated basis for depository institutions, depository holding companies, and firms designated by the Financial Stability Oversight Council (FSOC) as systemically significant. These requirements must be no lower than those that were set for depository institutions as of the date of enactment (July 2010). One example of the effect of this provision is that bank holding companies will no longer be able to include trust-preferred securities in Tier I capital. These requirements are phased in over time, and certain small firms are exempted.

Section 115(c) requires the Financial Stability Oversight Council to study the feasibility of implementing a contingent capital requirement for systemically significant firms. Contingent capital is debt that can be converted into equity by the issuing firm under certain circumstances. Following the study, if the FSOC recommends, the Fed may impose contingent capital requirements on systemically significant firms.

Table A-1. Capital Standards for Federally Regulated Depository Institutions

Agency	Capital Standard	Source
OCC (bank charters)	Minimum risk-based capital ratio of 8%. (The ratio measures bank capital against assets, with asset values risk-weighted, or adjusted on a scale of riskiness.) In addition, banks must maintain Tier 1 capital[a] in an amount equal to at least 3.0% of adjusted total assets. (A simple definition of Tier 1 capital is stockholders' equity, or the net worth of the institution.) The 3% total assets leverage ratio applies to the most highly rated banks, which are expected to have well-diversified risks, including no undue interest rate risk exposure, excellent control systems, good earnings, high asset quality, high liquidity, and well managed on-and off-balance sheet activities. In general, they should be considered strong banking organizations, with a rating of 1 under CAMELS[b] rating system of banks. For other banks, the minimum Tier 1 leverage ratio is 4%.	12 CFR §3.6 ("Minimum capital ratios")
FDIC	The FDIC requires institutions to maintain the same minimum leverage capital requirements (ratio of Tier 1 capital to assets) as the OCC, that is, 3% for the most highly rated institutions and 4% for others.	12 CFR §325.3 ("Minimum leverage capital requirement")
Federal Reserve	State banks that are members of the Federal Reserve System must meet an 8% risk-weighted capital standard, of which at least 4% must be Tier 1 capital (3% for strong banking institutions rated "1" under the CAMELS rating system of banks). In addition, the Fed establishes levels of reserves that depository institutions are required to maintain as part of monetary policies. Changing reserve requirements could also affect potential bank lending in a way analogous to changing capital requirements. These reserves include vault cash (currency) or deposits at the nearest regional Federal Reserve branch, held against the bank's deposit liabilities, primarily checking, saving, and time deposits (CDs). The size of these reserves places a ceiling on the amount of deposits that financial institutions can have outstanding, and ties deposit liabilities to the amount of assets (loans) these institutions can acquire.	12 CFR §208.4, Regulation H ("Membership of State Banking Institutions in the Federal Reserve System") and 12 CFR §204.9 (Reserve requirements)

Agency	Capital Standard	Source
OCC (thrift charters)	Risk-based capital must be at least 8% of risk-weighted assets. Federal statute requires that thrift capital regulations be no less stringent than the OCC's regulations for banks. Tangible capital must exceed 1.5% of adjusted total assets. The leverage ratio (Tier 1 capital to assets) must be 4% of adjusted total assets (3% for thrifts with a composite CAMELS rating of 1).	12 CFR §167
NCUA	Credit unions must maintain a risk-based net worth of 7%, as a minimum to be considered well capitalized.	NCUA Regulations (Section 702, Subpart A)

Source: CRS from statutes and legislation.

[a] Tier 1 capital or core capital means the sum of common stockholders' equity, noncumulative perpetual preferred stock, and minority interests in consolidated subsidiaries, minus all intangible assets, minus identified losses, minus investments in certain financial subsidiaries, and minus the amount of the total adjusted carrying value of nonfinancial equity investments that is subject to a deduction from Tier 1 capital.

[b] See Appendix C for a broader discussion of the CAMELS rating system.

Section 165(j) requires the Federal Reserve to impose leverage limits on bank holding companies with assets over $50 billion and on the systemically important non-bank financial companies that it will supervise. When this section is implemented, such firms will be required to maintain a debt-to-equity ratio of no more than 15-to-1.

Title VI requires the federal banking regulators to make capital "requirements countercyclical, so that the amount of capital required to be maintained ... increases in times of economic expansion and decreases in times of economic contraction, consistent with ... safety and soundness."[42]

APPENDIX B. FORMS OF BANKING ORGANIZATIONS

The structure of banks can be complex. Currently, the regulator of a particular activity of a bank or its subsidiary depends in part on the activity of the subsidiary or its charter, as described previously. The following flow charts provide simplified representations of various bank structures. In some cases, the umbrella bank and its subsidiaries may have different regulators.

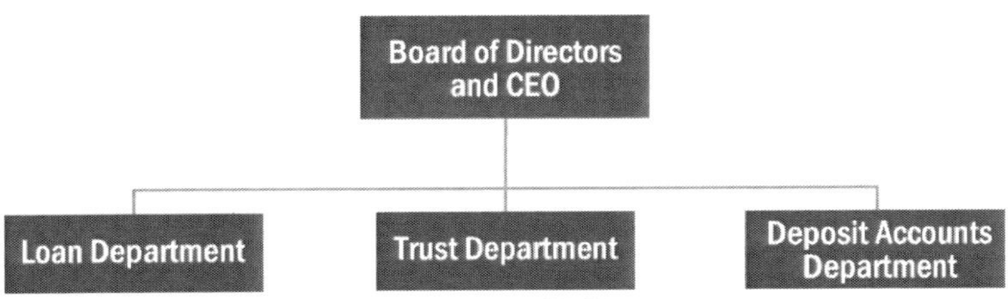

Source: The Congressional Research Service (CRS).

Figure B-1. National Bank.

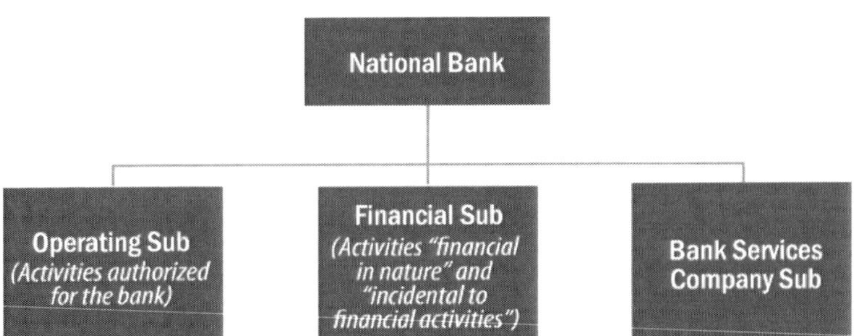

Source: CRS.

Figure B-2. National Bank and Subsidiaries.

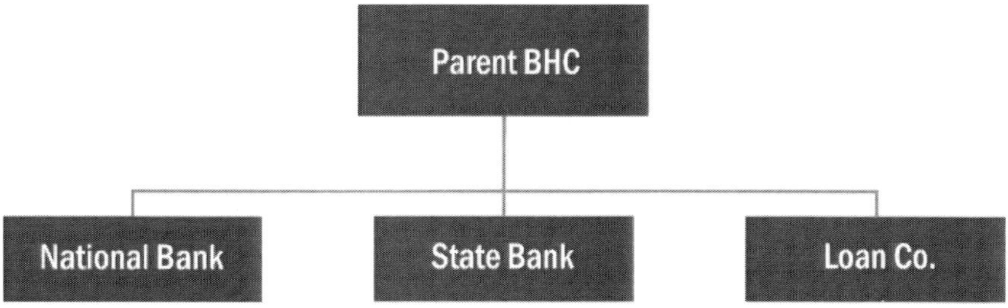

Source: CRS.

Figure B-3. Bank Holding Company.

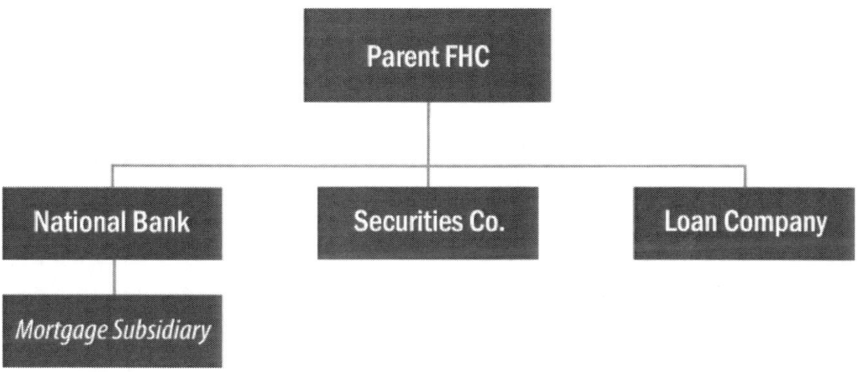

Source: CRS.

Figure B-4. Financial Holding Company.

APPENDIX C. BANK RATINGS: UFIRS AND CAMELS

Federal bank regulators conduct confidential assessments of covered banks. The Federal Financial Institutions Examination Council (FFIEC) helps coordinate the ratings system used by bank examiners so that there is some consistency to the examinations, although the ratings do take into account differences in bank size, sophistication, complexity of activities, and risk profile. The FFIEC adopted the Uniform Financial Institutions Rating System (UFIRS) in 1979. The system was revised in 1996 and is often referred to as the CAMELS rating system. CAMELS stands for **C**apital adequacy, **A**sset quality, **M**anagement, **E**arnings, **L**iquidity, and **S**ensitivity to market risk. These are measures used to evaluate the safety and soundness of banks. A description of the CAMELS system is found in the Comptrollers Handbook:

Bank Supervision Process, provided by the Office of the Comptroller of the Currency (OCC).[43] Market factors can affect more than one category in the CAMELS ratings.

Capital Adequacy

This component assesses the level of capital held by the institution in relation to the risks that it takes. Capital adequacy can be affected by a number of factors, including changes in credit risk, market risk, and the institution's financial condition. Increases in problem assets would require increased capital. Capital adequacy is also supposed to reflect potential risks even if they are technically off of the bank's balance sheet.

Asset Quality

Asset quality refers to existing and potential credit risk associated with a bank's portfolio. Like capital adequacy, this component is supposed to reflect risk even if it is not technically on the bank's balance sheet. Asset quality can include changes in loan default rates, investment performance, exposure to counterparty risk, and all other risks that may affect the value or marketability of an institution's assets.

Management Capability

The governance of the bank, including management and board of directors, is assessed in relation to the nature and scope of the bank's activities. This rating is affected by the level and quality of management oversight. It also includes legal compliance, responsiveness to auditor recommendations, and similar issues.

Earnings Quantity and Quality

The rating of a bank's earnings takes into account current earnings and the sustainability of future earnings. Earnings that rely on favorable tax effects and nonrecurring events receive lower ratings. Similarly, inadequate controls for expenses can reduce the rating for earnings. Difficulties in forecasting and managing risks can also reduce the earnings rating.

Liquidity

Liquidity includes the ability of a bank to meet its expected funding needs. For a given institution size and complexity, this factor assesses the ability of the firm to fulfill its financial obligations in a timely manner. Liquidity refers to the ability to meet short-term funding needs without incurring excessive losses, which might occur if assets had to be sold at a steep discount in a time-pressure situation (or "fire sale"). Liquidity also includes assessments of specific financial categories, such as the trend and stability of deposits, and the expected ability to securitize and sell pools of assets.

Sensitivity to Market Risk

Market risk includes potential changes in the prices of financial assets, such as movements in interest rates, foreign exchange rates, commodity prices, and stock prices. The nature and scope of a bank's activities can affect the markets that it is exposed to; therefore, market risk is closely related to the other CAMELS factors. This rating takes into account management's ability to identify and manage the risks that can arise from the bank's trading activities in financial markets. It also takes into account interest rate risk from nontrading positions, such as any duration mismatch in loans held to maturity.

Appendix D. Regulatory Structure before the Dodd-Frank Act

Regulatory Agency	Institutions Regulated	Emergency/Systemic Risk Powers	Other Notable Authority
Federal Reserve (The Fed)	Bank holding companies,[a] financial holding companies, state banks that are members of the	Lender of last resort to member banks (through discount window lending). In "unusual and exigent circumstances" the	The Fed issues consumer protection regulations under various federal laws,

Appendix D. (Continued)

Regulatory Agency	Institutions Regulated	Emergency/Systemic Risk Powers	Other Notable Authority
	Federal Reserve System, U.S. branches of foreign banks, foreign branches of U.S. banks	Fed may lend to "any individual, partnership, or corporation"	including the Truth-in-Lending Act
Office of the Comptroller of the Currency (OCC)	National banks, U.S. federal branches of foreign banks		
Federal Deposit Insurance Corporation (FDIC)	Federally insured depository institutions, including state banks that are not members of the Federal Reserve System	After making a determination of systemic risk, the FDIC may invoke broad authority to use the deposit insurance funds to provide an array of assistance to depository institutions	
Office of Thrift Supervision (OTS)	Federally chartered and insured thrift institutions, savings and loan holding companies		
National Credit Union Administration (NCUA)	Federally chartered or insured credit unions	Serves as a liquidity lender to credit unions experiencing liquidity shortfalls through the Central Liquidity Facility	Operates a deposit insurance fund for credit unions, the National Credit Union Share Insurance Fund (NCUSIF)

Regulatory Agency	Institutions Regulated	Emergency/Systemic Risk Powers	Other Notable Authority
Securities and Exchange Commission (SEC)	Securities exchanges, brokers, and dealers; mutual funds; investment advisers. Registers corporate securities sold to the public	May unilaterally close markets or suspend trading strategies for limited periods	Authorized to set financial accounting standards which all publicly traded firms must use
Commodity Futures Trading Commission (CFTC)	Futures exchanges, brokers, pool operators, advisers	May suspend trading, order liquidation of positions, or raise margins in emergencies	
Federal Housing Finance Agency (FHFA)	Fannie Mae, Freddie Mac, and the Federal Home Loan Banks	Acting as conservator (since Sept. 2008) for Fannie and Freddie	

Source: CRS.

Note: Provisions in italics were repealed by Dodd-Frank. a. See Appendix B.

APPENDIX E. ACRONYMS

AICPA	American Institute of Certified Public Accountants
BIS	Bank for International Settlements
CAMELS	Capital Adequacy, Asset Quality, Management, Earnings, Liquidity, Sensitivity to Market Risk
CFTC	Commodity Futures Trading Commission
CSE	Consolidated Supervised Entities
DIF	Deposit Insurance Fund
EESA	Emergency Economic Stabilization Act
FASB	Financial Accounting Standards Board
FCM	Futures Commission Merchant
FDIC	Federal Deposit Insurance Corporation
FDICIA	The FDIC Improvement Act of 1991

FFIEC	Federal Financial Institution Examination Council
FHFA	Federal Housing Finance Agency
FHFB	Federal Housing Finance Board
FINRA	Financial Industry Regulatory Authority
FIRREA	The Financial Institutions Reform, Recovery, and Enforcement Act of 1989
FRB	Federal Reserve Board
FSOC	Financial Stability Oversight Council
FSLIC	Federal Savings and Loan Insurance Corporation
FX	Foreign Exchange
GLBA	Gramm-Leach-Bliley Act
GAAP	Generally Accepted Accounting Principles
GSE	Government-Sponsored Enterprise
NCUA	National Credit Union Administration
OCC	Office of the Comptroller of the Currency
OFHEO	Office of Federal Housing Enterprise Oversight
OFR	Office of Financial Research
OTS	Office of Thrift Supervision
PCS	Payment, Clearing, and Settlement Systems
PWG	President's Working Group on Capital Markets
SEC	Securities and Exchange Commission
SIPC	Securities Investor Protection Corporation
SRO	Self Regulatory Organization
UFIRS	Uniform Financial Institutions Rating System

APPENDIX F. GLOSSARY OF TERMS

This glossary has been compiled from several earlier CRS reports, the CFTC and SIFMA websites, and other sources.

Affiliate—A corporate relationship of control. Two companies are affiliated when one owns all or a large part of another, or when both are controlled by a third (holding) company. (See "Subsidiary.") All subsidiaries are affiliates, but affiliates that are less than 50% controlled are usually not treated as subsidiaries.

Agency relationship—A business relationship of two parties in which one represents the other in transactions with third parties. The agent negotiates on behalf of the party actually at risk, who is known as the "principal." A commission goes to the agent who does not take on the risk of the transaction; the profit or loss goes to the principal.

Asset-backed security—A bond that represents a share in a pool of debt obligations or other assets. The holder is entitled to some part of the repayment flows from the underlying debt. (See "Securitization.") Mortgage-backed securities and asset backed commercial paper are examples of this.

Bank holding company—A business incorporated under state law, which controls through equity ownership ("holds") one or more banks and, often, other affiliates in financial services as allowed by its regulator, the Federal Reserve. On the federal level, these businesses are regulated through the Bank Holding Company Act.

Bank Holding Company Act—The federal statute under which the Federal Reserve regulates bank holding companies and financial holding companies (FHC). Besides the permissible financial activities enumerated in the Gramm-Leach-Bliley Act (P.L. 106-102), the law provides a mechanism between the Federal Reserve and the Department of the Treasury to decide what is an appropriate new financial activity for FHCs.

Basel Accords—International banking agreements coordinated through the Basel Committee on Bank Supervision (BCBS), which provides recommendations on banking regulations among participating countries.

Blue sky laws—State statutes that govern the offering and selling of securities.

Broker/dealer—An individual or firm that buys and sells securities for itself as well as for customers. Broker/dealers are registered with the Securities and Exchange Commission.

Bubble—Self-reinforcing process in which the price of an asset exceeds its fundamental value for a sustained period, often followed by a rapid price decline. Speculative bubbles are usually associated with a "bandwagon" effect in which speculators rush to buy the commodity (in the case of futures, "to take positions") before the price trend ends, and an even greater rush to sell the commodity (unwind positions) when prices reverse.

Capital requirements—Capital is the owners' stake in an enterprise. It is a critical line of defense when losses occur, both in banking and nonbanking enterprises. Capital requirements help assure that losses that might occur will accrue to the institution incurring them. In the case of banking institutions experiencing problems, capital also serves as a buffer against losses to the federal deposit insurance funds.

Charter conversion—Banking institutions may, with the approval of their regulators, switch their corporate form between: commercial bank or savings institution, National or State charter, and to stockholder ownership from depositor ownership. Various regulatory conditions may encourage switching.

Clearing Organization—An entity through which futures and other derivative transactions are cleared and settled. A clearing organization may be a division or affiliate of a particular exchange, or a freestanding entity. Also called a clearing house, multilateral clearing organization, or clearing association.

Collateralized debt obligation (CDO)—A bond created by the securitization of a pool of asset-backed securities.

Collateralized mortgage obligation (CMO)—A multiclass bond backed by a pool of mortgage pass-through securities or mortgage loans.

Commercial bank—A deposit-taking institution that can make commercial loans, accept checking accounts, and whose deposits are insured by the Federal Deposit Insurance Corporation. National banks are chartered by the Office of the Comptroller of the Currency; state banks, by the individual states.

Commodity Futures Modernization Act of 2000 (CFMA; P.L. 106-554, 114 Stat. 2763)— Overhauled the Commodity Exchange Act to create a flexible structure for the regulation of futures and options trading, and established a broad statutory exemption from regulation for OTC derivatives. Largely repealed by the Dodd-Frank Act.

Community financial institution—As provided for in the Gramm-Leach-Bliley Act, a member of the Federal Home Loan Bank System whose deposits are insured under the Federal Deposit Insurance Act and which has assets of less than $500 million (calculated according to provisions in the law, and in succeeding years to be adjusted for inflation). Such institutions may become members without meeting requirements with regard to the percentage of total assets that must be in residential mortgage loans and may borrow from the Federal Home Loan Banks for small business and agriculture.

Conservatorship—When an insolvent financial institution is reorganized by a regulator with the intent to restoring it to an ongoing business.

Counterparty—The opposite party in a bilateral agreement, contract, or transaction, such as a swap.

Credit Default Swap (CDS)—A tradeable contract in which one party agrees to pay another if a third party experiences a credit event, such as default on a debt obligation, bankruptcy, or credit rating downgrade.

Credit Risk—The risk that a borrower will fail to repay a loan in full, or that a derivatives counterparty will default.

Credit union—A nonprofit financial cooperative of individuals with one or more common bonds (such as employment, labor union membership, or residence in the same neighborhood). May be state or nationally chartered. Credit unions accept deposits of members' savings and transaction balances in the form of share accounts, pay dividends (interest) on them out of earnings, and primarily provide consumer credit to members. The federal regulator for credit unions is the National Credit Union Administration (NCUA).

Dealer—An individual or financial firm engaged in the purchase and sale of securities and commodities such as metals, foreign exchange, etc., for its own account and at its own risk as principal (see broker). Commercial banks are typically limited to acting as dealers in specified high-quality debt obligations, such as those of the federal government.

Depository institution—Customarily refers to commercial banks, savings institutions, and credit unions, since traditionally the greater part of their funding has been in the form of deposits. Deposits are a customer's funds placed with an institution according to agreed-upon terms and conditions and represent a credit to the depositor.

Derivatives—Financial contracts whose value is linked to the price of an underlying commodity or financial variable (such as an interest rate, currency price, or stock index). Ownership of a derivative does not require the holder to actually buy or sell the underlying interest. Derivatives are used by hedgers, who seek to shift risk to others, and speculators, who can profit if they can successfully forecast price trends. Examples include futures contracts, options, and swaps.

Discount window—Figurative term for the Federal Reserve facility for extending credit directly to eligible depository institutions. It may be used to relieve temporary cash shortages at banks and other depository institutions. Borrowers are expected to have tried to borrow elsewhere first and must provide collateral as security for loans. The term derives from the practice whereby bankers would come to a Reserve Bank teller window to obtain credit in the early days of the Federal Reserve System.

Dual banking system—The phrase refers to the fact that banks may be either federally or state-chartered. In the case of state-chartered banks, the state is the primary regulator; for national banks, the Office of the Comptroller of the Currency is the primary regulator.

Electronic fund transfer (EFT) systems—A variety of systems and technologies for transferring funds electronically rather than by paper check.

Exchange—A central marketplace with established rules and regulations where buyers and sellers meet to trade futures and options contracts or securities.

Federal Home Loan Banks—Twelve regional member-owned federally sponsored organizations that extend credit to their member banking institutions, largely to finance mortgages made to homeowners. The 12 FHLBs make up a single government-sponsored enterprise.

Federal safety net—A broad term referring to protection of banking institutions through deposit insurance, discount window credit, other lender of last resort support, and certain forms of regulations to reduce risk. Commercial and industrial companies generally lack any of these cushions against loss.

Financial businesses—In discussions about financial services modernization, usually refers to commercial banks and savings institutions, securities firms, and insurance companies and agents, as contrasted with commercial and industrial firms.

Financial holding company—A form of bank holding company authorized by the GrammLeach-Bliley Act that may control one or more banks, securities firms, and insurance companies.

Financial institution—An enterprise that uses its funds chiefly to purchase financial assets such as loans and debt securities, as opposed to tangible property. Financial institutions are differentiated by the manner in which they invest their funds: in loans, bonds, stocks, or some combination; as well as by their sources of funds. Depository financial institutions are differentiated in that they may accept deposits which are federally insured against loss to the depositor. Nondepository financial institutions such as life and property/casualty insurance companies, pension funds, and mutual funds obtain funds through other types of receipts, whose values may fluctuate with market conditions.

Financial subsidiary—Under the Gramm-Leach-Bliley Act, both national and state-chartered banks are authorized to form financial subsidiaries to engage in activities that would not otherwise be permitted within the bank itself, subject to certain limits. Besides the permissible financial activities enumerated in P.L. 106-102, the law provides a mechanism between the U.S. Department of the Treasury and the Federal Reserve to decide what is an appropriate new financial activity for a financial subsidiary.

Firewalls—Barriers to the flow of capital, information, management, and other resources among business units owned by a common entity. In case of financial distress of one operation ("fire"), the "walls" are intended to prevent the spread of loss to the other units—especially to banking units. Example:

losses in a securities subsidiary of a holding company could not be covered by any of the holding company's bank subsidiaries.

Foreign bank—Banks and their holding companies headquartered in other countries may have a variety of financial operations in the United States: U.S.-chartered subsidiary banks, agencies, branches, and representative offices. Their primary federal regulator is the Federal Reserve, under the International Banking Act of 1978 as amended. States and the Office of the Comptroller of the Currency may also regulate them, depending on whether they have a state or federal charter.

Forward Contract—A cash transaction in which a buyer and seller agree upon delivery of a specified quality and quantity of goods at a specified future date.

Functional regulation—Regulatory arrangements based on activity ("function") rather than organizational structure. The Gramm-Leach-Bliley Act called for more functional regulation than in the past.

Futures Contract—An agreement to purchase or sell a commodity for delivery in the future: (1) at a price that is determined at initiation of the contract; (2) that obligates each party to the contract to fulfill the contract at the specified price; (3) that is used to assume or shift price risk; and (4) that may be satisfied by delivery or offset.

Glass-Steagall Act—Part of the Banking Act of 1933; divided the commercial and investment banking industries. The Gramm-Leach-Bliley Act repealed two sections of the act dealing with the relationship between banks and securities firms.

Government-sponsored enterprise (GSE)—GSEs are private companies with government charters. Government sponsorship typically gives them a funding advantage over purely private competitors, while their charters restrict the kinds of businesses they may conduct.

Gramm-Leach-Bliley Act of 1999—P.L. 106-102, also known as the Financial Services Modernization Act, authorized increased affiliations between banks, securities firms, and insurers. Permitted the establishment of financial holding companies, under the regulation of the Federal Reserve. Also addressed privacy protection for consumers' financial data.

Haircut—In computing the value of assets for purposes of capital, segregation, or margin requirements, a percentage reduction from the stated value (e.g., book value or market value) to account for possible declines in value that may occur before assets can be liquidated.

Hedge funds—Hedge funds are essentially unregulated mutual funds. They are pools of invested money that buy and sell stocks and bonds and many other assets, including precious metals, commodities, foreign currencies, and derivatives (contracts whose prices are derived from those of other financial instruments). Hedge funds are limited to qualified investors with high net worth.

Hedging—Investing with the intention of reducing the impact of adverse movements in interest rates, commodities, or securities prices. Typically, the hedging instrument gains value as the hedged item loses value, and vice versa.

Insolvent—A firm whose liabilities exceed its assets.

Institutional regulation—Regulation that is institution-specific as contrasted with activity-specific (see functional regulation).

Investment bank—A financial intermediary, active in the securities business. Investment banking functions include underwriting (marketing newly registered securities to individual or institutional investors), counseling regarding merger and acquisition proposals, brokerage services, advice on corporate financing, and proprietary trading.

Investment bank holding company—A holding company for securities firms authorized under the Gramm-Leach-Bliley Act. Such holding companies are subject to regulation by the Securities and Exchange Commission.

Issuer—A person or entity (including a company or bank) that offers securities for sale. The issuing of securities, where the proceeds accrue to the issuer, is distinct from the secondary, or resale, market, where securities are traded among investors.

Lender of last resort—Governmental lender that acts as the ultimate source of credit in the financial system. In the United States, the Federal Reserve has this role.

Leverage—In derivatives markets, leverage (or "gearing") often refers to the ability to control large dollar amounts of a commodity or security with a comparatively small amount of capital. In banking, the term leverage is often used to describe the amount of a bank's assets that are funded with debt rather than equity. In banking, leverage is typically the ratio of lending to equity.

Limited-purpose bank—Although generally commercial firms may not conduct a banking business, some exceptions exist. Examples: Nonbank banks are banks that either accept deposits or make commercial loans but cannot do both. Such banks grew up through a loophole in the law, which was closed by the Competitive Equality Banking Act of 1987 (CEBA). Credit card banks conduct credit card operations. Industrial loan companies in a few states may offer restricted banking services.

Liquidity—The ability to trade an asset quickly without significantly affecting its price, or the condition of a market with many buyers and sellers present. Also, the ability of a person or firm to access credit markets.

Liquidity risk—The possibility that the market for normally-liquid assets will suddenly dry up, leaving firms unable to convert assets into cash. Also, the risk that other firms will refuse to extend credit on any terms to a firm that is perceived as distressed.

Market risk—The risk that the price of a tradeable security or asset will decline, resulting in a loss to the holder.

Merchant banker—A European style investment banker concentrating on corporate deals, in which it may invest its own funds.

Money market mutual fund (MMF)—A form of mutual fund that pools funds of individuals and other investors for investment in high-grade, short-term debt and bank deposits paying market rates of return. Examples of these money market instruments include U.S. Treasury bills, certificates of deposit, and commercial paper. In addition to the investment features, most MMFs offer check-writing redemption features.

Moral hazard—The tendency of people to take more risks once another party has agreed to provide protection. Regulatory interventions to bail out failing firms are often said to create moral hazard, on the assumption that others will expect to be saved from their mistakes, too.

Mortgage-backed security (MBS)—A bond backed by a pool of mortgage loans. The bondholders receive a share of the interest and principal payments on the underlying mortgages. The cash flows may be divided among different classes of bonds, called tranches.

Mutual fund—An investing company that pools the funds of individuals and other investors, and uses them to purchase large amounts of debt or equity obligations of businesses and sometimes debt obligations of governments. The owners of the mutual fund hold proportional shares in the entire pool of securities in which a fund invests. Owners pay taxes on their distributions from a fund; the mutual fund itself is not normally subject to federal or state income taxation.

Naked option—The sale of a call or put option without holding an equal and opposite position in the underlying instrument.

Operational risk—The possibility that a financial institution will suffer losses from a failure to process transactions properly, from accounting mistakes, from rogue traders or other forms of insider fraud, or from other causes arising inside the institution.

Over-the-counter (OTC)—Trading that does not occur on a centralized exchange or trading facility. OTC transactions can occur electronically or over the telephone.

Ponzi Scheme—Named after Charles Ponzi, a man with a remarkable criminal career in the early 20th century, the term has been used to describe pyramid arrangements whereby an enterprise makes payments to investors from the proceeds of a later investment rather than from profits of the underlying business venture, as the investors expected, and gives investors the impression that a legitimate profit-making business or investment opportunity exists, where in fact it is a mere fiction.

Prompt corrective action (PCA)—A framework of bank regulation in which banks with insufficient capital must undertake remedial action to improve their capital positions. In the United States, the PCA framework has five categories of bank capitalization. Financially troubled banks are required to take prompt action as directed by the relevant agencies to remedy identified deficiencies.

Receivership—When an insolvent financial institution is taken over with the intent to liquidate its assets.

Regulatory Arbitrage—If different contract types or firm charters can be used to achieve similar ends, but have different regulatory treatment, then regulatory arbitrage refers to attempts to receive the least burdensome regulatory treatment for a given activity. In economics, arbitrage is the practice of taking advantage of a price difference between two or more markets.

Resolution Trust Corporation (RTC)—The agency set up to resolve savings and loans declared failed beginning in 1989. Between 1989 and mid-1995, the Resolution Trust Corporation closed or otherwise resolved 747 thrifts with total assets of $394 billion.

Repurchase Agreement (Repo)—A contract in which one party sells a contract (typically a bond or other debt contract) to buyer, with a commitment to repurchase the contract on a future date at a specified price. In economics, repurchase agreements have similar characteristics to collateralized lending.

Savings association—A savings and loan association, mutual savings bank, or federal savings bank, whose primary function has traditionally been to encourage personal saving (thrift) and home buying through mortgage lending. In recent years, such institutions' charters have been expanded to allow them to provide commercial loans and a broader range of consumer financial services. The federal regulator for most savings associations is the

Office of Thrift Supervision. Also known as savings and loans, thrifts, and mutual savings banks.

Securities Investor Protection Corporation (SIPC)—A private nonprofit membership corporation set up under federal law to provide financial protection for the customers of failed brokers and/or dealers. SIPC is a liquidator; it has no supervisory or regulatory responsibilities for its members, nor is it authorized to bail out or in other ways assist a failing firm.

Securitization—The process of transforming a cash flow, typically from debt repayments, into a new marketable security. Holders of the securitized instrument receive interest and principal payments as the underlying loans are repaid. Types of loans that are frequently securitized are home mortgages, credit card receivables, student loans, small business loans, and car loans.

Self-regulatory organizations (SROs)—National securities or futures exchanges, national securities or futures associations, clearing agencies and the Municipal Securities Rulemaking Board are all authorized to make and enforce rules governing market participants. The respective federal regulatory agency has authority in connection with SROs and may require them to adopt or modify their rules. Examples of SROs in the securities industry include the Financial Industry Regulatory Authority (FINRA), and the New York Stock Exchange.

Shadow banking—The funding of loans through firms that do not have bank charters, through securities markets, or the funding of banks with sources other than deposits. Often, the term shadow banking is used to describe financial intermediation with at least one deviation from a model in which banks raise all of their funds from sources with government guarantees (such as deposit insurance) and banks have access to emergency government lending facilities, such as the Federal Reserve's discount window.

Special-purpose entities (SPEs)—Also referred to as off–balance-sheet arrangements, SPEs are legal entities created to perform a specific financial function or transaction. They isolate financial risk from the sponsoring institution and provide less-expensive financing. The assets, liabilities, and cash flows of an SPE do not appear on the sponsoring institution's books.

Speculation—A venture or undertaking of an enterprising nature, especially one involving considerable financial risk on the chance of unusual profit.

State regulation—Under the dual system of bank regulation, states as well as the federal government may charter, regulate, and supervise depository institutions. States are the primary regulators in the insurance field. States also have authority over securities companies, mortgage lending companies, personal finance companies, and other types of companies offering financial services.

Structured debt—Debt that has been customized for the buyer, often by incorporating complex derivatives.

Subordinated debt—Debt over which senior debt takes priority. In the event of bankruptcy, subordinated debt holders receive payment only after senior debt claims are paid in full.

Subsidiary—A company whose controlling shares are owned 50% or more by another ("parent") corporation. Like companies with less than 50% ownership, it is an affiliate of the controlling company. A subsidiary is usually consolidated for regulatory and reporting purposes with its parent.

Swap—The exchange of one asset or liability for a similar asset or liability for the purpose of lengthening or shortening maturities, or otherwise shifting risks. For example, parties could exchange a fixed interest rate stream of income for a floating rate stream of income, or a stream of income based on one currency's exchange rate for a stream of income based on another currency's exchange rate.

Systemic Risk—The term *systemic risk* does not have a single, agreed-upon definition. Some define systemic risk as the risk an institution faces that it cannot diversify against. In other circumstances, systemic risk is defined as the risk that the linkages between institutions may affect the financial system as a whole, through a dynamic sometimes referred to as contagion.

Thrift holding company—Also known as a savings and loan holding company, a business that controls one or more savings associations. These holding companies are regulated under the Home Owners' Loan Act by the Office of Thrift Supervision.

Too-big-to-fail doctrine—An implicit regulatory policy holding that very large financial institutions must be rescued by the government, because their failure would destabilize the entire financial system. (See "Moral Hazard.")

Umbrella supervision—The term applied to comprehensive regulation of a holding company and its parts by one or more holding company regulator(s).

Underwriter—For securities markets, see investment bankers. For insurance, underwriters are the life, health and property-casualty companies that receive premiums and pay off losses and other risks as they occur. The underwriters bear the risks of losses and expenses exceeding receipts.

Unitary thrift holding company (UTHC)—A holding company that owns a single thrift institution. A distinction between UTHCs and other thrift holding companies has been that a UTHC could be involved in any lines of business, whereas the others have been restricted to certain activities primarily financial in nature. The Gramm-Leach-Bliley Act limits the commercial activities and affiliations of new UTHCs.

Universal bank—An organizational model typical of some foreign countries whereby a bank can exist as an operating enterprise and own directly a variety of other businesses. (See "Subsidiary.") It contrasts with the banking model typical in the United States where the parent holding company owns several different businesses, all structurally separate. (See "Affiliate.") In practice, the two approaches are not exclusive.

Volcker Rule—Section 619 of the Dodd-Frank Act, which prohibits insured depository banks and their affiliated firms from engaging in proprietary trading or affiliating with hedge funds.

End Notes

[1] A fifth agency, the Office of Thrift Supervision (OTS), was abolished in 2010, and its responsibilities were spread among other agencies. Its prudential regulation of thrift depositories was transferred to the Office of the Comptroller of the Currency. Its prudential regulation of thrift holding companies was transferred to the Federal Reserve.

[2] The Federal Reserve also provides prudential regulation to certain nonbank financial companies and financial-market utilities that are designated as systemic.

[3] Although the distinction between prudence-based regulators and disclosure-based regulators may be true in general, bank regulators can regulate the disclosures of their chartered firms and securities and derivatives regulators do have some prudential responsibilities. For example, Section 731 of the Dodd-Frank Act instructs derivatives regulators to set capital requirements for major swap participants.

[4] The term *agency* is being used to describe the functional relationship and does not imply any contractual obligation.

[5] The term *agent* is being used to describe the functional relationship, not any contractual obligations.

[6] See, e.g., U.S. Department of the Treasury, *Blueprint for a Modern Financial Regulatory Structure*, March 2008, which called for a three-agency structure: a systemic risk regulator, a markets supervisor, and a consumer regulator.

[7] "Competition Among Bank Regulators," John Weinberg, *Economic Quarterly*, Fall 2002, available at http://www.richmondfed.org/publications/research/economic_quarterly/2002/fall/pdf/weinberg.pdf.

[8] Illustrations of several forms of depository organization are presented in Appendix B.

[9] Historically, "banks" also referred to firms with special charters that issued debt, which often circulated as currency. The Bank of England had been granted a monopoly on this form of banking (note issue), which was determined not to extend to depository banking in the nineteenth century.

[10] As described in a *Wall Street Journal* article, available at http://online.wsj.com/article/SB10000872396390444433504577649971326432962.html.

[11] This report will not track the ultimate fate of the ice cream shop. The owner reportedly changed the name to remove the word bank. Regulatory interaction is likely to be ongoing. For example, see "Pittsburgh ice cream bank owner says regulators are backing off," WTAE News, available at http://www.wtae.com/news/local/allegheny/Pittsburgh-icecream-bank-owner-says-regulators-are-backing-off/-/10927008/19522712/-/asy08i/-/index.html.

[12] Regulatory uses of "capital" include more specific definitions and classifications.

[13] See CRS Report R42744, *U.S. Implementation of the Basel Capital Regulatory Framework*, by Darryl E. Getter.

[14] Bank for International Settlements, "About the Basel Committee," January 23, 2013, available at http://www.bis.org/ bcbs/about.htm.

[15] Section 135 of the Emergency Economic Stabilization Act of 2008 (EESA; P.L. 110-343).

[16] CRS Report R41718, *Federal Deposit Insurance for Banks and Credit Unions*, by Darryl E. Getter.

[17] FDICIA created a new Section 13(c)(4) of the Federal Deposit Insurance Act, 12 USC §1823(c)(4)(G).

[18] FDIC, "FDIC Announces Plan to Free Up Bank Liquidity," press release, October 14, 2008, http://www.fdic.gov/ news/news/press/2008/pr08100.html.

[19] For more detail, see CRS Report R41384, *The Dodd-Frank Wall Street Reform and Consumer Protection Act: Systemic Risk and the Federal Reserve*, by Marc Labonte.

[20] A counter example would be SEC's net capital rule as discussed below in "The SEC's Net Capital Rule."

[21] See CRS Report RL34420, *Bear Stearns: Crisis and "Rescue" for a Major Provider of Mortgage-Related Products*, by Gary Shorter.

[22] See CRS Report RL34427, *Financial Turmoil: Federal Reserve Policy Responses*, by Marc Labonte.

[23] SEC, "Holding Company Supervision Program Description: Consolidated Supervised Entities ("CSEs")," http://www.sec.gov/divisions/marketreg/hcsupervision.htm.

[24] The Market Reform Act of 1990 permits the SEC to collect certain financial information from unregulated affiliates of broker/dealers, under the Broker-Dealer Risk Assessment Program. The impetus for the CSE program was a European Union requirement that investment banks operating in Europe be subject to consolidated financial supervision.

[25] Some argue that CSE allowed the investment banks to hold less capital and increase their leverage. For two views on this issue, see Stephen Labaton, "Agency's '04 Rule Let Banks Pile Up New Debt, and Risk," *New York Times*, October 3, 2008, p. A1, and Testimony of SEC Chairman Christopher Cox, House Oversight and Government Reform Committee, October 23, 2008. (Response to question from Rep. Christopher Shays.)

[26] By becoming bank holding companies, Morgan Stanley and Goldman Sachs placed themselves under Federal Reserve regulation, presumably to signal to the markets that their financial condition was being monitored and to gain access to the Fed's lending facilities.

[27] SEC, "Chairman Cox Announces End of Consolidated Supervised Entities Program," press release 2008-230.

[28] For more on GSEs and their regulation, see CRS Reports CRS Report R40800, *GSEs and the Government's Role in Housing Finance: Issues for the 113th Congress*, by N. Eric Weiss.

[29] See CRS Report R42760, *Fannie Mae's and Freddie Mac's Financial Status: Frequently Asked Questions*, by N. Eric Weiss.

[30] See CRS Report R41338, *The Dodd-Frank Wall Street Reform and Consumer Protection Act: Title X, The Consumer Financial Protection Bureau*, by David H. Carpenter. CRS Report

R42615, *A Brief Overview of Actions Taken by the Consumer Financial Protection Bureau (CFPB) in Its First Year*, by Sean M. Hoskins.

[31] See CRS Report R41384, *The Dodd-Frank Wall Street Reform and Consumer Protection Act: Systemic Risk and the Federal Reserve*, by Marc Labonte.

[32] P.L. 95-630, 92 STAT. 3641.

[33] Executive Order 12631, March 18, 1988, 53 FR 9421.

[34] President's Working Group on Financial Markets, "Policy Statement on Financial Market Developments," March 2008, http://www.ustreas.gov/press/releases/reports/pwgpolicy statemktturmoil_03122008.pdf.

[35] Securities and Exchange Commission, "President's Working Group Report on Money Market Fund Reform," Release No. IC-29497; File No. 4-619, available at http://www.sec.gov/ rules/other/2010/ic-29497.pdf.

[36] See Sections 1142 and 1143 of the Housing and Economic Recovery Act of 2008, P.L. 110-289.

[37] This is an example of the SEC regulation for the risk that a firm takes, as alluded to in the description of the SEC.

[38] National Futures Association, *NFA Manual/Rules*, Section 7001, http://www.nfa.futures.org/ nfaManual/manualFinancial.asp#fins1.

[39] Bank for International Settlements, *Triennial Central Bank Survey of Foreign Exchange and Derivatives Market Activity*, September 2010, http://www.bis.org/publ/rpfxf10t.htm.

[40] See http://www.newyorkfed.org/aboutthefed/fedpoint/fed02.html.

[41] Federal Reserve Bank of New York, "Federal Reserve Announces Establishment of Primary Dealer Credit Facility," Press Release, March 16, 2008, http://www.newyorkfed.org/ newsevents/news/markets/2008/rp080316.html.

[42] Dodd-Frank Act, Section 616.

[43] The Comptrollers handbooks are occasionally updated. The handbook for the Bank Supervision Process can be found at http://www.occ.gov/handbook/banksup.pdf.

In: U.S. Financial Regulatory Structure ISBN: 978-1-63485-636-2
Editor: Laurence Watson

Chapter 2

FINANCIAL REGULATION: COMPLEX AND FRAGMENTED STRUCTURE COULD BE STREAMLINED TO IMPROVE EFFECTIVENESS*

United States Government Accountability Office

WHY GAO DID THIS STUDY

The U.S. financial regulatory structure has evolved over the past 150 years in response to various financial crises and the need to keep pace with developments in financial markets and products in recent decades.

GAO was asked to review the financial regulatory structure and any related impacts of fragmentation or overlap. This report examines the structure of the financial regulatory system and the effects of fragmentation and overlap on regulators' oversight activities. GAO reviewed relevant laws and agency documents on their oversight responsibilities; held discussion groups with former regulators, industry representatives, and experts; and interviewed agency officials.

* This is an edited, reformatted and augmented version of a United States Government Accountability Office, Publication No. GAO-16-175, dated February 2016.

What GAO Recommends

Congress should consider whether changes to the financial regulatory structure are needed to reduce or better manage fragmentation and overlap. Congress should also consider whether legislative changes are needed to align FSOC's authorities with its mission to respond to systemic risks. GAO also recommends that OFR and the Federal Reserve (1) jointly articulate individual and common goals for their systemic risk monitoring activities and engage in collaborative practices to support those goals; and (2) regularly and fully incorporate their monitoring tools, assessments, or results of monitoring activities into Systemic Risk Committee deliberations. Federal Reserve and OFR agreed with GAO's recommendations.

What GAO Found

The U.S. financial regulatory structure is complex, with responsibilities fragmented among multiple agencies that have overlapping authorities. As a result, financial entities may fall under the regulatory authority of multiple regulators depending on the types of activities in which they engage (see figure 2 in this chapter). While the Dodd-Frank Wall Street Reform and Consumer Protection Act (Dodd-Frank Act) made a number of reforms to the financial regulatory system, it generally left the regulatory structure unchanged.

U.S. regulators and others have noted that the structure has contributed to the overall growth and stability in the U.S. economy. However, it also has created challenges to effective oversight. Fragmentation and overlap have created inefficiencies in regulatory processes, inconsistencies in how regulators oversee similar types of institutions, and differences in the levels of protection afforded to consumers. GAO has long reported on these effects in multiple areas of the regulatory system. For example,

- **Depository institutions.** Inconsistencies in examination activities of the depository institution regulators can result in different conclusions regarding the safety and soundness of an institution and difficulties identifying emerging trends.

- **Securities and derivatives markets.** Securities and derivatives markets have become increasingly interconnected, and regulation of these markets by separate agencies has created challenges. For example, regulation of entities that engage in similar activities is at times duplicative and at other times inconsistent.
- **Insurance.** Insurance regulation is primarily state-based, and a lack of uniformity, including inconsistencies in the licensing of insurance agents and the approval of insurance products, has resulted in uneven consumer protection and increased costs to insurers.

In 2009, GAO established a framework for evaluating regulatory reform proposals and noted that an effective regulatory system would need to address certain structural shortcomings created by fragmentation and overlap. While changes made by the Dodd-Frank Act were consistent with some of the characteristics identified in this framework, the existing regulatory structure does not always ensure (1) efficient and effective oversight, (2) consistent financial oversight, and (3) consistent consumer protections. As a result, negative effects of fragmented and overlapping authorities persist throughout the system. For example, regulation of the swaps and security-based swaps markets by separate agencies creates potential market inefficiencies because of differences in certain of the agencies' rules for each product. GAO has previously made suggestions to Congress to modernize and improve the effectiveness of the financial regulatory structure. Without congressional action it is unlikely that remaining fragmentation and overlap in the U.S. financial regulatory system can be reduced or that more effective and efficient oversight of financial institutions can be achieved.

The 2007-2009 financial crisis highlighted the lack of an agency or mechanism responsible for monitoring and addressing risks across the financial system. The Dodd-Frank Act tried to address this gap in systemic risk oversight by placing this responsibility on a collective group of financial regulators and other entities through the creation of the Financial Stability Oversight Council (FSOC) and the Office of Financial Research (OFR). However, collaborative efforts have not been sufficient, and FSOC's authorities are limited and unclear. Specifically:

- The Board of Governors of the Federal Reserve System (Federal Reserve) and OFR have been developing systemic risk monitoring efforts with similar goals, but have not effectively engaged in key collaboration practices that GAO has previously identified. As a result, OFR and the Federal Reserve could miss opportunities to benefit from each other's work and may conduct unnecessarily duplicative analyses.

- FSOC's Systemic Risk Committee has improved interagency collaboration on systemic risk monitoring among regulators, but its process for identifying new threats continues to be based on participants' expert views and is not fully informed by OFR or the Federal Reserve's systemic risk monitoring efforts. Federal internal control standards call for the use of relevant, reliable, and timely information to achieve the entity's responsibilities. Without better access to existing systemic risk monitoring tools and other outputs, the committee may miss some risks or not identify them in a timely manner.
- Although FSOC's mission is to respond to systemic risks, which may involve multiple entities, its recommendations are not binding and do not guarantee regulatory response. FSOC has authorities to designate certain entities or activities for enhanced supervision by a specific regulator, but these authorities may not allow FSOC to address certain broader risks that are not specific to a particular entity. For such risks, FSOC can recommend but not compel action. GAO's 2009 framework states that financial systems should include a mechanism for managing risks regardless of the source of the risks, and international best practices for systemic risk oversight state that macroprudential entities require authorities to foster the ability to act and ensure regulatory responses. Because of the limitations in FSOC's authorities, without congressional action FSOC may not have the tools it needs to carry out its mission to comprehensively respond to systemic risks, and it may be difficult to hold the council accountable for doing so.

ABBREVIATIONS

AIG	American International Group, Inc.
Basel Committee	Basel Committee on Banking Supervision
BSA	Bank Secrecy Act
CEA	Commodity Exchange Act

CFPB	Consumer Financial Protection Bureau
CFTC	Commodity Futures Trading Commission
CSBS	Conference of State Banking Supervisors
CSE	consolidated supervised entities
Dodd-Frank Act	Dodd-Frank Wall Street Reform and Consumer Protection Act
FDIC	Federal Deposit Insurance Corporation
Federal Reserve	Board of Governors of the Federal Reserve System
FFIEC	Federal Financial Institutions Examination Council
FHFA	Federal Housing Finance Agency
FinCEN	Financial Crimes Enforcement Network
FINRA	Financial Industry Regulatory Authority
FIO	Federal Insurance Office
FSB	Financial Stability Board
FSOC	Financial Stability Oversight Council
FTC	Federal Trade Commission
GLBA	Gramm-Leach-Bliley Act of 1999
IAIS	International Association of Insurance Supervisors
IMF	International Monetary Fund
IOSCO	International Organization of Securities Commissions
MOU	memorandum of understanding
MSRB	Municipal Securities Rulemaking Board
NAIC	National Association of Insurance Commissioners
NCUA	National Credit Union Administration
NRSRO	nationally recognized statistical rating organization
OCC	Office of the Comptroller of the Currency
OFHEO	Office of Federal Housing Enterprise Oversight
OFR	Office of Financial Research
OIG	Office of the Inspector General
OTS	Office of Thrift Supervision
PCS	payment, clearing, or settlement
SEC	Securities and Exchange Commission
SRO	self-regulatory organization
Treasury	Department of the Treasury

February 25, 2016

Congressional Requesters

While a fully functioning financial system is critical to the well-being of our citizens and overall economic growth, financial services activities can, at times, cause significant harm, as evidenced in the 2007-2009 financial crisis. In response to this experience and past crises, the U.S. financial regulatory structure has evolved into an extremely complex system. Reforms eliminated some agencies but created others with the intent of more appropriately overseeing ever-evolving financial markets. Most recently, the Dodd-Frank Wall Street Reform and Consumer Protection Act (Dodd-Frank Act) abolished one regulatory agency, created a new regulatory agency, and expanded the authorities of some existing agencies, among other things.[1] The act also established the Financial Stability Oversight Council (FSOC), a council of the heads of the federal financial regulatory agencies, as well as representatives from state regulatory agencies and others in charge of identifying and responding to systemic risks.[2]

You asked us to review the current financial regulatory structure and any effects of fragmentation or overlap. In addition, Congress included a provision in statute for GAO to identify and report to Congress on federal programs, agencies, offices, and initiatives—either within departments or government-wide—that have duplicative goals or activities. This report examines the following: (1) the overall structure of the U.S. financial regulatory system, (2) effects of fragmentation and overlap on agencies' oversight activities, and (3) the collaborative efforts and relevant authorities of agencies involved in systemic risk oversight.

To examine the overall structure of the financial regulatory system, we reviewed financial regulatory statutes, including the Dodd-Frank Act. We divided the financial regulatory structure into the following sectors based on agencies' missions: (1) safety and soundness oversight of depository institutions, (2) consumer protection oversight, (3) securities and derivatives markets oversight, (4) insurance oversight, and (5) systemic risk oversight. In addition, for each sector we reviewed agencies' documents to identify the financial institutions and entities under their jurisdictions and the types of oversight activities each conducts. We also interviewed agency officials and representatives of industry and policy organizations that represent a range of experiences, views, and perspectives. We used procedures outlined in GAO's *Fragmentation, Overlap, and Duplication: An Evaluation and Management*

Guide to help us analyze the information we obtained and identify areas of fragmentation and overlap in the U.S. financial regulatory structure.[3]

To identify the effects of fragmentation and overlap on agencies' oversight activities, we held four discussion groups, reviewed past GAO reports, and reviewed reports from U.S. agencies and international regulatory bodies. The discussion groups, which consisted of a diverse group of former regulatory officials, industry and advocacy group representatives, and experts, covered the following areas:

- the supervision of bank and thrift holding companies and their depository subsidiaries by the Federal Deposit Insurance Corporation (FDIC), Board of Governors of the Federal Reserve System (Federal Reserve), Office of the Comptroller of the Currency (OCC), and state banking supervisors;
- consumer protection oversight conducted by the Bureau of Consumer Financial Protection, also known as the Consumer Financial Protection Bureau (CFPB), and the federal prudential regulators—FDIC, the Federal Reserve, the National Credit Union Administration (NCUA), and OCC;
- the regulation of swaps and security-based swaps by the Commodity Futures Trading Commission (CFTC) and the Securities and Exchange Commission (SEC);[4] and
- the supervision of insurance groups by state insurance regulators and the Federal Reserve.

We chose these topics because either the Dodd-Frank Act altered the regulatory structure in the area or the issue had been widely identified as a potential cause of the 2007-2009 financial crisis. In each discussion group, we asked participants to help identify (1) areas of fragmentation and overlap in agencies' responsibilities for the specific topic and the effects of fragmentation and overlap on agencies' oversight activities and (2) possible approaches to help mitigate any negative effects from the fragmentation and overlap. Our discussion groups were not designed to achieve agreement or consensus among participants. Rather, we sought participants' help to identify areas of fragmentation and overlap and the effects they have in each of the four topic areas. We interviewed relevant agency officials after the discussion groups were held to get their perspectives on the areas identified by discussion group participants. We also reviewed our previous reports to identify instances in which we have reported on fragmentation and overlap in the financial regulatory structure and its effects. Additionally, we reviewed recent assessments of the U.S. regulatory structure conducted by the Financial Stability Board (FSB), the International Monetary Fund (IMF), and the Federal Insurance Office (FIO).[5] Finally, we assessed the current regulatory structure and the effects of fragmentation and overlap within it against the characteristics of an effective and efficient regulatory structure that we identified in a January 2009 report in which we developed a framework for evaluating proposals for reforming the regulatory structure.[6]

To examine the collaborative efforts and relevant authorities of agencies involved in systemic risk oversight—which includes monitoring the financial system to identify systemic risks and mitigating those risks—we first identified agencies with explicit systemic risk authorities, goals, or activities by reviewing the Dodd-Frank Act, our previous reports, and agencies' strategic plans, websites, and other documents, and by interviewing federal and state financial agencies. We consequently focused our assessment on the systemic risk monitoring and identification activities of FSOC's Systemic Risk Committee, as the FSOC committee where interagency staff meet to identify, monitor, and analyze systemic risks; the Office of Financial Research (OFR); and the Federal Reserve; as those were the three entities that were actively monitoring the broader financial system with the purpose of identifying and analyzing potential systemic risks. We analyzed, among other things, annual reports, strategic documents, bylaws, and other public and internal documents from FSOC, OFR, and the Federal Reserve from 2011 to 2015, as well as agendas and presentations from monthly FSOC Systemic Risk Committee meetings held between July 2012 and August 2014. We evaluated these three agencies' actions against federal internal control standards and our key interagency collaboration practices, as well as best practices identified by IMF on systemic risk monitoring.[7] In addition, we interviewed staff from FSOC member agencies who participated in Systemic Risk Committee discussions, including staff from OFR and the Federal Reserve. We also interviewed academics and industry experts who served on OFR's Financial Research Advisory Council. Finally, to assess FSOC's and FSOC member agencies' authorities to mitigate identified systemic risks, we reviewed the Dodd-Frank Act, FSOC annual report recommendations, and FSOC's proposed Section 120 recommendation.[8] We also interviewed participants in FSOC's Financial Market Utilities and Payment, Clearing, and Settlement Activities Committee to understand FSOC's authority to designate payment, clearing, or settlement (PCS) activities as systemically important and actions the committee has taken to implement this authority. We evaluated FSOC's authorities against our

January 2009 framework and against IMF's best practices for systemic risk oversight.[9] Appendix I contains a detailed description of our scope and methodology.

We conducted this performance audit from April 2014 to February 2016 in accordance with generally accepted government auditing standards. Those standards require that we plan and perform the audit to obtain sufficient, appropriate evidence to provide a reasonable basis for our findings and conclusions based on our audit objectives. We believe that the evidence obtained provides a reasonable basis for our findings and conclusions based on our audit objectives.

BACKGROUND

The federal laws related to financial regulation set forth specific authorities and responsibilities for regulators. Although these authorities typically do not explicitly link such responsibilities to overall goals of financial regulation, we have grouped them into four broad categories based on the principal goal of the regulatory activity:

- *Monitor the safety and soundness of institutions.* Because markets sometimes lead financial institutions to take on excessive risks that can have significant negative effects on consumers, investors, and taxpayers, regulators oversee, among other things, risk-taking activities to promote the safety and soundness of financial institutions.
- *Ensure adequate consumer and investor protections.* Financial institutions' incentives to maximize profits can in some cases lead to sales of unsuitable or fraudulent financial products, or unfair or deceptive acts or practices. In response, regulators take steps to address informational disadvantages that consumers and investors may face, ensure consumers and investors have sufficient information to make appropriate decisions, and oversee business conduct and sales practices to prevent fraud and abuse.
- *Ensure the integrity and fairness of markets.* Some market participants may seek to manipulate markets to obtain unfair gains in a way that is not easily detectable by other participants. In response, regulators set rules for and monitor markets and their participants to

prevent fraud and manipulation, limit problems in asset pricing, and help ensure efficient market activity.

- *Act to ensure the stability of the overall financial system.* Because shocks to the system or the actions of financial institutions can lead to instability in the broader financial system and real economy, regulators act to reduce systemic risk.

Although these goals have traditionally been their primary focus, financial regulators are also often tasked with achieving other goals as they carry out their activities. These goals can include promoting economic growth, capital formation, and competition in our financial markets. Regulators have also taken actions with an eye toward helping ensure that regulated U.S. financial institutions are competitive with institutions in other sectors or with others around the world. In other cases, financial institutions may be required by law or regulation to foster social policy objectives, such as fair access to credit and increased homeownership.

Overview of GAO's Fragmentation, Overlap, and Duplication Work

In 2010, Congress included a provision in statute for GAO to identify programs, agencies, offices, and initiatives with duplicative goals and activities within departments and government-wide and report to Congress annually.[10] Since March 2011, we have issued annual reports to Congress in response to this requirement.[11] The annual reports describe areas in which we found evidence of fragmentation, overlap, or duplication among federal programs. As shown in figure 1, fragmentation refers to circumstances in which more than one federal agency is involved in the same broad area of national need and opportunities exist to improve service delivery. In this case, the broad area of national need is regulation of the financial system (which also includes oversight by state regulators and industry self-regulatory organizations (SRO)).[12] Overlap occurs when multiple agencies or programs have similar goals, engage in similar activities or strategies to achieve them, or target similar beneficiaries. In the context of financial regulation, overlap in the regulatory structure could refer to several circumstances, such as when multiple regulatory bodies (federal, state, or SROs)

- are involved in the same financial regulatory goal (e.g., safety and soundness or consumer protection);
- engage in similar activities or strategies, such as writing regulations or examining financial institutions to achieve the same financial regulatory goal; or
- perform related regulatory functions for the same or similar financial institutions or entities.

Duplication occurs when two or more agencies or programs are engaged in the same activities or provide the same services to the same beneficiaries. In the case of financial regulation, duplication would occur when more than one agency oversees the same financial institution or entity and engages in the same activities. As in all of GAO's work in this area, overlap and fragmentation might not necessarily lead to actual duplication, and some degree of overlap and duplication may at times be justified.

Fragmentation refers to those circumstances in which more than one federal agency (or more than one organization within an agency) is involved in the same broad area of national need and opportunities exist to improve service delivery.

Overlap occurs when multiple agencies or programs have similar goals, engage in similar activities or strategies to achieve them, or target similar beneficiaries.

Duplication occurs when two or more agencies or programs are engaged in the same activities or provide the same services to the same beneficiaries.

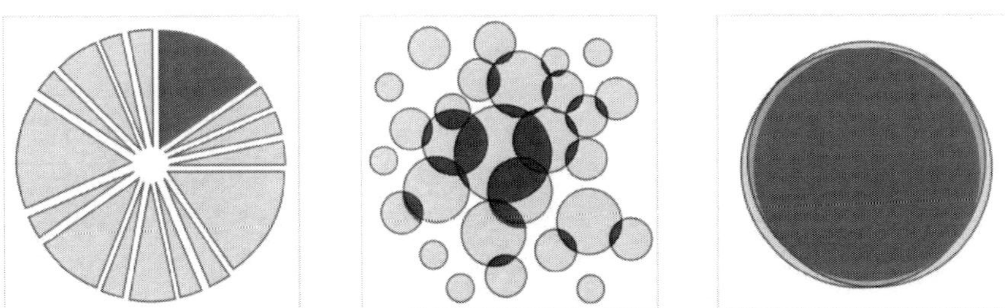

Source: GAO. | GAO-16-175.

Figure 1. Definitions of Fragmentation, Overlap, and Duplication.

The Financial Regulatory Structure Is Fragmented among Multiple Agencies with Overlapping Regulatory Authorities

The United States financial regulatory system is fragmented and complex. Today's financial regulatory system was built over more than a century, evolving over time in response to financial crises and market developments.[13] Most recently, in response to the 2007-2009 financial crisis, the Dodd-Frank Act took a number of steps intended to, among other things, promote the stability of the financial system and expand protections for consumers and investors. In doing so, the act (1) abolished the Office of Thrift Supervision (OTS), the former regulator of thrifts and thrift holding companies, and transferred its authorities to other depository institution and holding company regulators; (2) created CFPB, a new federal consumer financial protection regulator; (3) created FSOC; and (4) created OFR and FIO, two additional nonregulatory offices housed in the Department of the Treasury (Treasury) with mandates that include certain responsibilities related to monitoring systemic risk.[14]

After approximately 150 years of piecemeal changes, the U.S. financial regulatory structure is fragmented among multiple agencies with varying primary missions. These missions can generally be categorized as safety and soundness oversight, consumer protection oversight, securities and derivatives markets oversight, insurance oversight, systemic risk oversight, and consolidated supervision.[15] Table 1 provides a description of these broad regulatory missions.

Table 1. Broad Financial Regulatory Missions

Safety and soundness of depository institutions. Safety and soundness refer to a broad range of issues that relate to the health of a financial institution, including capital requirements, risk management, the quality and diversification of an institution's portfolio, liquidity and funds management, and adequate procedures for internal controls. To achieve their safety and soundness goals, regulators establish capital requirements and conduct on-site examinations and off-site monitoring to assess an institution's financial condition, operational security, and governance, and monitor compliance with applicable laws, regulations, and guidance. Regulators also take enforcement actions, and those who charter institutions may close them based on statutory grounds that include insolvency, illiquidity, and unsafe and unsound condition to transact business.

Consumer protection oversight. Consumer protection oversight generally involves ensuring that consumers have access to markets for consumer financial products and services and that these markets are fair, transparent, and competitive. Regulation covers the offering and provision of consumer financial products and services under consumer protection laws. Depository institutions and certain nondepository institutions are subject to examination by federal, and sometimes state, regulators to help ensure their compliance with consumer protection laws and regulations.

Securities and derivatives markets oversight. Much of the regulation of the securities markets (i.e., debt and equities markets) focuses on integrity of the capital-raising process for companies, resolving conflicts of interest in that process, and requiring full disclosure of material information in order to protect investors and other market users. The prices of stocks traded on the exchanges are generally not regulated; rather, the organization and membership of the exchanges and trading activities are regulated in an attempt to prevent fraud, maintain the integrity of the markets, protect investors, and facilitate capital formation. Securities markets oversight also includes regulation of the asset management industry which includes investment companies and investment advisers in order to protect investors, promote informed investment decisions, and facilitate appropriate innovation in investment products and services. Oversight also includes the establishment and maintenance of standards for fair, orderly, and efficient markets; the facilitation of prompt and accurate clearance and settlement of securities transactions; and the safeguarding of securities and funds. As such, securities market participants, including broker-dealers, self-regulatory organizations (such as stock exchanges and clearing agencies), and transfer agents, are regulated.

Much of the regulation of the derivatives markets (i.e., futures and swaps markets) focuses on protecting the integrity of price discovery and risk transfer (i.e., hedging) for financial instruments as well as commodities (such as energy and agricultural commodities). Derivatives prices are generally not regulated except in emergency situations. The organization and membership of the trading platforms and clearinghouses, rules for trading and clearing, conflicts of interest, or price manipulation by market participants are regulated in an attempt to prevent fraud, maintain the integrity of the prices publicly reported, and the risks transferred through these markets.

Insurance oversight. Insurance regulation is structured around several key functions, including company licensing, producer licensing, product regulation, market conduct, solvency and capital requirements, prudential regulation, and consumer services. U.S. insurers are subject to regulation in their state of domicile and in the other states where they are licensed to sell insurance. State regulators protect consumers by ensuring that insurance policy provisions comply with state law, are reasonable and fair, and do not contain major gaps in coverage that might be misunderstood by consumers and leave them unprotected. Periodic financial examinations investigate a company's accounting methods, procedures, and financial statement presentation, and they verify and validate what is presented in the company's annual statement to ascertain whether the company is in good financial standing. In addition, examinations help to identify issues that may develop in the future at the insurer. Market regulation attempts to help ensure fair and reasonable insurance prices, products, and trade practices in order to protect consumers.

Systemic risk oversight and consolidated supervision. Systemic risk oversight includes monitoring the financial system to identify and analyze threats to financial stability and mitigating those threats. This oversight can include enhanced supervision of financial institutions and other financial entities that may present a threat to financial stability.

The goal of consolidated supervision, among other things, is to provide a comprehensive and enterprisewide approach to supervision that extends beyond legal entity-based supervision of certain subsidiaries. Consolidated supervision can provide for an understanding of the financial and managerial strength and risks within the consolidated organization as a whole, and it provides the ability to address significant management, operational, capital, or other deficiencies within the overall organization before they pose a threat to subsidiary depository institutions or to U.S. financial stability, in certain instances. Holding companies may have subsidiaries such as banks, thrifts, securities firms, commodities trading firms, or insurers.

Source: GAO. | GAO-16-175.

Under the current regulatory structure (see fig. 2), financial institutions or entities may fall under the regulatory authority of multiple regulators within and across these oversight categories.

Although the regulatory structure is complex, U.S. regulators and financial market participants have noted it also has provided some benefits. For example, they have noted that the structure has contributed to the development of U.S. capital markets and to overall growth and stability in the U.S. economy. Some noted that the presence of multiple regulators for depository institutions can also lead to competition among them, which helps promote regulatory innovation, providing businesses with an opportunity to move to regulators whose approaches better match the businesses' operations. In addition, in some cases, potential benefits might result from having multiple regulators overseeing an institution. For example, representatives of state banking and credit union regulators, and consumer advocacy organizations, have noted that concurrent jurisdiction—between two federal regulators or a federal and state regulator—can provide needed checks and balances against individual financial regulators who have not always reacted appropriately and in a timely way to address problems at institutions. They also noted that states may move more quickly and more flexibly to respond to activities causing harm to consumers. Further, banking officials have stated that having multiple federal banking regulators in the U.S. system has resulted in diversity, inventiveness, and flexibility in the banking system, which are important for responding to changes in market share and in technology. Fragmentation and overlap, however, can lead to inefficiencies and inconsistencies in oversight and regulatory gaps, which we examine later in this report. The following sections describe the fragmentation and overlap that exist in this complex regulatory structure.

Safety and Soundness and Consumer Protection Oversight

Depository Institutions

As shown in figure 2, currently four federal prudential regulators—the Federal Reserve, OCC, FDIC, and NCUA—as well as state banking regulators oversee their respective depository institutions for safety and soundness. CFPB regulates the offering and provision of consumer financial products or services. For depository institutions with over $10 billion in assets and their affiliates, CFPB, pursuant to the Consumer Financial Protection Act of 2010 (Title X of the Dodd-Frank Act), has exclusive examination authority as well as primary enforcement authority for the Federal consumer financial laws.[16] CFPB has rulemaking authority for these statutes. The regulation of safety and soundness for depository institutions depends on the type of charter an institution chooses (commercial bank, thrift, or credit union) and the origin of the charter (federal or state). Table 2 explains the basic functions of the four federal prudential regulators.

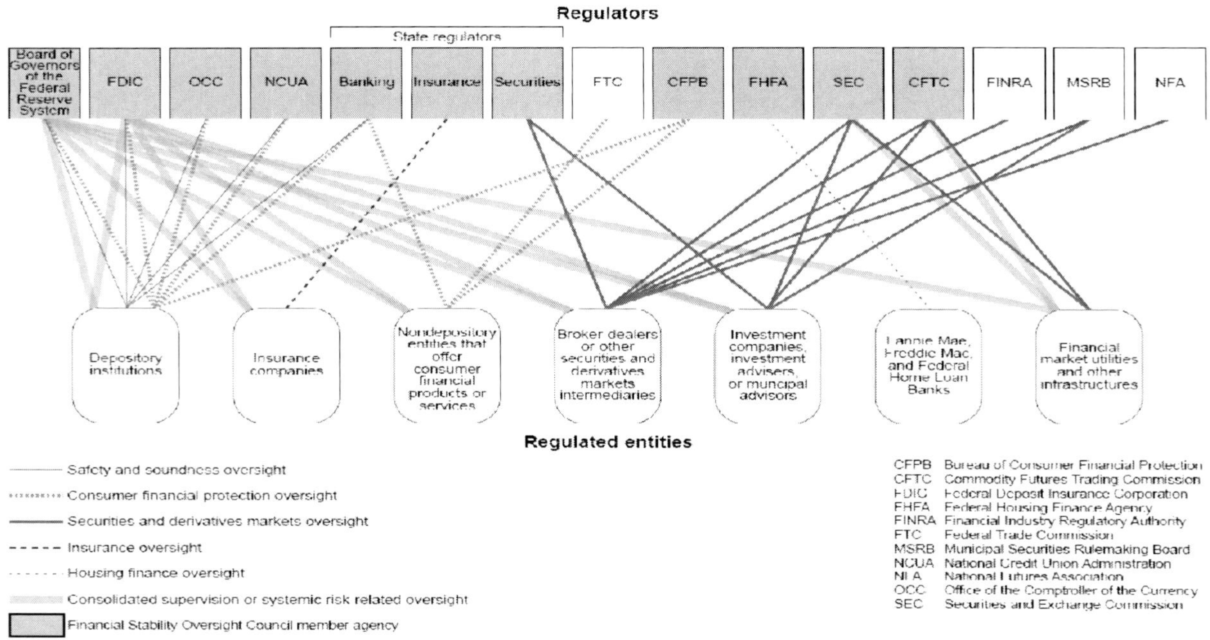

Source: GAO. | GAO-16-175.

Note: This figure depicts the primary regulators in the U.S. financial regulatory structure, as well as their primary oversight responsibilities. "Regulators" generally refers to entities that have rulemaking, supervisory, and enforcement authorities over financial institutions or entities. There are additional agencies involved in regulating the financial markets and there may be other possible regulatory connections than those depicted in this figure.

Figure 2. U.S. Financial Regulatory Structure, 2016.

Table 2. Federal Prudential Regulators and Their Basic Functions

Agency	Basic function
Office of the Comptroller of the Currency	Charters and supervises national banks, federal thrifts, and federally-chartered branches and agencies of foreign banks.
Board of Governors of the Federal Reserve System	Supervises state-chartered banks that opt to be members of the Federal Reserve System; bank and thrift holding companies, and the nondepository institution subsidiaries of those institutions; and nonbank financial companies designated by the Financial Stability Oversight Council for consolidated supervision and enhanced prudential standards. Supervises state-licensed branches and agencies of foreign banks and regulates the U.S. nonbanking activities of foreign banking organizations. Supervises Edge corporations pursuant to the Edge Act and certain designated financial market utilities (such as a clearinghouse) pursuant to the Dodd-Frank Act.[a]
Federal Deposit Insurance Corporation	Supervises state-chartered banks that are not members of the Federal Reserve System, as well as state savings banks and thrifts; insures the deposits of all banks and thrifts that are approved for federal deposit insurance; has the authority to conduct backup examinations for any insured institution; resolves all failed insured banks and thrifts and, if appointed receiver by the Secretary of the Treasury, has authority to resolve certain large bank holding companies and nonbank financial companies.
National Credit Union Administration	Charters and supervises federally-chartered credit unions and insures savings in federal and most state-chartered credit unions.

Source: GAO. | GAO-16-175.

[a]Edge Act corporations are established as separate legal entities and may conduct a range of international banking and other financial activities in the United States. Pub. L. No. 66-106, 41 Stat. 378 (1919) (codified as amended at 12 U.S.C. § 611).

The Dodd-Frank Act reduced fragmentation in the safety and soundness oversight of depository institutions by eliminating OTS and transferring its oversight responsibilities for federal thrifts to OCC, for state-chartered thrifts to FDIC, and for thrift holding companies to the Federal Reserve.[17] Before the Dodd-Frank Act implementation, the prudential regulators regulated depository institutions for both safety and soundness and consumer protection. Two major criticisms of this consumer protection system were raised by proponents for consolidation of the authority to regulate consumer financial protection. First, proponents noted that the regulatory system allowed financial institutions to choose the charter type so that they would be regulated by the most accommodating regulator. Second, proponents maintained that banking regulators were primarily concerned with safety and soundness, and only secondarily with consumer protection. The Dodd-Frank Act helped to reduce fragmentation in consumer financial protection oversight by consolidating authority for a number of consumer financial protection laws that had been handled by seven different agencies.[18] Unlike the prudential regulators, CFPB has the primary mission of consumer protection. However, the Dodd-Frank Act also limits the authority of CFPB to regulate certain institutions. For example, the act fragmented consumer protection supervision and enforcement for depository institutions, based on a depository institution's size. Specifically, while most consumer protection oversight responsibilities were transferred from the prudential regulators to CFPB for depository institutions with more than $10 billion in assets and their affiliates, prudential regulators retained authority for certain consumer protection laws for these institutions. In addition, the prudential regulators continue to supervise institutions with assets of $10 billion or less for consumer protection.[19] This allocation of authority based on size was apparently grounded in policy considerations including concerns with the disruption that additional examinations may cause for smaller depositories and the greater effect that compliance costs could have for smaller institutions.[20] Finally, the Dodd-Frank Act provided that state banking regulators can bring proceedings against institutions chartered, incorporated, or licensed in their states to enforce the Consumer Financial Protection Act of 2010 and CFPB rules issued thereunder.[21] State banking regulators also have authority to enforce state consumer protection laws.

Multiple forms of overlap exist among the agencies that perform safety and soundness and consumer protection oversight of depository institutions. For example, state banking regulators share oversight of the safety and soundness of state-chartered banks with FDIC and the Federal Reserve.[22] Further, FDIC administers the Deposit Insurance Fund, which insures the deposits of all banks and thrifts that are approved for federal deposit insurance. In this role, FDIC has backup supervisory authorities over all banks and thrifts that are federally insured. This responsibility creates overlap between FDIC's authorities and those of the Federal Reserve and OCC as the primary prudential regulators of insured institutions.[23] While NCUA supervises only federally-chartered credit unions, it is the deposit insurer for both federal credit unions and most state-chartered credit unions. Therefore, its role as deposit insurer creates overlap with state credit union regulators.[24] Overlap also exists in the consumer protection oversight of depository institutions with more than $10 billion in assets. That is, because the primary federal prudential regulator (FDIC, the Federal Reserve, NCUA, or OCC) of these institutions retained authority to oversee their compliance with certain consumer protection laws, two federal agencies are responsible for reviewing these institutions' compliance with consumer protection laws.[25] Additionally, overlap exists because state regulators have authority to enforce the provisions of the Consumer Financial Protection Act of 2010 or regulations issued under those provisions, with respect to state-chartered entities or entities licensed to do business in the state, which may also be overseen by their prudential regulator or CFPB for the same purpose. Finally, the Federal Reserve has consolidated supervision authorities over most holding companies that own or control a bank or thrift and their subsidiaries.[26] Consolidated supervision authorities create additional overlap because, among other things, the Federal Reserve can provide oversight to the holding company's subsidiary depository institutions, in addition to the oversight provided by the depository institution's primary prudential regulator.[27] Figure 3 shows some examples of regulatory overlap for safety and soundness and consumer protection purposes for three types of depository institutions: (1) a national bank with more than $10 billion in assets; (2) a state-member bank that is not a member of the Federal Reserve system, is not an affiliate of a depository institution with more than $10 billion in assets, and has less than $10 billion in assets; and (3) a state-chartered bank that is a member of the Federal Reserve system and has more than $10 billion in assets.

Nondepository Entities

Responsibilities for overseeing certain nondepository financial entities, which can offer consumers financial products and other services similar to those provided by banks, is fragmented among CFPB, the Federal Trade Commission (FTC), and state banking regulators.[28] With the creation of CFPB, the Dodd-Frank Act closed a gap in consumer protection oversight by providing supervisory oversight to CFPB for certain nondepository financial entities, including certain kinds of mortgage market participants, private student lenders, and payday loan lenders, for the purposes of enforcing the consumer financial protection laws. Such entities generally lacked federal supervisory oversight prior to the act and generally are not overseen by federal prudential regulators for safety and soundness purposes, but some are subject to federal consumer financial and state consumer protection laws. In addition, the Dodd-Frank Act gave CFPB supervisory authority over "larger participants" in markets for consumer financial products or services as CFPB defines by rule.[29] FTC retained its consumer protection enforcement authorities over most nondepository entities, including mortgage companies, mortgage brokers, finance companies, auto dealers, payday lenders, debt collectors, and others.[30] Overlap exists between CFPB's and FTC's authorities for certain nondepository entities including those involved in mortgage servicing, lending, and assistance; debt collection; and payday lending. In addition, state banking regulators may also license and conduct oversight of certain nondepository financial entities, such as those engaged in mortgage origination and servicing, for consumer protection purposes.[31] State banking regulator oversight creates additional overlap in the consumer protection oversight of nondepository entities. Figure 4 provides an example of the overlap that can exist among agencies involved in overseeing a nondepository mortgage servicer.

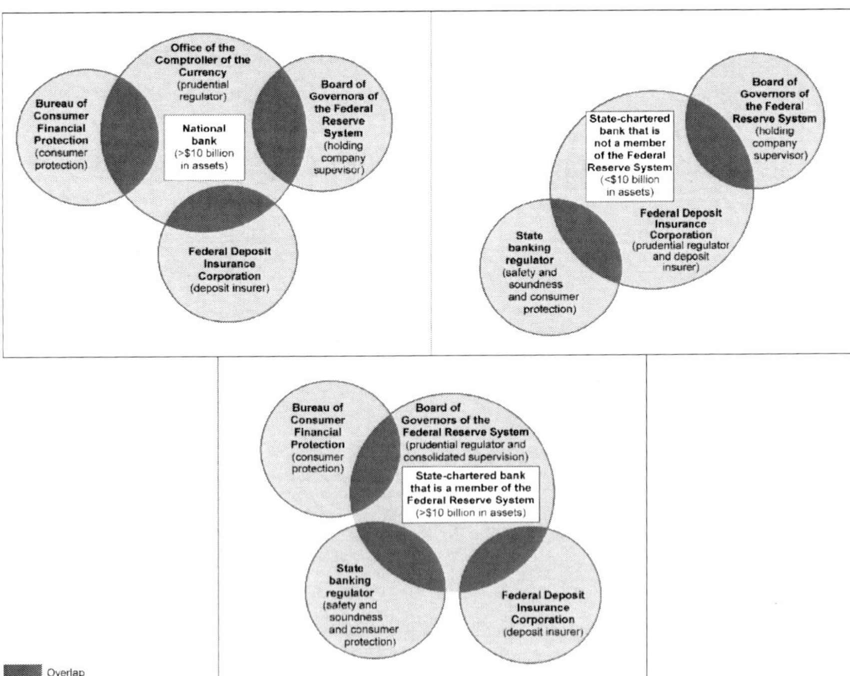

Source: GAO | GAO-16-175

Note: Depending on the types of financial activities in which a financial institution engages, additional financial regulators may be involved in their oversight.

Figure 3. Examples of Overlap in the Safety and Soundness and Consumer Protection Oversight for Certain Depository Institutions.

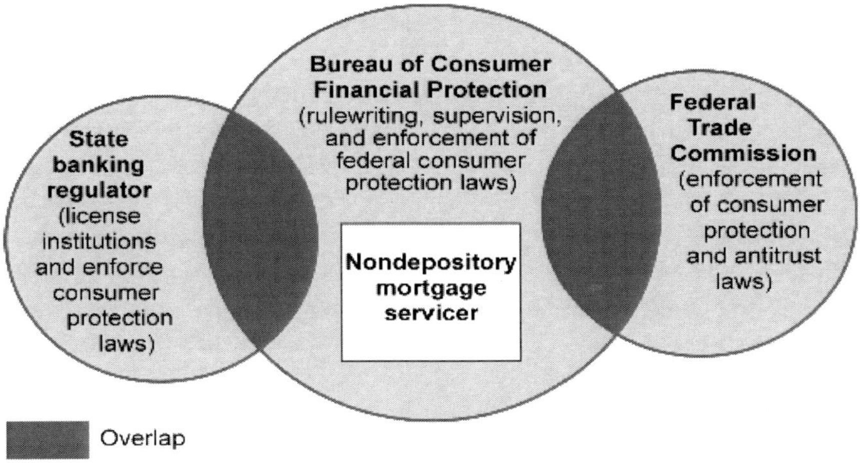

Source: GAO. | GAO-16-175.

Note: Depending on the types of financial activities in which a financial institution engages, additional financial regulators may be involved in their oversight.

Figure 4. Example of Overlap in Consumer Protection Oversight for a Nondepository Mortgage Servicer.

Securities and Derivatives Markets Oversight

The securities and derivatives markets are regulated under a combination of self-regulation (subject to oversight by the appropriate federal regulator) and direct oversight by SEC and CFTC, respectively. State securities regulators also play a role in overseeing the securities market.

SEC regulates the securities markets, including participants such as securities exchanges, broker-dealers, investment companies, and certain investment advisers and municipal advisors. SEC's mission is to protect investors; maintain fair, orderly, and efficient markets; and facilitate capital formation. SEC also oversees SROs—including securities exchanges, clearing agencies, and the Financial Industry Regulatory Authority (FINRA)—that have responsibility for overseeing securities markets and their members; establishing the standards under which their members conduct business; monitoring business conduct; and bringing disciplinary actions against members for violating applicable federal statutes, SEC's rules, and their own rules. In the securities markets, SROs, such as a national securities exchange or association, are regulators that have responsibility for much of the day-to-day oversight of the securities markets and broker-dealers under their jurisdiction. CFTC is the primary regulator of the derivatives markets and its mission is to protect market users and the public from fraud, manipulation, abusive practices, and systemic risk related to derivatives subject to the Commodity Exchange Act (CEA), and to foster open, competitive, and financially sound futures markets. CFTC oversees the registration of intermediaries and relies on SROs, including the futures exchanges and the National Futures Association, to establish and enforce rules governing member behavior.[32] The Dodd-Frank Act closed gaps that existed in the regulatory structure by expanding the jurisdictional authorities of CFTC and SEC and creating a new oversight regime for the swaps and security-based swaps markets. The act also required advisers to certain private funds—such as hedge funds and private equity funds—to register with SEC.

Overlap exists in the oversight of securities and derivatives markets in several ways, including the entities being overseen and those providing the oversight.

- *Investment adviser oversight.* Oversight of investment advisers is divided between SEC and state securities regulators depending on the amount of assets an investment adviser manages.[33] Investment advisers who manage $100 million or more in assets generally must register with SEC and are subject to SEC regulation. Most small and mid-sized investment advisers who manage up to $100 million in assets are overseen by state securities regulators. State securities regulators' authorities for these small and mid-sized advisers may also overlap because the advisers may be required to register with and be subject to oversight by one or more state securities regulators.
- *Security futures oversight.* CFTC and SEC have overlapping authority for security futures products, which generally refers to futures on single securities and narrow-based security indexes. Both agencies jointly regulate this product.
- *Swaps and security-based swaps oversight.* Regulation of the swaps and security-based swaps market is generally divided between CFTC and SEC, respectively. The Dodd-Frank Act authorizes CFTC to regulate swaps and SEC to regulate security-based swaps and both agencies are responsible for issuing rules for their respective products and market participants. However, CFTC's and SEC's authorities to regulate mixed swaps—security-based swaps that have a commodity component—overlap. The agencies share authority over mixed swaps and issue joint rules for this product.

- *SRO oversight.* SRO oversight creates overlap with the authorities of SEC and CFTC because market participants are subject to the oversight of both their relevant federal regulator and one or more SRO. The Municipal Securities Rulemaking Board (MSRB) is another SRO that, among other things, develops rules for broker-dealers engaged in underwriting, trading, and selling municipal securities with the goals of protecting investors and issuers and promoting a fair and efficient marketplace.[34] MSRB also writes rules regulating municipal advisors that, among other things, provide advice to or on behalf of municipal entities with respect to the issuance of municipal securities. MSRB's authorities overlap with those of FINRA and SEC because it relies on both of them to examine municipal securities broker-dealers and to enforce its rules because it does not have the authority to enforce the rules it writes. Further, both MSRB and SEC register municipal securities broker-dealers.
- *State securities regulator oversight.* Some state securities regulators' authorities overlap with those of SEC. State securities regulators are responsible for, among other things, licensing securities firms and investment professionals, such as broker-dealers and investment advisers; registering certain securities offerings; and, along with SEC, investigating securities fraud.[35]
- *Other oversight.* Additional overlap with the Federal Reserve may exist for derivatives and securities market participants overseen by CFTC or SEC that operate as part of a bank or thrift holding company under consolidated supervision by the Federal Reserve.

Insurance Oversight

The business of insurance is regulated primarily at the state level in the United States and, therefore, is fragmented among 56 state insurance regulators.[37] State regulators oversee insurers for financial solvency and policyholder protection, among other things. The National Association of Insurance Commissioners (NAIC) is the voluntary association of the heads of insurance departments from the 56 insurance jurisdictions. While NAIC does not regulate insurers, it does provide services to the insurance regulators, including providing data to help regulators analyze insurance sales and practices and coordinating regulatory efforts by providing guidance, model laws and regulations, and information-sharing tools, among other things. Both FIO and the Federal Reserve also have authorities related to the U.S. insurance sector, which creates overlap. The Dodd-Frank Act created FIO, which does not have general supervisory or regulatory authority over the business of insurance. However, it does have targeted authority under the Dodd-Frank Act to monitor all aspects of the insurance industry, including identifying issues or gaps in the regulation of insurers that could contribute to a systemic crisis in the insurance industry or the U.S. financial system.[38] FIO also coordinates federal efforts and develops federal policy on prudential aspects of international insurance matters, among other things.[39] The Federal Reserve can oversee insurance companies that are owned by bank or thrift holding companies, that are bank or thrift holding companies, or have been designated by FSOC for enhanced supervision by the Federal Reserve. Insurance companies designated by FSOC are subject to consolidated supervision by the Federal Reserve and enhanced prudential standards.[40] In these cases, overlap exists between the Federal Reserve and the state insurance regulator.[41] Figure 6 shows examples of regulatory overlap that can exist for an insurance company that is part of a thrift holding company and an insurance company that has been designated by FSOC for enhanced supervision by the Federal Reserve.

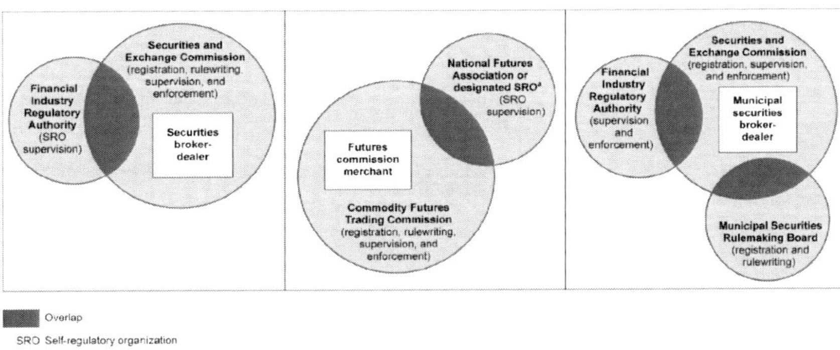

Source: GAO. | GAO-16-175.

Note: Depending on the types of financial activities in which a financial institution engages, additional financial regulators may be involved in their oversight.

[a]When a futures commission merchant is a member of more than one SRO, the SROs may decide among themselves which of them will assume primary responsibility for these regulatory duties and, upon approval of the plan by CFTC, be appointed the "designated self-regulatory organization" for that futures commission merchant.

Figure 5. Examples of Overlap in the Securities and Derivatives Markets Oversight for Certain Market Intermediaries.

Figure 5 illustrates examples of the regulatory overlap that exists for securities and futures market intermediaries, including a securities broker-dealer, a futures commission merchant, and a municipal securities broker-dealer.[36]

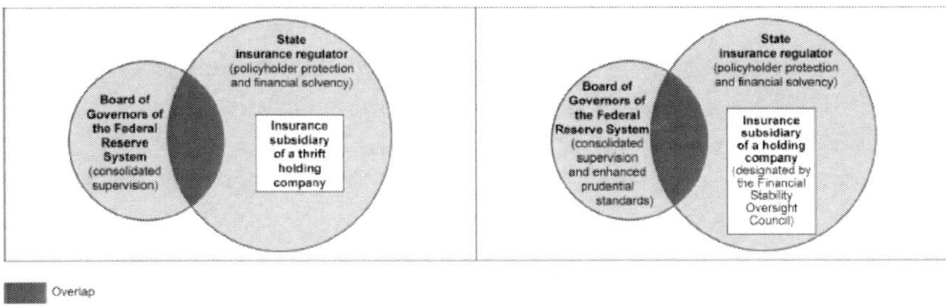

Source: GAO. | GAO-16-175.

Note: Depending on the types of financial activities in which a financial institution engages, additional financial regulators may be involved in their oversight.

Figure 6. Examples of Overlap in Oversight for Certain Types of Insurance Company Subsidiaries.

Systemic Risk Oversight and Consolidated Supervision

The Dodd-Frank Act established a systemic risk oversight framework within the fragmented regulatory structure. The act generally did not assign systemic risk oversight authorities to any existing agency; rather, it placed responsibility for identifying and responding to systemic risks with the collective group of regulators through the creation of FSOC. FSOC is chaired by the Secretary of the Treasury and its members include the heads of CFPB, CFTC, FDIC, the Federal Reserve, the Federal Housing Finance Agency (FHFA), NCUA, OCC, SEC, OFR, and FIO; representatives from the state banking, securities, and insurance regulators; and an insurance expert appointed by the President of the United States.[42] The Dodd-Frank Act also created OFR to support FSOC's activities and, similar to FIO, gave it certain systemic risk monitoring mandates. We discuss both OFR's and FIO's activities in more detail later in this report.

The Dodd-Frank Act also aimed to address systemic risks from large, complex financial institutions through consolidated supervision by the Federal Reserve and the imposition of enhanced prudential standards. Prior to the enactment of the Dodd-Frank Act, the Federal Reserve had consolidated supervision authorities for all bank holding companies, and with the elimination of OTS, the Federal Reserve also became responsible for the supervision of thrift holding companies. The act also expanded the Federal Reserve's consolidated supervision authorities for systemic risk purposes by (1) giving it consolidated supervision authority over nonbank financial companies designated by FSOC, (2) requiring it to establish enhanced prudential standards for nonbank financial companies designated by FSOC and bank holding companies with $50 billion or more in total consolidated assets, and (3) requiring these standards to be more stringent than those applicable to financial companies that do not present similar risks to U.S. financial stability. All forms of consolidated supervision by the Federal Reserve create overlap with authority of the primary regulators of the holding company's regulated subsidiaries. These subsidiaries may include banks, thrifts, securities firms, commodities trading firms, or insurers which are already overseen by other regulators, as described earlier.

The Dodd-Frank Act gives FDIC certain authorities to effectively plan and manage an orderly resolution of a failing financial company that poses a significant risk to the financial stability of the United States, which creates overlap. For example, the act requires bank holding companies that have total consolidated assets of $50 billion or more as well as nonbank financial companies designated by FSOC to periodically submit resolution plans and credit exposure reports to the Federal Reserve and FDIC for review. The Federal Reserve and FDIC must each review the information in the plans and if they arrive at a joint determination that their plans are not credible or would not facilitate an orderly resolution in bankruptcy, the agencies can jointly impose sanctions.[43] Second, the act also gives FDIC authority, if appointed receiver by the Secretary of the Treasury, to liquidate or resolve certain systemically important firms—including those under Federal Reserve consolidated supervision—whose failure and resolution under otherwise applicable law would have serious adverse effects on U.S. financial stability.

Lastly, the Dodd-Frank Act also gave FSOC the authority to designate financial market utilities and PCS activities as systemically important. Financial market utilities include payment systems, central securities depositories, and central counterparties that provide the infrastructure to clear and settle payments and other financial transactions, some of which are overseen by SEC and CFTC.[44] Under the Dodd-Frank Act, the Federal Reserve must prescribe (or consult in the establishment of) enhanced risk-management standards for operations related to PCS activities conducted by a designated financial market utility and the conduct of designated activities by financial institutions. The act also allows either SEC or CFTC to prescribe such standards for designated clearing agencies and financial institutions engaged in designated activities when the agency is the primary supervisor, but the agency must consult with the Federal Reserve and FSOC before doing so.[45] Generally, the act provides the Federal Reserve with an enhanced role with respect to designated financial market utilities and entities conducting designated PCS activities for which it is not the primary supervisor. Consequently, such designations can create overlap. For example, the Federal Reserve has the authority to participate in any examination of a designated financial market utility led by the entity's primary supervisor and to review proposed changes to a designated financial market utility's rules, procedures, or operations that could materially affect the nature or level of risk presented by the designated financial market utility.

Complex Structure Creates Inefficiencies and Inconsistencies and Limits International Coordination

Extensive fragmentation and overlap in the regulatory structure create various inefficiencies and inconsistencies in regulators' oversight activities. Prior to the passage of the Dodd-Frank Act, we reported on numerous examples of the negative effects of fragmentation and overlap in safety and soundness, consumer protection, securities and derivatives markets, and insurance oversight. In 2009, we established a framework for evaluating regulatory reform proposals that describes nine characteristics that should be reflected in a new regulatory system.[46] While changes made by the Dodd-Frank Act were consistent with some of these characteristics, the act did not address three that would likely help to reduce the negative effects of fragmentation and overlap in the structure. In particular, the current regulatory structure does not always ensure (1) efficient and effective oversight, (2) consistent financial oversight, and (3) consistent consumer and investor protections.[47] Because regulatory reforms, including the Dodd-Frank Act, have not fully addressed these characteristics and fragmentation and overlap remain, challenges persist in each sector.[48] In most of the examples cited below from our previous work, agencies have taken actions to help mitigate the negative effects of fragmentation and overlap that we identified and have addressed our previous concerns. However, the past examples, coupled with more recent examples of the negative effects of fragmentation and overlap, demonstrate a pattern of inconsistencies and inefficiencies that continue to persist because of the fragmented regulatory structure. We and others have suggested changes that could help to mitigate the negative effects of fragmentation and overlap that exist in the regulatory structure.

Multiple Regulators Can Result in Inefficient and Inconsistent Safety and Soundness and Consumer Protection Oversight

Since the mid-1990s, we have stated that having multiple depository institution regulators can cause inconsistencies and inefficiencies in the oversight of these institutions. Inconsistent practices can result in different conclusions about the safety and soundness of an institution, difficulties tracking violations and identifying emerging trends, and different levels of protection provided to consumers. Further, fragmentation in safety and soundness and consumer protection oversight has delayed regulatory action on matters of emerging risk because of difficulties regulators face in reaching agreement and the time it takes for them to coordinate their efforts. While the regulators do coordinate in many areas to try to reduce the negative effects of fragmentation and overlap, the fragmented structure continues to create a significant responsibility on the part of the regulators to cooperate and effectively coordinate their activities.[49]

Inconsistent Oversight

Our past work evaluating regulators' examination activities has shown inconsistencies in their efforts. For example, from 1990 through 1993, we identified significant inconsistencies in examination policies and practices among FDIC, OCC, OTS, and the Federal Reserve, including differences in examination scope, frequency, and documentation and examination guidance and regulations. We found that methods for assessing loan loss reserves varied among the regulators and the lack of a generally accepted method for assessing loss reserves made it difficult for the regulators to successfully challenge management's estimates when the examiners thought reserves were inadequate.[50] As a result, we recommended that the federal bank and thrift regulatory agencies establish examination policies, as applicable, to develop and implement a sound methodology for evaluating the adequacy of loan loss reserves and reserving methods.[51] In 2006 we also found that although the federal prudential regulators had worked to develop interagency procedures to help ensure consistency for Bank Secrecy Act (BSA) examinations, the regulators' guidance and terminology for the classification of BSA compliance problems differed. We found that these differences could, among other things, make it difficult for banking regulators to have a comprehensive overview of BSA compliance at their institutions and for Treasury's Financial Crimes Enforcement Network (FinCEN)—the overall administrator of BSA—to have a comprehensive overview across regulators.[52] We recommended that FinCEN and the prudential regulators jointly assess the feasibility of developing a uniform classification system for BSA noncompliance.[53]

We have also found inconsistencies in the prudential regulators' oversight of compliance with federal consumer protection laws prior to the passage of the Dodd-Frank Act.[54] For example, in 2009 we reported that the federal prudential regulators' fair lending oversight programs differed in their oversight procedures.[55] We found that each regulator used different approaches to screen data to identify lenders that may have violated fair lending laws. We also identified significant differences in the practices that the federal prudential regulators employed to make referrals to the Department of Justice and in the number of referrals they made. We concluded that despite the federal prudential regulators' having issued joint interagency fair lending examination guidance and having engaged in various coordination efforts, federal enforcement agencies and prudential regulators faced challenges in consistently, efficiently, and effectively overseeing and enforcing fair lending laws due in part to the fragmented U.S. financial regulatory structure. We suggested that Congress may wish to take steps to help ensure that consumers are adequately protected by, among other things, addressing the potentially inconsistent oversight provided by the federal prudential regulators.[56]

While Congress addressed some of our concerns through consolidating rulemaking and other authorities over consumer financial products and services under CFPB, the Dodd-Frank Act maintained a divided consumer protection regulatory regime for depository institutions. As a result, the potential for inconsistencies continues to exist in the way depository institutions are overseen for compliance with consumer protection laws and the level of protections provided to consumers. In particular, CFPB and the federal prudential regulators have similar but different regulatory authorities related to unfair or deceptive acts or practices. Prudential regulators enforce Section 5 of the Federal Trade Commission Act, which prohibits unfair or deceptive acts or practices for depository institutions of any size that they supervise. The Dodd-Frank Act prohibits unfair, deceptive, or abusive acts or practices and CFPB enforces this for depository institutions with more than

$10 billion in assets.[57] This means that for depository institutions with more than $10 billion in assets that are overseen by both CFPB and a prudential regulator, both regulators can enforce their respective authorities and conflicts may arise in how the two regulators interpret and apply them. Further, because CFPB and each of the prudential regulators can enforce their respective authorities against their regulated institutions, participants in our consumer protection discussion group stated that the potential for differences in interpretations and applications of the authorities can occur, which could result in depository institutions being held to different standards. Officials from the Federal Reserve, FDIC, OCC, and CFPB told us that they coordinate on issues related to unfair or deceptive acts or practices prior to or during examinations, or when enforcement actions are necessary. FDIC officials also noted that they were not aware of any instances in which interpretations of these authorities differed between CFPB and the prudential regulators.

Inefficient Oversight

Inefficiency is another principal concern with the regulatory structure for safety and soundness and consumer protection oversight. For example, a long-standing issue in this area involves the overlapping authorities of the Federal Reserve and the primary prudential regulator in holding company examinations. In its holding company examinations, the Federal Reserve, to the fullest extent possible, relies on reports and other supervisory information that the bank holding company or any subsidiary has provided to other regulatory agencies.[58] However the potential exists for the Federal Reserve, as supervisor of the holding company, to duplicate the work of the primary regulator of the subsidiary depository institution, which can result in an inefficient use of federal resources and increased regulatory burden for the institution. In 1994, we found that overlapping authority was a particularly significant problem in bank holding company regulation and that although the Federal Reserve and the primary regulators tried to coordinate their supervision and examination responsibilities, the efforts were not always successful.[59] In addition, in a 2007 report on consolidated supervision we found some duplication in the examinations of financial holding companies, despite OCC's and the Federal Reserve's efforts to coordinate.[60] Further, we found that while the Federal Reserve and OCC had and generally followed procedures to resolve differences, one firm had initially received conflicting information from the Federal Reserve and OCC about the firm's business continuity provisions. As a result of these findings, we recommended in March 2007 that the Federal Reserve identify additional ways to more effectively collaborate with primary bank and other functional supervisors (e.g., developing appropriate mechanisms to better define responsibilities and to monitor, evaluate, and report jointly on results).[61] However, in its September 2015 report on the Federal Reserve's major management challenges, the Federal Reserve Office of the Inspector General noted that the Federal Reserve still faces challenges in coordinating with other federal supervisory agencies in its role as the consolidated supervisor for bank, financial, and thrift holding companies.[62]

Further, participants in our discussion groups noted that they see overlap in agencies' data collection activities. In particular, participants noted overlap between the Federal Reserve and OCC and CFPB and OCC. For example, they explained that the Federal Reserve's data requests can be very similar to OCC's requests and that often the two requests will ask for the same data but in different formats. They said that providing data in multiple formats may be inefficient for an institution because often its information systems do not capture the data in the format requested, which can require staff to go to data files to create a dataset from scratch. Federal Reserve officials told us that in the agency's role as a consolidated supervisor, it first attempts to obtain any needed information from the primary regulator and only requests information from a depository institution subsidiary if the primary regulator does not have the information. CFPB staff told us that they are aware of the data that already exist from the primary prudential regulator of their supervised depository institutions. In addition, in our September 2014 report on consumer financial data collections, we found that CFPB has coordinated with the prudential regulators and shared consumer financial data through various formal agreements.[63] For example, in May 2012, CFPB and the prudential regulators entered into a memorandum of understanding (MOU) on supervisory coordination to facilitate their compliance with the Dodd-Frank Act's coordination requirements (described in more detail below) and, in 2013, CFPB entered into an agreement with OCC covering any sharing of information from their respective credit card collections.[64]

However, in our September 2014 report, we also found that despite the regulators' coordination efforts, some overlap still existed in agencies' collections of consumer financial data.[65] For example, four institutions that provided credit card data to CFPB also provided the same types of data to the Federal Reserve. In addition, we found overlap in the data collections of OCC and the Federal Reserve. Fifteen of the 16 national banks submitting credit card data to OCC submit similar data through eight holding companies to the Federal Reserve. We also found that 48 national bank affiliates that report mortgage data to OCC also report these data through their eight holding companies to the Federal Reserve.

Participants also noted that the Dodd-Frank Act's changes to the regulatory oversight of the thrift industry have created some additional regulatory burden for thrifts and thrift holding companies. Thrifts are now subject to oversight by two regulators—their primary prudential regulator (FDIC or OCC) and the Federal Reserve as their holding company regulator—rather than the sole oversight OTS provided to both the thrift and the holding company. They also said that this new regulatory overlap creates the same types of challenges for thrifts and thrift holding companies as those described previously for bank and bank holding companies. FDIC and OCC officials explained that they try to manage these new overlapping authorities with the Federal Reserve on thrift and thrift holding company examinations by using the same coordination processes that they use for bank and bank holding company examinations. For instance, they share supervisory strategies and data requests with each other prior to beginning examinations in an effort to reduce duplication in examination activities and, in some cases, conduct joint examinations.

Fragmentation in consumer protection oversight between the prudential regulators and CFPB may result in inefficiencies such as duplication in examinations.[66] For example, examiners from both the prudential regulators and CFPB examine the compliance management systems of depository institutions under their mutual supervision.[67] In addition to reviewing these systems as part of their safety and soundness examination activities, prudential regulators also examine them as part of their efforts to help ensure compliance with other financial laws and provisions, including the Bank Secrecy Act and anti-money-laundering requirements. CFPB's Supervision and Examination Manual states that CFPB conducts its own independent compliance management system assessment to help ensure that its regulated entities maintain effective compliance management systems. Regulatory officials explained that differences can exist in the scope of compliance management system reviews by prudential regulators and CFPB, which can result in inconsistences in regulators' ratings of the systems.[68] Differences in ratings can cause confusion for a depository institution regarding the effectiveness of its system. Officials told us that the prudential regulators and CFPB are working on ways to clarify how an institution should interpret each regulator's assessment and that, to the extent possible, the agencies are trying to coordinate their discussions of findings with supervised institutions.

Delays in Regulatory Action

In addition, a fragmented regulatory structure for safety and soundness and consumer protection can create difficulties for agencies in trying to reach consensus on various issues. We testified in March 1994 that the practice of trying to reduce inconsistency in regulators' oversight by having all the bank regulatory agencies adopt a common rule or guidance resulted in a cumbersome interagency process for developing new rules and guidance.[69] Although regulatory officials acknowledged the need for agency coordination, we also found that the efforts to develop uniform policies and procedures took months, involved scores of people, and still failed to result in uniformity. Further, in some cases, regulators' efforts to respond to increased risks were slowed in part because of the need for multiple regulators to reach agreement and coordinate their response. This was the case in the mid 2000s, when regulators began to recognize the increased risks associated with new mortgage products. We found that prudential regulators began crafting regulatory guidance to strengthen lending practices and improve disclosures for these loan products in late 2005.[70] The regulators completed their first set of such standards in September 2006, with respect to the disclosure of risks associated with nontraditional mortgage products, and a second set, applicable to subprime mortgage loans, in June 2007.[71] Some industry observers and consumer advocacy groups criticized the amount of time it took for regulators to reach agreement and issue these changes, noting that the second set of guidance was released well after many subprime lenders had already gone out of business.

Agencies Engage in Coordination in an Effort to Manage Fragmentation

The prudential regulators, CFPB, FTC, and state banking regulators also engage in a variety of coordination activities, such as establishing interagency groups to facilitate coordination and communicating informally on a variety of issues. Some of the main coordination mechanisms the regulators use for safety and soundness and consumer protection oversight include the following:

- Prudential regulators, CFPB, and state banking regulators formally coordinate examination policies through the Federal Financial Institutions Examination Council (FFIEC).[72] FFIEC is a forum for the development of uniform standards and principles and it can make recommendations to promote uniformity in the supervision of financial institutions. It also serves as a forum for dialogue between federal and state bank supervisory agencies. Prudential regulators also engage in a number of coordination activities to avoid duplication that could result from their overlapping examination authorities. For example, when exercising its backup examination authority, FDIC coordinates with the primary federal prudential regulator and generally participates with them during its onsite examination activities. In addition, as mentioned previously, the Federal Reserve is required to rely on reports of examination made by other regulatory agencies in its role as the holding company supervisor. The Federal Reserve is also required to consult with regulators before commencing an examination of a subsidiary and to avoid, to the fullest extent possible, duplication of examination activities. The Federal Reserve also coordinates with the federal prudential regulators by engaging in information sharing agreements and coordinating examination schedules, among other things.

- The Riegle Community Development and Regulatory Improvement Act of 1994 required the prudential regulators to coordinate examinations with each other and with state banking regulators in order to minimize the disruptive effect of examinations resulting from multiple examinations. The Federal Reserve, FDIC, and the Conference of State Banking Supervisors (on behalf of state banking departments) signed an agreement aimed at providing a seamless supervisory process and minimizing regulatory burden, among other things.[73] The agreement allows for examinations to be conducted jointly by state and federal regulators, although they also can alternate examination responsibilities. In 2013, the Conference of State Banking Supervisors and CFPB also developed a supervisory coordination framework that establishes the process for how state regulators and CFPB will share supervision of nondepository financial services providers and covered depository institutions with more than $10 billion in assets.
- Agencies sometimes develop formal agreements and MOUs. For example, CFPB and the prudential regulators have an MOU on supervisory coordination which specifies various ways in which CFPB and the prudential regulators are to coordinate their examination activities, including establishing guidelines for coordinated examinations and expectations for sharing information. CFPB and FTC also have an MOU to coordinate efforts to protect

consumers and to help reduce duplication of federal law enforcement and regulatory efforts.

Separate but Interconnected Markets Create Challenges for Regulation of Products

Over time, separate regulation of the securities and futures markets has created confusion about which agency has jurisdiction and has raised concerns about duplicative or inconsistent regulation of entities that engage in similar activities. These concerns, in turn, have raised questions about whether separate regulatory agencies remain appropriate. The U.S. securities and futures markets are regulated by different agencies—SEC and CFTC, respectively—in part because they are separate markets serving different primary purposes. However, we have long reported that, although their primary purposes still differ, the securities and futures markets have become increasingly interconnected, and the distinction between a financial product as a security or a future has become increasingly difficult to determine as more and more products are developed that combine characteristics of both securities and futures.[74]

As early as the 1970s, the emergence of derivative products with characteristics of both securities and futures led to periodic disputes concerning which agency should have regulatory jurisdiction over them. These disputes have at times consumed significant agency resources and resulted in lengthy delays in introducing product innovations to the markets. For example, in January 2005 the Chicago Board Options Exchange filed a proposal with SEC to list and trade a new option on an exchange-traded fund holding investments involving gold, but introduction of this product was delayed by over 3 years as CFTC and SEC could not reach agreement on jurisdiction.[75] Moreover, in April 2010, we found that the futures and securities markets had also increasingly overlapped in terms of market participants, raising concerns about duplicative or inconsistent regulation of entities that engage in similar activities.[76] For example, exchanges that list and trade security futures are subject to the jurisdiction of both CFTC and SEC, and financial intermediaries generally must register with both CFTC and SEC if they serve investors trading in instruments subject to the jurisdiction of the two agencies.

In addition, in its June 2009 white paper on financial regulatory reform, Treasury noted that the regulatory structure can cause economically equivalent instruments to be regulated differently, depending on which agency has jurisdiction.[77] For example, many futures products and financial options regulated as securities are functionally similar. Further, Treasury noted that jurisdictional distinctions may have unnecessarily limited competition between markets and exchanges. Under existing law, financial instruments with similar characteristics may be forced to trade on different exchanges that are subject to different regulatory regimes. Given the challenges created by the bifurcated regulation of the two similar markets, Treasury stated that the broad public policy objectives of futures and securities regulation are the same and that many of the differences in the regulation of the markets are no longer justified.

CFTC and SEC have worked together to resolve jurisdictional disputes and address other emerging areas of overlap in their respective oversight of futures and securities markets. For example, in 1981 CFTC and SEC developed the Shad-Johnson Jurisdictional Accord, which was enacted into law in 1983 and clarified the agencies' jurisdictions over securities-based options and futures. Among other things, the accord confirmed SEC's jurisdiction over securities-based options, including stocks and stock indexes; provided CFTC with jurisdiction over futures (and options thereon) on certain securities and securities indexes; and prohibited futures trading on single stocks, as well as on securities indexes that did not meet specific requirements.[78] Similarly, pursuant to the Commodity Futures Modernization Act of 2000, the two agencies worked together to jointly create margin requirements for single stock futures when the act lifted the ban on futures on single stocks and narrow-based securities indexes, allowing them to be traded on securities or futures exchanges but subject to joint regulation of CFTC and SEC. Another example is an MOU the two agencies developed in 2008 with the goal of creating a closer relationship on a broad range of issues affecting their jurisdictions.[79] The MOU identified points of contact for coordination, outlined a protocol for addressing novel derivative products, and generally contemplated enhanced information sharing between the two agencies on areas of mutual interest.

As previously discussed, the Dodd-Frank Act closed a regulatory gap by establishing a new regulatory framework for swaps and security-based swaps, which expanded the responsibilities of both agencies.[80] The act authorizes CFTC to regulate swaps—which represent the vast majority of the market—and SEC to regulate security-based swaps, and the agencies share authority over mixed swaps—security-based swaps that have a commodity component. Both agencies are responsible for issuing rules to address the act's requirements, as well as jointly defining terms relating to jurisdiction, such as swap and security-based swap, and terms relating to market intermediaries, and issuing joint rules for mixed swaps. To help ensure regulatory consistency and comparability across the rules, the Dodd-Frank Act required SEC and CFTC to coordinate and consult with each other and prudential regulators, to the extent possible, before starting a rulemaking or issuing an order on swaps, security-based swaps, swap entities, or security-based swap entities.[81] In December 2014 we found that CFTC and SEC coordinated on their swaps and security-based swaps rulemakings as required by the Dodd-Frank Act.[82] However, we also found substantive differences exist between certain of the agencies' rules.[83] For example, CFTC and SEC have issued guidance and rules, respectively, specifying the cross-border application of provisions in the Dodd-Frank Act. Among other things, CFTC guidance and SEC rules address the scope of the term "U.S. persons." Although their definitions are similar in several areas, there are several differences. To illustrate, CFTC and SEC similarly consider a legal entity, such as a partnership, corporation, or trust, that is organized or incorporated under U.S. laws or that has its principal place of business in the United States as a U.S. person. However, CFTC also considers U.S. persons to include collective investment vehicles that are majority owned by U.S. persons, but SEC includes only collective investment vehicles established in the United States.

We also found a lack of coordination between CFTC and SEC in the timetables for finalizing their swaps rulemakings. For example, as of December 2015, CFTC had adopted rules covering most areas of its regulatory framework for swaps.[84] In contrast, SEC had finalized rules covering fewer areas.[85] Market participants said that the differences in the timing of rules and the differences in the rules themselves between the two agencies could lead to operational challenges for market participants, as well as uncertainty and regulatory inefficiencies and burden. The mitigation of any negative market effects resulting from differences in the agencies' rules will likely require that CFTC and SEC continue to coordinate after all of the rules are finalized. Officials from CFTC told us that they intend to evaluate the effect of their final rules on the market and plan to revisit their rules if they find conflicts arising from differences between their rules and those of SEC.

Participants in our discussion group questioned the utility of having separate regulatory regimes for swaps and security-based swaps, particularly given that CFTC regulates the vast majority of the market (over 90 percent according to their estimates). Further, they noted that market participants do not distinguish between the two products because they are functionally identical and can be used for similar purposes. Participants expressed concern that inconsistency in the regulatory regimes for these products might present market participants with market and operational challenges, as market participants use the same trading and compliance systems to trade both swaps and security-based swaps. For example, participants could see no benefit to differences in how swaps and security-based swaps are cleared and traded and said that these systems should be identical. However, participants told us that firms will likely have to spend more resources to comply with both rules than they would spend complying with one set of rules, creating opportunities for regulatory and economic inefficiencies.

Participants in our discussion group told us firms have spent large amounts of time and money putting their systems in place to comply with CFTC's rules. Because SEC has not finalized all of its major rules yet, the extent to which they will differ from CFTC's rules is uncertain. If SEC's final rules include different requirements than CFTC's rules, market participants will have to further revise their infrastructure, trading systems, and documentation systems. Further, one industry association we spoke with noted that if firms are unable to use the systems they have already built after SEC issues its rules, they might avoid security-based swap transactions. For example, firms might decide they are better off handling certain trades in the futures markets rather than the swaps markets because of differences in the way the markets may end up being regulated. While some participants thought that joint rulemaking would have helped to solve these issues, others pointed out that it would have taken too long for the regulators to agree on the rules and that the systemic risks present before the financial crisis would have continued to exist.

CFTC's and SEC's efforts to develop the regulatory framework for swaps illustrate the same types of challenges the agencies have faced historically in separately regulating the interconnected markets. In its March 2008 white paper on financial regulatory reform, Treasury noted that the realities of the current marketplace have significantly diminished, if not entirely eliminated, the original reason for the regulatory bifurcation between the futures and securities markets.[86] It stated that product and market participant convergence, market linkages, and globalization have rendered regulatory bifurcation of the futures and securities markets untenable, potentially harmful, and inefficient. To address this issue, it recommended that CFTC and SEC should be merged to provide unified oversight and regulation of the futures and securities industries. In addition, in its November 2012 report investigating the bankruptcy of MF Global—a large, globally active company with a commodity and securities broker-dealer—the House of Representatives Committee on Financial Services, Subcommittee on Oversight and Investigation, found that SEC and CFTC failed to share critical information about the company with one another.[87] The report states that the failure to coordinate regulatory oversight of the company meant that the agencies missed several opportunities to share critical information with one another. The subcommittee recommended that, given this failure to coordinate and the reality that futures products, markets, and market participants have converged, Congress explore whether customers and investors would be better served if SEC and CFTC streamline their operations or merge into a single agency that would have oversight of the securities and derivatives markets as a whole. Similarly, over a decade ago, in 1995, we suggested that Congress should analyze the benefits and risks of merging the two agencies and noted that a merger could increase regulatory effectiveness and efficiency.[88]

Fragmentation Has Created Inefficiency in Insurance Oversight and Could Hinder Effective Insurance Group Supervision

Fragmentation in the insurance regulatory structure has, in some instances, led to inefficient oversight of individual insurers and could create challenges to the effective oversight of insurance groups.[89] We have reported in the past on ways in which the state-based insurance regulatory structure has resulted in inefficient oversight of insurers, including uneven consumer protection and increased costs. State insurance regulators and NAIC have attempted to address these inefficiencies in oversight through initiatives aimed at achieving uniformity and reciprocity, such as through state adoption of NAIC model laws, but not all states have fully participated in these efforts.[90] Further, as a result of the financial crisis, concerns arose as to state insurance regulators' ability to comprehensively oversee all risks posed to insurance companies, particularly those originating in subsidiaries of a multijurisdictional insurance group. Although states have adopted, or are expected to adopt, NAIC model laws and regulations intended to help expand state regulators' authority over insurance groups, questions exist as to whether these efforts will grant insurance regulators consistent and effective authority over these entities.

Uneven Consumer Protection and Increased Costs to Insurers

The fragmented regulatory structure can be inefficient, resulting in increased costs to industry participants and consumers. For example, we have found that the product review and approval processes for certain types of insurance products that are sold on a multistate or nationwide basis were not uniformly conducted.[91] As a result, we found that the lack of uniform product approval processes makes it difficult for insurers that operate in multiple states to achieve timely and cost-effective approval because they must submit applications with different requirements in each state in which they wish to operate. This creates inefficiencies, which may result in higher costs for insurers and, in turn, consumers, and may also inhibit the introduction of new products. In 2002, to improve the speed and efficiency of product approval, NAIC and state regulators developed an interstate agreement to standardize procedures for approval for certain lines of insurance and for participating states. In April 2009, we found that while the agreement provided for a more centralized and streamlined process, several key states had not joined the agreement because, according to industry officials, those states believed that their product approval processes provided better consumer protections than those of the agreement. As a result, we recommended that NAIC and state regulators work with the insurance industry to further identify differences in the ways state regulators review and approve product filings.[92] Although NAIC and state regulators have taken steps to address the lack of uniformity in product approval, NAIC cannot force states to adopt its initiatives, and the success of any of its initiatives is reliant upon the common consent of the states. While 10 more jurisdictions have joined the agreement since our 2009 report, as of December 2015, seven states, the District of Columbia, and four U.S. territories continued to operate outside of the agreement.[93]

Producer licensing—the licensing of agents and brokers who sell insurance—is also an area of the insurance industry where fragmentation has led to inefficient oversight as well as uneven consumer protection. Since 2002, we have reported that the processes for licensing producers have varied across states, resulting in increased costs for insurers because they must follow different application processes and standards to meet individual state requirements.[94] To improve reciprocity in producer licensing, NAIC developed the Producer Licensing Model Act in 2000, which set licensing standards for states to follow.[95] However, we found in April 2009 that several key states had generally not accepted licenses granted by states with less stringent licensing standards.[96] For example, while criminal background checks are not required for reciprocal licensing arrangements between states, state insurance regulators have responsibility to review insurance applications and prevent criminals from being licensed. We found that some states that conduct background checks that include fingerprinting have been unwilling to reciprocate with states that conduct background checks that do not include fingerprinting. These regulators told us that they would be weakening consumer protections by accepting the licensing decisions of states that do not perform background checks that include fingerprinting. Although NAIC's producer licensing initiatives have resulted in increased reciprocity among states over time, neither universal reciprocity nor uniformity in producer licensing has been achieved through NAIC initiatives and common consent of the states. We found that while the lack of uniformity and reciprocity did not preclude producers from obtaining a license in multiple states, producers experienced increased costs and inefficiencies because they had to follow different application processes and standards to meet individual state requirements. In response to these findings, we suggested that Congress may wish to explore ways to ensure that all state insurance regulators could conduct nationwide criminal background checks as part of their producer licensing and consumer protection functions.[97] In 2015, congressional intervention was taken to try to achieve reciprocity. The National Association of Registered Agents and Brokers Reform Act of 2015 was enacted in January 2015 and created a national clearinghouse for producers licensed in one state to operate in all states through a membership system. The act stipulates that the establishment and membership in the association will take effect no sooner than January 2017.

Challenges to Comprehensive Risk Oversight

While actions taken by state and federal regulators and NAIC helped to limit the effects of the 2007-2009 financial crisis on insurers and policyholders, concerns arose as to state insurance regulators' ability to comprehensively oversee all risks posed to insurance companies, particularly those originating in subsidiaries of a multijurisdictional insurance group.[98] In particular, the state-based insurance regulatory structure may potentially limit state insurance regulators' ability to comprehensively oversee all risks posed to insurance companies. Insurance supervision in the United States is generally at the legal entity level where the contract with the policyholder is held, rather than the holding company or group level, in cases where a company owns one or more insurance companies. Therefore, although state insurance regulators have the authority to supervise individual insurance companies in their states, they have traditionally lacked the legal authority to directly supervise a company that might own an insurer, or to directly supervise a noninsurance affiliate or any affiliate domiciled and operating outside of the state. Instead, states approach group supervision through a review of the holding company system. Although NAIC has revised its insurance holding company model law several times since first passing it in 1969, the general principles of group supervision have remained the same. Described as a "windows and walls" approach, group supervision provides state regulators "windows" to scrutinize group activity and assess its potential effect on the ability of the insurer to pay its claims and "walls" to protect the capital of the insurer by requiring the insurance commissioner's approval of material related-party transactions. However, concerns about the effectiveness of group supervision arose during the 2007-2009 financial crisis when a number of insurers received extraordinary financial support from governmental entities. For example, one of the largest U.S. holding companies that had substantial insurance operations, American International Group, Inc. (AIG), suffered large losses. These losses were driven in large part by certain activities conducted by noninsurance affiliates and life insurance subsidiaries.[99] In its insurance modernization report, FIO said that inherent limitations of state law, stemming from the lack of legal authority to supervise noninsurance affiliates or those located outside of the state, have constrained state regulators in conducting oversight over or obtaining information on the operations of subsidiaries in a multijurisdictional insurance group.[100]

Since the crisis, steps have been taken to enhance authorities in this area. First, the Dodd-Frank Act partly addresses this limitation by requiring the Federal Reserve to establish enhanced prudential standards for nonbank financial companies—including insurance organizations— that FSOC designates for supervision by the Federal Reserve.[101] Second, NAIC developed initiatives in 2010 intended to enhance state regulators' "windows" to scrutinize group activity. These initiatives include revisions to NAIC's Insurance Holding Company System Regulatory Act and the Insurance Holding Company System Model Regulation with Reporting Forms and Instructions (holding company model laws) of 2010—and the introduction of another model law, the Risk Management and Own Risk and Solvency Assessment Model Act. The holding company model laws revisions are aimed at (1) expanding state regulators' ability to look at all entities in an insurance group; (2) enhancing state regulators' rights to access information, especially regarding the examinations of entities within the group; (3) enhancing state regulators' ability to participate in supervisory colleges; and (4) requiring insurers to identify and report their enterprise risk within the entire holding company system to the regulator in an annual filing.[102] Additional risk reporting is required from all U.S. insurers or their holding company through the Risk Management and Own Risk and Solvency Assessment Model Act, which sets out legal requirements for the development of a risk management framework. It also requires insurers to analyze all reasonably foreseeable and relevant material risks, such as underwriting, credit, and liquidity risks, that could affect an insurer's ability to meet its consumer obligations and to disclose those risks to state regulators by submitting an own risk and solvency assessment summary report. To encourage states to adopt the revised model laws, NAIC made adoption a requirement for states to maintain their NAIC accreditation effective January 1, 2016, for the revised Insurance Holding Company System Regulatory Act and effective January 1, 2018, for the Risk Management and Own Risk and Solvency Assessment Model Act.[103] NAIC officials stated that they have found that, while model laws establish the standards for state regulators to follow, its accreditation program has helped to successfully drive uniformity among states in certain areas.

As of January 2016, NAIC determined that all 56 U.S. insurance jurisdictions had adopted the revised Insurance Holding Company System Regulatory Act, 34 jurisdictions had adopted the revisions to the Insurance Holding Company System Model Regulation with Reporting Forms and Instructions, and 35 jurisdictions had implemented the Own Risk and Solvency Assessment requirement. NAIC staff noted that the Insurance Holding Company System Regulatory Act is the model law that provides states with the authority to carry out group supervision and the Insurance Holding Company System Model Regulation with Reporting Forms and Instructions provides details on how insurers should format certain reports that they submit to insurance regulators. NAIC staff noted that not all jurisdictions have adopted the Insurance Holding Company System Model Regulation with Reporting Forms and Instructions, but NAIC staff said that this should not affect the effectiveness of group supervision since they believe that the act provides broad authority for the state to examine any information on the insurer and any other entities within the holding company structure.

Opinions vary on how likely NAIC's initiatives are to improve state insurance regulators' effectiveness in overseeing all risks posed to insurance companies. Some participants in our discussion group said that regulators should be able to more proactively supervise insurance companies at the group level once the initiatives are implemented. However, despite their adoption by states, it is not clear whether the model laws will grant state insurance regulators the authority to oversee affiliates because one state's laws do not extend beyond its borders to entities in another state. For example, FIO, in its insurance modernization report, questioned whether the initiatives will grant insurance regulators effective authority over noninsurance affiliates or holding companies, given that direct state regulatory authority is limited to the state-licensed legal entity.[104] NAIC officials disagreed with this perspective, stating that while questions may exist as to whether states have direct regulatory authority over noninsurance affiliates, they can still drive changes in behavior with their authorities, such as requirements for approval of material transactions. Further, the effectiveness of NAIC's initiatives is uncertain because of differences that may arise in the specific ways states may implement them. For example, states may make changes to NAIC's model laws, and the specific provisions of states' insurance laws may limit or alter states' ability to obtain information on noninsurance affiliates of the insurance group, limiting their ability to fully evaluate risks. NAIC officials noted that they do not expect the revisions states have made to the model laws to affect the effectiveness of the intent of the model laws. They noted that the revisions have been minor—for example, revisions have been made to accommodate state statutory drafting conventions.

In recent assessments of U.S. insurance regulation and supervision, FSB, IMF, and FIO made observations on the negative effects of the fragmented insurance regulatory structure. For example, FSB's 2013 assessment of the post-Dodd-Frank U.S. regulatory structure found that, among other things, significant additional work is needed to promote greater regulatory uniformity in the insurance sector.[105] It noted that because NAIC is not a supervisory authority and state laws must only be "substantially similar" to NAIC's model laws, divergent approaches between states can occur, which may affect the consistency of supervision applied to large insurance groups with national and international reach. Similarly, FIO stated that the state-based system of insurance regulation in the United States is inherently limited in its ability to regulate uniformly and efficiently, and IMF pointed out that NAIC continues to promote uniform standards of state regulation but that it cannot enforce convergence.[106] While we have made recommendations to NAIC and state insurance regulators to improve uniformity and reciprocity in the past, the costs and benefits of further increases in reciprocity and uniformity must be considered. Regulators, insurers, and consumers may not benefit if achieving uniformity occurred by simply lowering standards across states. At the same time, it may not be feasible to achieve reciprocity and uniformity across states by meeting the highest standard achieved by any one state.

Several suggestions have been made by both U.S. agencies and international bodies that Congress should consider pursuing reforms to the insurance regulatory system that would promote more regulatory consistency at the national level. While many options include an expanded federal role, variations exist in the suggested level of federal involvement. In both its 2008 and 2009 white papers on financial regulatory reform, Treasury recommended creating an optional federal charter for insurers to increase uniformity in insurance regulation.[107] An optional federal charter could provide for a system of federal chartering, licensing, regulation, and supervision. It could also provide that the current state-based regulation of insurance would continue for those not electing to be regulated at the national level. FIO has also said that federal involvement of some kind in insurance regulation is necessary and would improve uniformity, efficiency, and consistency, but that the ideal solution would not necessarily be for the federal government to displace state regulation completely. Rather, it stated that consideration should be given to whether there are areas in which federal involvement in regulation under the state-based system is warranted and what kind of federal involvement would best provide for attaining policy objectives.[108] In their assessments of the U.S. regulatory structure, both FSB and IMF also noted that increased federal involvement may help improve uniformity. FSB said that consideration should be given to a more federal and streamlined structure and IMF suggested that expanding the federal role by assigning regulatory responsibilities to an independent agency with a national mandate might help improve consistency in insurance regulation.

Regulatory Structure Complicates U.S. Coordination Internationally

The U.S. regulatory structure can also complicate regulators' efforts to coordinate internationally with other regulators. In 2004, we found that a key development that has significantly challenged the existing regulatory structure was the increasingly global nature of financial markets over the past few decades.[109] Globalization of financial markets has required U.S. regulators to coordinate with each other and with their international counterparts to effectively adapt to industry changes. However, coordination and consensus among U.S. regulators has sometimes been difficult to achieve, in part, because the regulatory structure consists of multiple regulators in each financial sector with differing regulatory perspectives based on their statutory missions. To assist international coordination efforts, international bodies consisting of regulators from numerous countries develop financial reforms and set industry standards.[110] Multiple U.S. financial regulators participate in a variety of international bodies, including the Basel Committee on Banking Supervision (Basel Committee), the International Association of Insurance Supervisors (IAIS), and the International Organization of Securities Commissioners (IOSCO). The Basel Committee is the primary global standard-setter for the prudential regulation of banks, and FDIC, the Federal Reserve, and OCC are members. IAIS is responsible for developing principles and standards for the supervision of the insurance sector, and U.S. members include NAIC, FIO, the Federal Reserve, each of the 50 U.S. state insurance regulators, and regulators from the District of Columbia and the 5 U.S. territories.[111] IOSCO sets global standards for the securities sector to protect investors; ensure fair, efficient, and transparent markets; and reduce systemic risks. Both CFTC and SEC are members of IOSCO.

We have previously reported on instances in which the fragmented U.S. regulatory structure has precluded the ability of financial regulators to convey a single U.S. position in international discussions. For example, in the Basel Accords process for developing international capital standards for banks, each federal regulator involved oversees a different set of institutions and represents an important regulatory perspective, which made reaching domestic consensus on some issues difficult. Although U.S. regulators generally agreed on the broad underlying principles at the core of Basel II, including increased risk sensitivity of capital requirements and capital neutrality, in an October 2004 report we found that they sometimes had difficulty agreeing on certain aspects of the process.[112] We also found that the sometimes conflicting views expressed by U.S. regulators made it difficult for other countries to understand the U.S. position and that Congress had informed the bank regulatory agencies that it thought that the discord surrounding Basel II had weakened the U.S. negotiating position. Congress believed this resulted in an agreement that was less than favorable to U.S. financial institutions. However, regulatory officials we spoke to for our 2004 report also told us that the final outcome of the Basel II negotiations was better than it would have been with a single U.S. representative because of the agencies' varying perspectives and expertise. More recently, one regulator told us that the additional capital safeguards embedded in the U.S. implementation of Basel II appear to have enabled U.S. institutions to recover more quickly from the crisis than some of their foreign counterparts.

Since the Dodd-Frank Act was enacted, U.S. regulators have continued to face challenges in their efforts to coordinate internationally. In addition to the individual state insurance regulators, the Federal Reserve is also involved in the supervision of insurance holding companies. Further, the Dodd-Frank Act established FIO and provided it authority to, among other things, represent the United States, as appropriate, at IAIS and to coordinate federal efforts and develop federal policy on prudential aspects of international insurance matters. As a result of this fragmentation, complications have arisen in efforts to effectively represent U.S. interests in international forums focused on the supervision of internationally active insurance groups.[113] In a June 2015 report examining the development of international capital standards for these groups, we found that initially, after the Federal Reserve and FIO joined IAIS, U.S. IAIS members did not collaborate effectively or speak with a unified voice on international capital standards for insurers.[114] Similarly, in 2015, IMF reported that state insurance regulators and the Federal Reserve had different focuses and potential conflicts between their objectives regarding group-wide supervision.[115] IMF found that the state insurance regulators focused on policyholder protection, while the Federal Reserve, in relation to insurance consolidated supervision, focuses on protecting depositors and risks to financial stability. IMF also noted that state regulators' objectives are not clearly and consistently defined in law and agency officials told us that when FIO and the Federal Reserve joined IAIS, they did not have official policies guiding their work in IAIS or in collaboration with other U.S. IAIS members on international capital standards. U.S. IAIS members and stakeholders pointed to areas of public disagreement between FIO and NAIC on issues including FIO's potential role in supervisory colleges and the general need for certain capital standards.

This lack of a unified U.S. view initially was thought by industry participants to have reduced U.S. influence in IAIS, and some insurers indicated that this was one factor that enabled foreign regulators to strongly influence initial IAIS work on capital standards. While we concluded in our 2015 report that U.S. IAIS members had increased their focus on collaborating with each other and with U.S. stakeholders, and were aiming to establish a more unified U.S. view, we stated that in the multilateral setting of IAIS, U.S. members could better advance U.S. interests and concerns with a more unified voice and that room for improvement remained. As a result, we recommended that FIO, the Federal Reserve, and NAIC enhance future collaborative interagency efforts by following additional leading practices for collaboration, such as taking steps to sustain leadership in the collaborative efforts over the long term.[116] We see this as particularly important, given that the tenure of high-level officials who participate in the U.S. collaborative efforts is not guaranteed through the upcoming implementation of international capital standards. Further, even with improved collaboration by FIO, the Federal Reserve, and NAIC, we found that there is some uncertainty about the legal mechanisms that would be used by states to implement the standards in the United States. NAIC officials told us that implementation of new capital standards in the United States would likely require individual states to pass legislation that incorporates the standards. As we discussed previously, fragmentation in U.S. insurance regulation complicates uniform adoption of standards among the states.

Concerns Have Not Been Fully Addressed

The Dodd-Frank Act has helped to mitigate some of the negative effects of fragmentation and overlap in the regulatory structure, but we and others continue to have concerns.[117] For example, depository institutions choose to operate under the state or federal charter that best accommodates their business and strategic needs and are allowed to change their charter if they have legitimate reasons for doing so. While we have noted that this can provide some benefits to depository institutions, in its June 2009 white paper on financial regulatory reform, Treasury stated that the presence of multiple federal supervisors and the ability of firms to easily change their charter can lead to weaker regulation.[118] For example, it stated that prior to the Dodd-Frank Act significant differences between thrift holding company and bank holding company supervision and regulation created arbitrage opportunities—that is, opportunities for institutions to exploit variations in how agencies implement regulatory responsibilities to minimize regulatory scrutiny. For example, although the Federal Reserve imposed leverage and risk-based capital requirements on bank holding companies, OTS did not impose any capital requirements on thrift holding companies, such as AIG.[119] AIG suffered significant financial losses during the crisis and required federal assistance to mitigate systemic risk concerns. According to Treasury, AIG (as well as some large U.S.-based investment banks) chose to own depository institutions—thrifts—that were not considered "banks" under the Bank Holding Company Act, thereby allowing them to avoid the more rigorous oversight regime applicable to bank holding companies.[120]

The Dodd-Frank Act and the prudential regulators have tried to address regulatory arbitrage concerns. First, the Dodd-Frank Act generally prohibits charter conversions by a national bank or a federal thrift to a state bank or state thrift, or by a state bank or thrift to a national bank or federal thrift, while a depository institution is subject to any formal enforcement action or memorandum of understanding that involves a significant supervisory matter.[121] Second, in 2009, FFIEC issued a statement restricting proposed conversions by institutions that have less than satisfactory examination ratings or are subject to serious enforcement actions, among other things.[122]

According to the prudential and state banking regulators, FFIEC's statement covers a broader range of circumstances than the Dodd-Frank Act does. Further, by eliminating OTS and placing thrift holding companies under consolidated supervision of the Federal Reserve, the Dodd-Frank Act removed the option for firms to choose their consolidated supervisor based on the type of depository institution subsidiary the firm owns. In addition, because the Dodd-Frank Act transferred oversight authorities for federal thrifts from OTS to OCC, the only remaining potential arbitrage opportunity for federally-chartered institutions is to switch to a state charter. While all of these actions help to reduce opportunities for regulatory arbitrage through charter conversions, depository institutions still have a choice between more than one primary regulator. This allows depository institutions in good standing to continue to choose among charter types, and it creates the potential for arbitrage risks to continue. According to IMF, a large number of well-rated depository institutions currently fall outside the scope of both the Dodd-Frank Act and FFIEC statement on charter conversions. IMF states that there continues to be a steady stream of conversions in both directions, although the numbers are not large in absolute terms.[123] For example, according to Reports of Condition and Income (Call Report) data, approximately 300 depository institutions out of more than 6,500 institutions went through a charter conversion from 2011 through 2014.[124]

Further, IMF found that the Dodd-Frank Act reforms did not fundamentally address the fragmented nature of the U.S. financial regulatory structure and that the problems inherent in a system with multiple regulators with distinct but overlapping mandates remain. While IMF's April 2015 assessment found that cooperation among the prudential regulators has improved, it also stated that the supervisory structure of safety and soundness regulators involves substantial duplication of supervisory effort, carries a significant burden of ensuring cooperation and coordination, and runs the ongoing risk of inconsistent messages from the regulators. Further, it noted that new challenges exist for the prudential regulators with delineating their responsibilities in relation to those of CFPB. For example, the division of responsibilities between safety and soundness and consumer protection does not allow the prudential regulators to fully focus on safety and soundness matters because they retained their consumer protection oversight responsibilities for depository institutions with assets of $10 billion or less, as well as for certain consumer protection issues in institutions above that threshold. IMF noted that in other countries and regions, the establishment of a specialized consumer regulator has freed the bank supervisor to focus on safety and soundness matters. In those jurisdictions, the bank supervisor responds to operational and reputational risks associated with a bank's poor performance in dealing with customers, but it does not generally become involved in particular consumer matters.

As evidenced by the examples in each financial sector described above, the U.S. regulatory structure historically has created and continues to create challenges to effectively overseeing the financial services industry. While agencies coordinate extensively to mitigate the effects of fragmentation and overlap, this coordination requires considerable effort that, in a more efficient system, could be directed toward other activities. Fragmentation and overlap limit the structure's ability to achieve three characteristics for an effective regulatory system that we identified in our framework for evaluating regulatory proposals. Our framework calls for a regulatory system that provides (1) efficient and effective oversight, (2) consistent financial oversight, and (3) consistent consumer and investor protections. The fragmented regulatory structure with overlapping authorities also makes it difficult to hold regulators accountable for meeting regulatory goals—an additional characteristic we identified in our framework.[125] In the past, we have suggested to Congress ways in which the financial regulatory structure could be altered to address the challenges stemming from fragmentation and overlap. In 1996, we suggested that the regulatory structure could be modernized by reducing the number of federal agencies with responsibility for the oversight of depository institutions, which we stated should help improve the consistency of oversight and reduce regulatory burden.[126] In 2004, we suggested that Congress consider ways to improve the regulatory structure and provided the following options.[127] First, the regulatory structure could be consolidated within "functional" areas, such as banking, securities, insurance, and futures.[128] The two changes at the federal level that would be needed to accomplish this restructuring would be the consolidation of the depository institution regulators and, if Congress wishes to provide a federal charter option for insurance, the creation of an insurance regulatory entity.[129] Second, the regulatory structure could be based on a regulation by objective, sometimes known as the "twin peaks model." This option would require consolidating financial regulatory authority into two regulators, whereby one regulator would oversee safety and soundness and another would be a conduct-ofbusiness regulator for financial institutions. The third option would be to combine all financial regulators into a single entity, creating one regulator to oversee all financial institutions. While the most recent regulatory reform—the Dodd-Frank Act—did make some changes to the regulatory structure, much of the structure remained the same. As a result, we continue to see negative effects created by fragmentation and overlap that challenge the effectiveness of the financial regulatory system.

LIMITATIONS IN AGENCIES' COLLABORATION AND FSOC'S AUTHORITIES MAY HINDER SYSTEMIC RISK OVERSIGHT EFFORTS

The Dodd-Frank Act addressed the lack of systemic risk oversight by placing responsibility for identifying and responding to threats to financial stability, or systemic risks, on a collective group of federal and state regulators and others through the creation of FSOC. The Dodd-Frank Act also created OFR to support FSOC's activities and gave it broad systemic risk monitoring mandates (see table 3). These reforms aim to create ways to monitor, identify, and mitigate systemic risks within a regulatory structure that continues to be fragmented among numerous agencies. As a result, they create the potential for unnecessary duplication in activities or gaps in systemic risk oversight. FSOC's Systemic Risk Committee is the council's main staff-level vehicle for collaboration on systemic risk monitoring and identification efforts across the many federal and state financial regulators. However, the committee does not have full and consistent access to existing monitoring tools or other outputs developed by OFR and Federal Reserve. These two agencies conduct broad-based systemic risk monitoring efforts that use quantitative and qualitative information to monitor the breadth of the financial system for potential threats to financial stability.[130] The agencies have articulated similar goals with respect to their systemic risk monitoring activities. However, they have engaged in these efforts largely independently and their actions have not been consistent with key practices for collaboration. While FSOC's mission includes responding to systemic risks, it has limited authorities to do so. The Dodd-Frank Act left financial regulatory agencies responsible for overseeing financial entities and activities. FSOC's designation authorities do allow FSOC to respond to risks arising from specific entities, but these authorities are limited with respect to risks that arise from financial activities spanning multiple entities. In these instances, FSOC can recommend but not compel regulatory action even with broad consensus among FSOC members. As a result, FSOC may lack the tools needed to comprehensively respond to systemic risks that may emerge.

Table 3. Financial Stability Oversight Council's (FSOC) and Certain Federal Agencies' Select Authorities/Missions Related to Systemic Risk Oversight

	Systemic risk monitoring and identification[a]	Systemic risk mitigation
FSOC[b]	• Identify risks to financial stability that could arise from the material financial distress or failure, or ongoing activities, of large, interconnected bank holding companies or nonbank financial companies. • Determine whether the failure or a disruption of a financial market utility or the conduct of a payment, clearing or settlement activity could create or increase the risk of significant liquidity or credit problems spreading among financial institutions or markets and thereby threaten the stability of the U.S. financial system. • Monitor the financial services marketplace in order to identify potential threats to financial stability. • Identify gaps in regulation that could pose risks to financial stability. • Issue an annual report to Congress that includes potential emerging threats to financial stability.	• Designate nonbank financial companies for consolidated supervision by the Board of Governors of the Federal Reserve System (Federal Reserve) and enhanced prudential standards. • Designate financial market utilities and payment, clearing, and settlement activities as or likely to become systemically important. Designated utilities and payment, clearing, and settlement activities become subject to certain robust risk management and safety and soundness standards under the oversight of a supervisory agency or the Federal Reserve. • Issue recommendations to primary financial regulatory agencies to apply new or heightened standards for a financial activity or practice conducted by bank holding companies or nonbank financial companies under the agencies' jurisdictions. • Make recommendations in its annual reports to, among other things, enhance financial market stability.
Office of Financial Research (OFR)	• Develop and maintain metrics and reporting systems for the risks to U.S. financial stability. • Monitor, investigate, and report on changes in systemwide risk to FSOC and to Congress. • Issue an annual report to Congress that includes potential emerging threats to U.S. financial stability.	N/A

	Systemic risk monitoring and identification[a]	Systemic risk mitigation
	• Evaluate and report on stress tests or other stability-related evaluations of financial entities overseen by FSOC member agencies.	
Federal Insurance Office (FIO)	• Monitor all aspects of the insurance industry, including identifying issues or gaps in the regulation of insurers that could contribute to a systemic crisis in the insurance industry or the U.S. financial system. • Recommend to FSOC that it designate an insurer as an entity subject to regulation as a nonbank financial company supervised by the Federal Reserve.	N/A
Federal Reserve	• May develop analytic techniques to identify, measure, and monitor risks to the financial stability of the United States, as part of its requirement to conduct supervisory stress-tests of certain financial companies.	• Supervise bank holding companies with $50 billion in assets or more and nonbank financial companies designated by FSOC, and establish enhanced prudential standards, such as stress tests and resolution plans, to prevent or mitigate risks to financial stability. • Prescribe (or consult in the establishment of) enhanced risk-management standards for a designated financial market utility or entity conducting designated payment, clearing, or settlement activities for which the Federal Reserve or another federal agency is the agency that has primary jurisdiction over the entity.
Federal Deposit Insurance Corporation (FDIC)		• With the Federal Reserve, review resolution plans from bank holding companies with $50 billion in assets or more and nonbank companies designated by FSOC. • Resolve large financial companies whose failure and resolution under otherwise applicable Federal or State law may have serious adverse effects on financial stability in the United States.

Table 3. (Continued)

	Systemic risk monitoring and identification[a]	Systemic risk mitigation
Commodity Futures Trading Commission (CFTC), Securities and Exchange Commission (SEC)		• May prescribe enhanced risk-management standards for a designated financial market utility or entity conducting a designated payment, clearing, and settlement activity for which it is has primary jurisdiction.

Source: Dodd-Frank Act and GAO analysis. | GAO-16-175

[a]As of January 2016, federal financial regulatory agencies other than the Federal Reserve did not conduct broad-based assessments of systemic risks. However, they did conduct their own assessments of risk within their own regulatory jurisdictions and participated in FSOC.

[b]FSOC members include the Secretary of the Treasury, who chairs the council, and the heads of the Bureau of Consumer Financial Protection, CFTC, FDIC, Federal Reserve, the Federal Housing Finance Agency, the National Credit Union Administration, the Office of the Comptroller of the Currency, SEC, FIO, and OFR; representatives from the state banking, securities, and insurance regulators; and an independent insurance expert. FSOC member agency staff participate in FSOC committees to help fulfill FSOC's mission to identify risks to financial stability and respond to emerging threats.

FSOC'S Systemic Risk Committee Has Improved Interagency Collaboration but Does Not Have Access to Key Information

Interagency Collaboration in Systemic Risk Monitoring

As mentioned earlier, through the creation of FSOC—whose members include the heads of the federal financial regulatory agencies and are collectively referred to as principals—the Dodd-Frank Act addressed the lack of systemic risk oversight by making financial regulators and others collectively responsible for identifying systemic risks. FSOC's functional committees help the council carry out its authorities.[131] FSOC's committees generally comprise staff from each of its member agencies. In addition to the functional committees, FSOC's Deputies Committee is made up of senior officials designated by principals and is responsible for overseeing the work of the other committees. Further, the FSOC Secretariat—a dedicated policy office in Treasury's Office of Domestic Finance—coordinates the work of the committees and assists FSOC's chairperson (the Secretary of the Treasury) in carrying out his or her responsibilities. The Systemic Risk Committee is FSOC's main staff-level vehicle for collaboration on systemic risk monitoring and identification efforts across federal and state financial regulators. The committee is tasked with (1) monitoring and analyzing financial markets, the financial system, and issues related to financial stability to support FSOC's mission to identify and respond to risks and emerging threats, (2) facilitating information sharing and coordination among FSOC member staff and member agencies to help identify and respond to risks to financial stability, (3) supporting FSOC's responsibilities to annually report to and testify before Congress, and (4) coordinating with other FSOC committees on issues of common interest, as appropriate.[132] Treasury has administrative responsibility for coordinating the activities of the Systemic Risk Committee, which generally holds monthly meetings.

The Systemic Risk Committee's process for identifying, monitoring, and reporting on systemic risks is consensus based (see fig. 7). FSOC member agency staff generally agreed that the committee provides a venue for a regular and collaborative exchange of ideas and information about particular risks and a unique opportunity to learn in greater depth about risks from the point of view of other regulators. They generally agreed that the agenda, set by FSOC Secretariat staff, is flexible and members feel free to bring up any topics they deem important for interagency discussion. Our review of committee documents from July 2012 through August 2014 found that member agency staff generally organized in working groups to analyze specific potential systemic risks or provided updates on certain issues using both quantitative and qualitative information. Analyses or updates may be related to risks addressed in past FSOC annual report recommendations. Additionally, since we reported on FSOC processes in 2012, the work of the Systemic Risk Committee has become more tightly integrated into FSOC's annual reports, as represented in figure 7.[133] Staff from several FSOC member agencies stated that they benefited from committee analyses and presentations, which can pool information on a given risk from across the financial regulatory spectrum. Member agencies also generally stated that participation in the Systemic Risk Committee and other FSOC activities helped them build informal communication channels and good working relationships among staff across the agencies, which was not always common before the creation of FSOC and the committee.

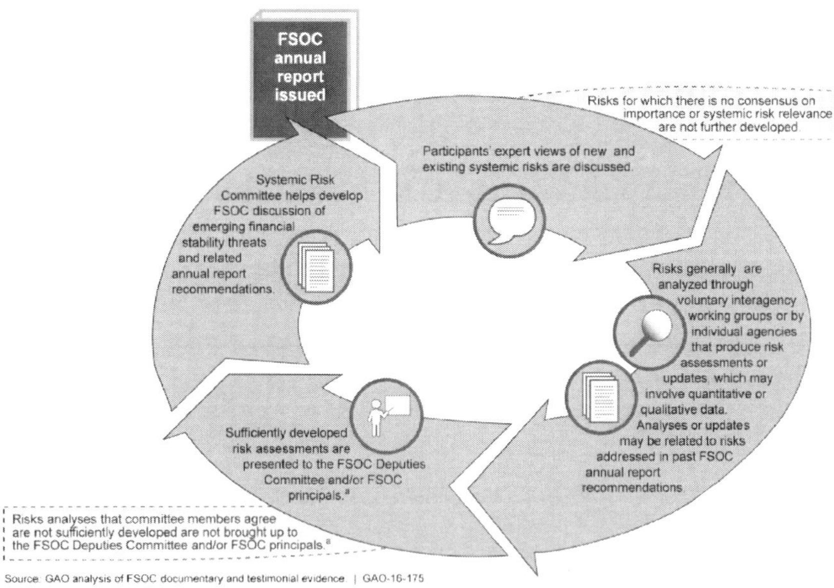

Source: GAO analysis of FSOC documentary and testimonial evidence. | GAO-16-175

[a]FSOC's Deputies Committee oversees the work of the other interagency staff committees. The members of the Deputies Committee are designated by each FSOC member. FSOC members are also referred to as principals and are generally the heads of each of the FSOC member agencies.

Figure 7. Financial Stability Oversight Council's (FSOC) Systemic Risk Committee Process for Identifying, Monitoring, and Reporting on Systemic Risks.

Use of Systemic Risk Monitoring Information

While FSOC's Systemic Risk Committee produces analyses of identified potential systemic risks using both quantitative and qualitative information, the current process for identifying potential new systemic risks continues to rely primarily on participants sharing their expert views on potential threats at the Systemic Risk Committee for consideration. That is, to identify new threats, Systemic Risk Committee members raise any new systemic risk concerns that they may have and, if there is sufficient consensus to study the issue further, they volunteer and organize in working groups to collaboratively produce risk assessments (see fig. 7).[134] However, as part of this process, the committee does not have full and consistent access to existing systemic risk monitoring tools or other outputs developed by OFR and the Federal Reserve, and legal data-sharing obstacles may impede access to additional monitoring information produced by OFR or other agencies.

Both OFR and the Federal Reserve conduct broad-based systemic risk monitoring efforts. In 2013, OFR released a prototype of its Financial Stability Monitor, a quantitative systemic risk monitoring tool that OFR describes as its benchmark tool for assessing risks across the system. The monitor uses publicly and commercially available data to provide a snapshot of potential weaknesses in broad areas of the financial system that may threaten financial stability. OFR shared early versions of the Financial Stability Monitor with the Systemic Risk Committee prior to its first public release in OFR's December 2013 annual report. Since that time, OFR has refined, broadened, and deepened the monitor and also began providing semiannual updates through its website and annual reports, but has only presented the updates and revised assessments to FSOC principals and the Deputies Committee and not the Systemic Risk Committee.

As seen in table 4, the Financial Stability Monitor is part of a suite of monitors that OFR is developing.[135] OFR staff said that to the extent that the monitors that are still in development contain disaggregated confidential information, they could not be shared widely with Systemic Risk Committee members even after they are completed. OFR staff and others stated that data-sharing agreements, which are designed to protect confidentiality and market integrity, generally include restrictions on how an agency may share information it receives from another agency with third parties. OFR staff said that at this time, monitors that use disaggregated confidential information could only be shared with certain FSOC member agency staff—generally FSOC deputies and principals— who sign specific agreements or where consent is given by the information provider. Several committee participants told us that Systemic Risk Committee meetings are open to any member agency staff, and OFR staff stated that current OFR agreements involving confidential information do not allow OFR to share such information with Systemic Risk Committee members at large unless it is anonymized or properly aggregated per the terms of the agreement. For example, even though OFR has authority to obtain data from FSOC member agencies, staff from SEC, which shares some of its data with OFR, stated that when providing data to OFR or others, SEC must ensure that its own statutory and other requirements for data sharing are followed.

The Federal Reserve also conducts frequent, broad-based systemic risk monitoring. However, the agency does not systematically share comprehensive results of its monitoring efforts with the Systemic Risk Committee, as these are intended for internal use to inform Federal Reserve policy, according to Federal Reserve staff. For example, Federal Reserve staff produce a quarterly assessment to provide the Federal Reserve Board with regular, confidential systemic risk assessments to inform Federal Reserve policy, including monetary policy.[136] Federal Reserve staff stated that such assessments or their underlying analyses may contain confidential supervisory information, including data from supervisory stress tests.

Federal internal control standards call for the use of relevant, reliable, and timely information from internal or external sources to achieve the entity's responsibilities.[137] In addition, according to IMF, efforts to monitor the financial system for systemic risks must be based on a continuous assessment of evolving risks that uses quality qualitative and quantitative information.[138] IMF guidance states that, because sources of systemic risk can shift and indicators cannot capture all information, systemic-riskrelated policy is generally better supported by guided discretion, where key indicators can help signal when adjustments might be appropriate but decisions are based on judgment that takes into account all available information. Such judgment requires access to both quantitative and qualitative information. In addition, our key collaboration practices call for identifying and addressing needs by leveraging resources, such as leveraging OFR's and Federal Reserve's broad-based systemic risk monitoring efforts for Systemic Risk Committee use.[139]

Table 4. Office of Financial Research (OFR) Monitors Related to Financial Stability, January 2016

Monitor	Frequency of updates and assessments	Description	Data informing the monitor
Financial Stability Monitor	Semiannual	Provides a snapshot of weaknesses in the financial system based on indicators in five functional areas of risk: macroeconomic, market, credit, funding and liquidity, and contagion. The monitor is not designed to predict the timing or severity of a financial crisis but to identify, at a high level, underlying vulnerabilities that may predispose the system to a crisis.	Public data, commercially acquired data, and industry analyses
Financial Markets Monitor	Monthly	Provides an overview of major developments and emerging trends in global capital markets.	Public data, commercially acquired data, and industry sources
Money Market Fund Monitor	Monthly	Examines individual funds and the industry as a whole on the basis of credit, interest rate, and liquidity risk. Each risk category is analyzed based on portfolio statistics and holdings.	Supervisory confidential information from the Securities and Exchange Commission (SEC), publicly available with a time lag[a]
Credit Default Swaps Monitor	To be determined	Provides analytics on various financial stability metrics in the credit default swap market, such as excessive market concentration and interconnectivity, through the use of risk metrics and visual assessment techniques.	Privately acquired confidential data from the Depository Trust and Clearing Corporation and commercially acquired data

Table 4. (Continued)

Monitor	Frequency of updates and assessments	Description	Data informing the monitor
Hedge Fund Monitor	To be determined	Provides analytics on potential risks that could arise out of the hedge fund industry.	SEC confidential supervisory information and commercially acquired data
Correlation Monitor	Daily	Explores cross asset correlations through interactive visualizations	Public data, commercially acquired data

Source: Office of Financial Research. | GAO-16-175

[a]According to OFR staff, OFR obtains form N-MFP information from SEC on monthly schedules of portfolio holdings of money market funds. As of January 2016, SEC published these data publicly with a 60 day lag. However, in August 2014 SEC eliminated the lag on public availability of these data, which OFR staff stated are intended to be publicly available in April 2016.

Note: According to OFR staff, as of January 2016, the Financial Stability Monitor and the Financial Markets Monitor are the only monitors in production. The remaining monitors are still under development.

Both OFR and the Federal Reserve officials stated that participation of key staff in the Systemic Risk Committee allows for the proper sharing of information on systemic risks identified by their respective efforts. OFR staff stated that by participating in the committee they are ensuring that staff assessments based on OFR monitors are being considered by all member agencies at Systemic Risk Committee meetings. Treasury and OFR staff also stated that once OFR finalized the Financial Stability Monitor, they deemed it more appropriate to present it to the FSOC principals and deputies, as risks are also discussed at those meetings. For their part, Federal Reserve staff stated that their participation in the Systemic Risk Committee is a built-in mechanism that helps ensure proper flow of information related to new risks between the Federal Reserve and the committee without the need to share the agency's internal assessments, reports, or other information. They stated that the Federal Reserve would have to carefully consider data confidentiality and other concerns when sharing such internal documents outside the agency. They also stated that when the Systemic Risk Committee analyzes specific threats that have been identified, Federal Reserve staff have shared analyses or metrics relevant to those threats.

However, participation of key OFR or Federal Reserve staff on the Systemic Risk Committee does not provide reasonable assurance that the committee has access to information that could better equip committee members to identify new potential risks to the system. For example, OFR staff presenting updated assessments of the Financial Stability Monitor or other systemic risk monitoring tools or outputs to FSOC principals or deputies is useful, but should not replace staff-level discussions of such information at the Systemic Risk Committee. Similarly, while sharing relevant metrics or specific analyses with the Systemic Risk Committee is appropriate, the committee is currently not fully benefitting from the frequent, broad-based systemic risk monitoring efforts already underway within the Federal Reserve. Systemic Risk Committee participants can dedicate time as a group to interpreting, assessing, and comparing existing financial stability assessments and can enrich the value of the monitors with their own points of view that, together, encompass regulatory perspectives over all regulated financial entities and activities. Such an exercise could, for instance, allow staff to identify information within their own agencies that could improve the monitoring efforts and make them more useful for the purposes of the committee. Lastly, if the nature of open participation of FSOC member agency staff at the Systemic Risk Committee presents serious impediments to meaningful sharing and discussion of confidential supervisory and other information, other arrangements may help overcome such impediments. OFR staff said that although legal constraints preclude them from sharing some monitors' underlying data widely at the Systemic Risk Committee, they could share this information with a small group, as they have done in other settings. For example, they could distribute numbered copies of the documents containing raw data if consistent with law and data-sharing agreements with the providing agencies. This could facilitate sharing information with a subset of the Systemic Risk Committee, but quality deliberation depends on the full participation of all relevant staff. The Systemic Risk Committee may not always require disaggregated, confidential information to carry out its responsibilities, but at times disaggregated data could be crucial for identifying systemically relevant interdependencies between financial entities or markets supervised by different regulators under the existing fragmented regulatory structure. Without better access to systemic risk monitoring tools and other outputs, the Systemic Risk Committee may identify and advance the analysis of only a subset of systemic risks in a timely manner and may identify others too late or miss others altogether.

OFR's and Federal Reserve's Collaboration in Their Systemic Risk Monitoring Activities Is Limited

OFR and Federal Reserve both conduct broad-based systemic risk monitoring activities that aim to identify threats across the financial system. However, the two agencies have developed these efforts largely independently from one another, leading to lost collaborative opportunities that could improve their ability to identify systemic risks and reduce the potential for unnecessary duplication. OFR is responsible for monitoring, investigating, and reporting on changes in systemwide risk levels and patterns to FSOC and to Congress, as well as developing and maintaining independent analytical capabilities and computing resources to be used, among other things, to monitor, investigate, and report on systemic risks.[140] OFR also has authority to collect data from financial institutions and receive data from FSOC member agencies, and one of its goals is to produce tools and analyses that are widely used and critical to monitoring and assessing financial stability. To address this goal, OFR developed the Financial Stability Monitor for assessing systemic risks across the system.

After the 2007-2009 financial crisis, the Federal Reserve expanded its strategic goals and activities around systemic risk monitoring. The Dodd-Frank Act gave the Federal Reserve the authority to develop analytic techniques needed to identify, measure, and monitor systemic risks as part of its stress testing responsibilities.[141] Federal Reserve senior officials have publicly stated that financial stability responsibilities are part of the agency's role as the central bank of the United States. The agency also highlighted the importance of expanding and improving its systemic risk monitoring capabilities in its 2012-2015 Strategic Framework. As a result, the Federal Reserve pooled staff expertise from across the agency and the Federal Reserve Banks and developed procedures to periodically produce internal assessments of financial stability that inform Federal Reserve policy.

In comparing OFR's Financial Stability Monitor to the Federal Reserve's financial stability monitoring program, we found that, while there are some differences in the analytical approaches and the implementation of their efforts, they also have many shared features and similar broad systemic risk goals.[142]

- The primary intent of both agencies' efforts is to identify weaknesses or vulnerabilities in the financial system that, given a shock or series of shocks, could result in material disruptions in financial and economic activity.[143] Both agencies' efforts measure vulnerabilities using, among other things, quantitative metrics (or indicators) that cover similar areas of the financial system and similar types of risk—for example, financial leverage and valuations in equity and property markets. OFR's Financial Stability Monitor uses public and commercially acquired data to provide a snapshot of vulnerabilities in the financial system generally by highlighting sharp movements of key risk indicators from their historical means. The monitor is visualized in a heat map based on indicators of five broad areas of risk: macroeconomic, market, credit, funding/liquidity, and contagion. OFR staff then conduct further analysis on areas of concern flagged by the monitor. Consequently, OFR's assessments of the monitor are accompanied by additional data to support deeper analysis on various potential risks. According to Federal Reserve staff, the Federal Reserve's financial stability monitoring program is also informed by indicators and consists of over a dozen input reports containing in-depth analyses of vulnerabilities in the banking, shadow banking, asset market, and nonfinancial sectors.[144] The reports use a broad range of metrics that focus on financial system vulnerabilities, including leverage, maturity transformation, interconnectedness, complexity, and pricing of risk. According to Federal Reserve staff, their program is informed by public and commercially available data, confidential supervisory data such as stress test data, as well as qualitative information on risks regarding entities the Federal Reserve oversees.

- Both agencies aim to understand how financial vulnerabilities could allow apparently isolated shocks to spread—or propagate—across the financial system. OFR officials stated that their systemic risk monitoring goals include understanding the propagation of threats, and OFR stated in its December 2014 annual report that it is working to improve the Financial Stability Monitor by incorporating methods that take into account channels that can transmit or amplify shocks through the financial system. Federal Reserve staff stated that they analyze how vulnerabilities could interact with relevant shocks. An official added that the efforts focus on vulnerabilities that the Federal Reserve can affect through its own policy or mitigation tools.
- Both OFR and the Federal Reserve aim to have forward-looking tools to identify where the build-up of vulnerabilities can provide early insight into emerging systemic risks. For example, OFR completed a

> back-testing exercise to assess the potential of the Financial Stability Monitor to capture extreme financial or market events, identify turning points, and provide early warning signals of stress.[145] The Federal Reserve's program is similarly intended to be forward-looking—that is, indicators in the Federal Reserve's program are designed to capture vulnerabilities before they materialize in the form of market stress or crisis.

OFR and the Federal Reserve also are engaged in distinct but related stress-testing activities stemming from the Dodd-Frank Act.[146] OFR is mandated to evaluate and report on stress tests. The Federal Reserve is mandated to conduct supervisory stress tests of nonbank financial companies designated by FSOC and bank holding companies with $50 billion or more in assets, as well as prescribe, or help prescribe, scenarios for company-run stress tests for these and other companies. The Federal Reserve issued its first round of Dodd-Frank Act mandated supervisory stress test results in March 2013, and OFR has since assessed the Federal Reserve's stress test activities in its annual reports and promoted research to advance stress testing methodologies.[147]

To some extent, OFR and the Federal Reserve have taken steps to share aspects of their financial stability monitoring programs with each other. For example, during the development phase of the Financial Stability Monitor, OFR staff stated that they sought expert input on the monitor from the Federal Reserve, among others, and periodically discussed the monitor with Federal Reserve staff once it was published in the 2013 OFR Annual Report. As explained earlier, OFR has presented updated assessments of its monitor to FSOC's Systemic Risk Committee, deputies, or principals, all of which include representatives from the Federal Reserve. Federal Reserve staff stated that both agencies coordinate on an ad hoc basis on their broad financial stability programs, as they encounter areas where additional information collection might be warranted. They added that staff involved in the Federal Reserve's financial stability monitoring program are also part of FSOC's Systemic Risk Committee and raise issues that are relevant or of interest to other FSOC member agencies as appropriate, including content from their assessments of financial stability. In addition, to address its mandate to evaluate stress tests, OFR is in the process of obtaining certain Federal Reserve stress test data, which it plans to use to advance research in this area.[148]

However, OFR and the Federal Reserve have developed and implemented their systemic risk monitoring efforts largely independently from one another. For example, OFR and Federal Reserve staff have not engaged in a formal process to learn from each other's detailed analytical and technical approaches for identifying vulnerabilities, measuring them, or modeling and measuring propagation channels given specific shocks to the financial system. The Federal Reserve has publicly released a conceptual framework for its monitoring program, but OFR does not have access to internal Federal Reserve assessments, underlying reports, or metrics.[149]

OFR's and the Federal Reserve's actions have not been consistent with our key collaboration practices.[150] These practices state, among other things, that to achieve a common outcome, agencies should establish mutually reinforcing or joint strategies and identify and address needs by leveraging resources. They further recommend that agencies engaging in collaborative efforts work together to define and agree on their respective roles and responsibilities.[151] OFR and the Federal Reserve believe the current nature and level of their collaboration are appropriate, and both agencies stated that they believe that their participation in FSOC's Systemic Risk Committee ensures communication between the two agencies about their systemic risk monitoring efforts.

Separate entities monitoring systemic risk from different perspectives could help reduce the likelihood that potential systemic risks will not be identified in time. As such, viewpoints, analytical tools, and conclusions need not be harmonized across agencies. Further, Federal Reserve staff said that multiple assessments of financial stability based on different assumptions and methodologies are useful in assessing systemic risks and can help avoid common blindspots shared by regulators and market participants. However, failure to use some key collaboration practices could result in OFR and the Federal Reserve missing opportunities to leverage each other's resources, including expertise, qualitative and market knowledge or insights, and distinct authorities (for example, authorities to receive supervisory data from financial regulatory agencies). It also could lead to unnecessarily duplicative analytical work. Further, by failing to collaborate more effectively, the agencies may miss opportunities to identify important and mutually beneficial ways to improve their current and planned systemic risk monitoring and identification activities and find ways to share useful tools or other outputs with FSOC's Systemic Risk Committee. Going forward, OFR and the Federal Reserve also could miss opportunities to leverage resources or act more strategically regarding other areas of growing common interest, such as research on stress testing and the propagation of risk. Engaging in certain collaborative practices, such as articulating individual and common goals for their systemic risk monitoring activities, could help the agencies make progress toward their goals and monitor that progress. This could formalize communications between the two agencies to help ensure comprehensiveness in systemic risk surveillance, intentional overlapping analyses or activities, sufficiently diverse analytical approaches, and reduced risk of duplication. It also could establish mechanisms to help ensure relevant new tools or other outputs are fully and consistently incorporated in FSOC Systemic Risk Committee deliberations.

FSOC's Systemic Risk Mitigation Authorities Are Limited and Remain Unclear

While FSOC's mission includes responding to systemic risks, it has limited authorities to do so. The Dodd-Frank Act left financial regulatory agencies responsible for overseeing financial entities and activities.[152] The act does allow FSOC to respond to certain potential systemic risks primarily through its authorities to designate certain entities or payment, clearing, and settlement (PCS) activities that may pose a threat to financial stability for enhanced supervision by a specific federal regulator (designation authorities).[153] However, FSOC's designation authorities, by statute, cannot be used to address certain types of risks, and the full scope of FSOC's designation authorities remains untested and unclear to date. FSOC has other nondesignation authorities that allow it to make recommendations to individual regulators to address specific risks, but these recommendations are nonbinding.

FSOC's nondesignation authorities include Section 120 recommendations and annual report recommendations.

- **Section 120 recommendations.** Per section 120 of the Dodd-Frank Act, FSOC may issue recommendations to a primary financial regulatory agency to apply new or heightened standards for a financial activity or practice conducted by financial companies under the regulator's jurisdiction. If no primary regulator exists, FSOC can recommend appropriate legislation to Congress. As of January 2016, FSOC had proposed to use this authority once. FSOC issued for public comment a proposed Section 120 recommendation to SEC to implement reforms in money market mutual funds in order to address structural weaknesses in this market.[154] This authority is broad in scope, as it can be used to address a financial activity or practice conducted by financial companies. The authority can provide clarity and public accountability for an identified risk by allowing FSOC to state which regulator should respond to the risk and how it should do so. However, the recommendations are nonbinding, and regulators can choose either to comply with FSOC's Section 120 recommendations or not to comply and explain the reason for noncompliance.[155]

- **Annual report recommendations.** The Dodd-Frank Act also requires FSOC to report annually and testify before Congress on recommendations to enhance financial stability, and FSOC has included such recommendations in its annual reports. FSOC annual report recommendations can be broad and do not necessarily identify specific systemic risk mitigation actions for member agencies on specific timelines, and identified agencies are not required to respond to them.

In addition, FSOC has three distinct designation authorities that, if invoked, require certain federal agencies to impose enhanced standards on designated entities or financial institutions conducting designated activities. FSOC can designate (1) nonbank financial companies for consolidated supervision by the Federal Reserve and enhanced prudential standards, (2) financial market utilities as systemically important, and (3) PCS activities as systemically important.[156] FSOC has a Nonbank Financial Companies Designations Committee and a Financial Market Utilities and PCS Activities Committee that develop analyses and conduct other work for such designations. As of January 2016, FSOC had designated four nonbank financial companies and eight financial market utilities. Federal Reserve must prescribe enhanced prudential standards for designated nonbank financial companies, and the Federal Reserve, SEC, or CFTC must prescribe enhanced risk management standards for designated financial market utilities.[157] These two entity-specific designation authorities help FSOC address fragmentation in systemic risk oversight by making one regulator primarily accountable for mitigating systemic risks from the designated entities and requiring enhanced supervision. While FSOC is a key player in the Dodd-Frank Act's mechanism to extend enhanced supervision over financial entities, the assigned federal financial regulator has the authority to impose requirements on designated entities and ultimately mitigate threats.

As of January 2016, FSOC had not yet designated any PCS activities as systemically important. Unlike the other designation authorities, such designation could apply to all financial institutions that engage in the designated activity and would require SEC, CFTC, or Federal Reserve to impose enhanced risk management standards on those financial institutions. However, the scope of FSOC's PCS activities designation authority (PCS designation authority) is limited by the statutory definition of PCS activities. The Dodd-Frank Act excludes certain pre-trade and other non-PCS activities from this definition, some of which could be associated with systemic risk.[158] Staff from SEC, CFTC, Federal Reserve, and Treasury told us that, to date, FSOC's Financial Market Utilities and PCS Activities Committee has focused on understanding risks from financial market utilities, such as central counterparty clearing agencies or organizations, monitoring these risks, and updating FSOC member staff on their status. They stated the committee has not yet discussed how FSOC would use this authority or the scope of this authority. Consequently, the extent to which statutory scope constraints on this authority could impair FSOC's ability to respond to certain threats involving multiple entities remains unclear. Staff from SEC, CFTC, and Federal Reserve stated that, thus far, they have been able to address identified risks primarily through their own supervisory authorities or FSOC's other designation authorities.

According to our framework for evaluating regulatory reform proposals, a financial system should include a mechanism for identifying, monitoring, and also managing risks to the financial system regardless of the source of the risk or the institutions from which the risk originates.[159] In addition, according to IMF, a strong institutional framework is essential to help ensure that macroprudential policy—policy that aims to enhance the stability of the financial system—can work effectively by, among other things, assigning an appropriate range and reach of policy tools to the macroprudential authority, in this case FSOC. Recognizing that financial systems evolve dynamically, IMF states that limiting systemic risks requires authorities that foster the ability to act. That is, the macroprudential authority needs powers to ensure regulatory responses and bring important entities into the financial regulatory umbrella as needed.[160]

Although FSOC's mission is to identify and mitigate systemic risks, FSOC's designation authorities have limited scope and represent a gap in the post-Dodd-Frank mechanisms for the mitigation of systemic risks. In particular, FSOC's collective designation authorities may not allow it to comprehensively address systemic risks that could arise from the financial activities of multiple entities. By statute, FSOC's PCS designation authority excludes certain types of activities, and its scope remains untested and unclear to date. Thus, there may be risks that arise from widely conducted financial activities that FSOC cannot address through its PCS designation authority and for which entity-by-entity designation may not be effective or feasible. In those cases, FSOC can recommend regulatory action, but it cannot act or compel action even with a broad consensus among FSOC members. In the event that regulators do not or cannot act to mitigate systemic threats, FSOC's authorities to respond are limited. As a result, FSOC may lack the tools needed to comprehensively address systemic risks that may emerge. In addition, without requisite authorities, holding FSOC accountable for addressing threats to financial stability will be difficult.

CONCLUSION

The U.S. financial regulatory structure is complex, with responsibilities fragmented among a number of regulators that have overlapping authorities. While the current structure allows for effective financial regulation in some key areas, recent changes may not have addressed long-standing fragmented and overlapping regulatory authorities and their effects on regulators' oversight activities. Fragmentation, overlap, and duplication also introduce significant challenges for efficient and effective oversight of financial institutions and activities. Fragmentation and overlap in the structure have resulted in inefficiencies in the regulatory process; inconsistencies in how regulators conduct oversight activities over similar types of institutions, products, and risks; the potential for duplication in regulators' oversight activities; and differences in the levels of protection provided to consumers. Further, the existence of multiple regulators makes it difficult to ensure that agencies are held accountable for failures to act in accordance with regulatory goals. The Dodd-Frank Act implemented a number of key reforms intended to address significant weaknesses and gaps in the regulatory system, including closing gaps in systemic risk and swaps oversight; consolidating supervision of large, complex institutions under the Federal Reserve; and expanding protections for consumers and investors. However, for the most part, the act left the regulatory structure unchanged. In the framework we developed in 2009 for evaluating regulatory reform proposals, we noted that an effective regulatory system would address certain structural shortcomings created by fragmentation and overlap. While coordination and collaboration among regulators help to manage some of the negative effects of fragmentation and overlap, the sheer number of regulatory bodies and differences in their regulatory approaches continue to make coordination challenging and time-consuming. In addition, issues related to fragmentation and overlap in the structure have continued to surface as new agencies created by the Dodd-Frank Act and existing agencies work together.

Within the area of systemic risk oversight, the Dodd-Frank Act addressed challenges by keeping the independence of the system's multiple regulators and by placing responsibility for identifying and responding to systemic risks on a collective group of regulators through the creation of FSOC. This approach to systemic risk oversight requires consistent and highly effective interagency collaboration. Further, although federal internal control standards and IMF guidelines for systemic risk monitoring call for the use of quality quantitative and qualitative information, FSOC's Systemic Risk Committee is not fully and consistently informed by OFR and the Federal Reserve's monitoring tools or other outputs. Both OFR and the Federal Reserve now monitor the financial system for systemic risk, with each agency devoting staff and resources to developing broad-based systemic risk surveillance efforts. However, despite having similar monitoring goals, OFR's and the Federal Reserve's actions have not been consistent with key practices for collaboration that we have previously identified. This limitation in their collaborative efforts represents lost opportunities for leveraging resources to further their systemic risk monitoring goals and improving their collective ability to identify new and emerging threats to the system. It also could lead to unnecessarily duplicative analytical work. We recognize the importance and value of the agencies' independent activities and conclusions regarding systemic risk and believe that this should be preserved as the agencies work to improve their collaborative efforts. Finally, as we have noted in the past, regulatory systems should include a mechanism for identifying, monitoring, and also managing risks to the financial system. In addition, IMF has stated that macroprudential entities require authorities to foster the ability to act and ensure regulatory responses. FSOC's designation authorities can bring certain entities or activities that may pose threats to financial stability into the regulatory purview and require enhanced oversight. However, limitations in its designation authorities raise questions about FSOC's ability to effectively respond to different kinds of systemic risks, particularly those whose origins are not entity-specific. These limitations also make it difficult to hold FSOC accountable for maintaining financial stability.

Matters for Congressional Consideration

We are suggesting two matters for congressional consideration. First, Congress should consider whether additional changes to the financial regulatory structure are needed to reduce or better manage fragmentation and overlap in the oversight of financial institutions and activities to improve (1) the efficiency and effectiveness of oversight; (2) the consistency of consumer and investor protections; and (3) the consistency of financial oversight for similar institutions, products, risks, and services. For example, Congress could consider consolidating the number of federal agencies involved in overseeing the safety and soundness of depository institutions, combining the entities involved in overseeing the securities and derivatives markets, transferring the remaining prudential regulators' consumer protection authorities over large depository institutions to CFPB, and the optimal role for the federal government in insurance regulation, among other considerations.

Second, Congress should consider whether legislative changes are necessary to align FSOC's authorities with its mission to respond to systemic risks. Congress could do so by making changes to FSOC's mission, its authorities, or both, or to the missions and authorities of one or more of the FSOC member agencies to support a stronger link between the responsibility and capacity to respond to systemic risks. In doing so, Congress could solicit information from FSOC on the effective scope of its collective designation authorities, including any gaps.

Recommendations for Executive Action

We are making three recommendations for executive action.

First, to help regulators address regulatory fragmentation and improve FSOC's ability to identify emerging systemic risks, we recommend that as OFR develops and refines its financial stability monitoring tools, it should work with FSOC to determine ways in which to fully and regularly incorporate current and future monitors and assessments into Systemic Risk Committee deliberations, including, where relevant, those that present disaggregated or otherwise confidential supervisory information.

Second, to help regulators address regulatory fragmentation and improve FSOC's ability to identify emerging systemic risks, we recommend that the Federal Reserve work with FSOC to regularly incorporate the comprehensive esults of its systemic risk monitoring activities into Systemic Risk Committee deliberations.

Third, to more efficiently and effectively monitor the financial system for systemic risks and reduce the risk of unnecessary duplication, we recommend that OFR and the Federal Reserve jointly articulate individual and common goals for their systemic risk monitoring activities, including a plan to monitor progress toward articulated goals, and formalize regular strategic and technical discussions around their activities and outputs to support those goals.

AGENCY COMMENTS

We provided a draft of this report to CFTC, CFPB, Federal Reserve, FDIC, FIO, FSOC, FTC, NAIC, NCUA, OCC, OFR, and SEC. CFTC, NCUA, Federal Reserve, and OFR provided written comments. CFTC noted that while the securities and derivatives markets are interconnected, they remain separate and serve distinct functions within the financial system. In addition, CFTC stated that it has worked and continues to work closely with SEC. Our report discusses areas that these agencies have worked together in the past to resolve jurisdiction disputes and address areas of overlap in the oversight of their respective markets, as well as recent examples of their coordination efforts on the swaps and security-based swaps rulemakings. However, the report also notes that, despite these efforts, there were still substantive differences between certain of the agencies' rules and in the timing of the rules, which create the potential for inefficiencies in the way the markets are overseen. For example, several differences exist in CFTC's and SEC's definition of the term "U.S. persons."

In written comments provided by NCUA, NCUA disagreed with our suggestion that Congress consider whether additional changes are needed to the regulatory structure and stated that consideration of changes to the regulatory structure would need to include a careful review of the costs and benefits. We maintain that changes to the regulatory structure could help to reduce and better manage fragmentation and overlap in the oversight of financial institutions and activities. The report documents several instances where the structure produced inconsistent, inefficient and ineffective oversight. The costs and benefits of any options for improving and modernizing the structure would have to be part of any consideration of additional changes to the regulatory structure but would not preclude considering other options as we suggest.

In written comments provided by the Federal Reserve and OFR, both agencies agreed with our recommendations to them. In response to our recommendation that the Federal Reserve work with FSOC to regularly incorporate the comprehensive results of its systemic risk monitoring activities into Systemic Risk Committee deliberations, the Federal Reserve stated that close collaboration with FSOC and the Systemic Risk Committee is essential to improving the council's ability to identify emerging systemic risks. The Federal Reserve also noted that it has actively participated in Systemic Risk Committee deliberations and has provided presentations, data, and staff observations relating to systemic risk matters to the committee since its inception. We note in the report that when the Systemic Risk Committee analyzes specific threats that have been identified, Federal Reserve staff have shared analyses or metrics relevant to those threats. While the sharing of such information is useful, the committee still lacks access to information from the broad-based systemic risk monitoring efforts at the Federal Reserve, which could better equip committee members in identifying new potential risks to the system. In response to our third recommendation that OFR and the Federal Reserve jointly articulate individual and common goals for systemic risk monitoring activities, the Federal Reserve also agrees that communication with OFR is a key aspect of monitoring the financial system for systemic risks, particularly given OFR's access to a broad range of data not available to other regulators. It noted that it has, and plans to continue to, consult with OFR, and it plans to continue to work with OFR to make the communication more formal. The Federal Reserve also noted that it did not understand the report's use of the word "tools" when referring to the systemic risk monitoring efforts of the Federal Reserve. Our use of this term was intended to simplify the many diverse systemic risk monitoring outputs of both OFR and the Federal Reserve. To clear up any confusion, where appropriate, we added "or other outputs" after the word "tools" in the report.

In its written comments, OFR agreed with our recommendation to work with FSOC to determine ways in which to fully and regularly incorporate current and future monitors and assessments into Systemic Risk Committee deliberations. OFR indicated that it has initiated conversations with Treasury FSOC staff on best practices for distribution of the results of current monitoring tools. It indicated that as future monitoring tools are finalized it plans to also work with FSOC staff to determine ways in which its tools can be incorporated into FSOC discussions. OFR noted that because certain data provided to supervisory regulators have legislatively mandated confidentiality requirements, tools developed using such data are only distributed to FSOC principals and deputies. As we noted in the report, OFR's efforts to share its tools outside of the FSOC principals and deputies may be constrained by current confidentiality requirements. However, our recommendation encourages OFR to seek ways in which such tools, or assessments resulting from those tools, can be fully and appropriately incorporated into Systemic Risk Committee discussions, without violating confidentially requirements. OFR also agreed with our recommendation that it and the Federal Reserve should improve the ways in which they collaborate on their systemic risk monitoring efforts. In response to the recommendation, OFR stated that it has also initiated discussion with the Federal Reserve on how best to address our recommendation while continuing to execute the agencies' respective missions.

In its written response, NCUA also noted that it had concerns with our recommendations to OFR and the Federal Reserve. Regarding our recommendations to OFR and the Federal Reserve that the agencies work with FSOC to determine ways in which to incorporate the results of their systemic risk monitoring activities into Systemic Risk Committee deliberations, NCUA said that our recommendations underestimate the costs and other issues relating to dissemination of supervisory data. NCUA stated that it believes this may be more costly than helpful to monitoring systemic risks. However, we maintain that it is vital that FSOC's Systemic Risk Committee—the council's main vehicle for collaboration on systemic risk monitoring and identification efforts—have access to the tools and other outputs developed by these agencies. The committee's leveraging of this information helps to reduce fragmentation in systemic risk monitoring and identification, and could help identify systemic risks that may otherwise be missed. NCUA also questioned the usefulness of our recommendation that the Federal Reserve and OFR jointly articulate individual and common goals for their systemic risk monitoring activities, and stated that wide disagreement remains within the financial community and across regulators about what constitutes financial stability and how it should be measured. NCUA believes that having a range of options provided to FSOC in this circumstance is an advantage, and not a cost. Our recommendation does not require OFR and the Federal Reserve to agree upon and choose one approach to systemic risk monitoring. Rather, we acknowledge in the report the importance and value of the agencies' independent activities and conclusions regarding systemic risk and note that this should be preserved as OFR and the Federal Reserve work to improve their collaborative efforts. However, in response to technical comments we received from Federal Reserve staff, we clarified the wording of the recommendation to clarify our intent. Initially, the recommendation stated that the Federal Reserve and OFR should work to develop and maintain a joint strategy for their systemic risk monitoring activities. Federal Reserve staff thought that the term "joint strategy" might imply that we intended for the two agencies to conduct a monitoring program jointly, which they believed would compromise the two agencies' independence in conducting their own work in this area. In response, we clarified the wording of the recommendation to emphasize that collaboration requires the agencies to jointly articulate both individual and common goals related to systemic risk monitoring.

CFPB, FDIC, the Federal Reserve, FIO, FTC, NAIC, OCC, OFR and Treasury FSOC Secretariat staff provided technical comments, which we have incorporated, as appropriate.

Lawrance Evans, Jr.
Director, Financial Markets and Community Investment

APPENDIX I: OBJECTIVES, SCOPE, AND METHODOLOGY

This report examines (1) the overall structure of the U.S. financial regulatory system, (2) effects of fragmentation and overlap on agencies' oversight activities, and (3) the collaborative efforts and relevant authorities of agencies involved in systemic risk oversight.

Structure of the U.S. Financial Regulatory System

To examine the overall structure of the U.S. financial regulatory system, we reviewed financial regulatory statues, including the Dodd-Frank Wall Street Reform and Consumer Protection Act (Dodd-Frank Act), and the Dodd-Frank Act legislative history. We divided the financial regulatory structure into the following sectors based on agencies' missions: (1) safety and soundness oversight of depository institutions, (2) consumer protection oversight, (3) securities and derivatives markets oversight, (4) insurance oversight, and (5) systemic risk oversight. This report does not include assessments of fragmentation and overlap in housing finance oversight as they relate to the supervisory duties of the Federal Housing Finance Agency because the agency generally does not share oversight responsibilities over the government-sponsored enterprises—Fannie Mae and Freddie Mac—and the Federal Home Loan Banks. Additionally, other entities and activities involved in housing finance markets are subject to consumer financial protection, safety and soundness, and securities and derivatives oversight, which we do analyze in the report. We also did not evaluate fragmentation and overlap in the farm credit system because the Farm Credit Administration is the sole regulator of the system. For each sector we reviewed the relevant financial agencies' websites and documents, including strategic plans, performance plans and annual reports, supervisory manuals, and rulemakings to identify financial institutions and entities under their jurisdictions and the types of oversight activities each conducts. We also reviewed reports on financial regulatory reform conducted by U.S. agencies, international regulatory bodies, policy organizations, and previous GAO reports that identified areas of fragmentation and overlap within the financial regulatory structure.[1] We interviewed agency officials, including officials from the Board of Governors of the Federal Reserve System (Federal Reserve), the Commodity Futures Trading Commission (CFTC), the Bureau of Consumer Financial Protection (CFPB), the Federal Deposit Insurance Corporation (FDIC), the Federal Insurance Office (FIO), the Federal Trade Commission, the U.S. Department of the Treasury (Treasury), the Office of the Comptroller of the Currency (OCC), the Office of Financial Research (OFR), the National Credit Union Administration (NCUA), and the Securities and Exchange Commission (SEC). We also interviewed officials from self-regulatory organizations (SRO) and associations of state supervisors, including the Financial Industry Regulatory Authority, the National Futures Association, the Conference of State Bank Supervisors, the North American Securities Administrators Association, and the National Association of Insurance Commissioners, and representatives of industry and policy organizations. We selected industry and policy organizations that represented the different areas of the financial system or had expertise in evaluating areas of the financial regulatory structure. We used procedures outlined in GAO's *Fragmentation, Overlap, and Duplication: An Evaluation and Management Guide* to help us analyze the information we obtained and identify areas of fragmentation and overlap in the U.S. financial regulatory structure.[2]

Effects of Fragmentation and Overlap on Oversight Activities

To identify the effects of fragmentation and overlap on agencies' oversight activities, we held four discussion groups, reviewed past GAO reports, and reviewed reports from U.S. agencies and international regulatory bodies. We held the discussion groups in November 2014 on the following four topics: (1) the supervision of bank and thrift holding companies and their depository subsidiaries by FDIC, the Federal Reserve, OCC, and state banking supervisors; (2) consumer protection oversight conducted by CFPB and the federal prudential regulators— FDIC, Federal Reserve, NCUA, and OCC; (3) the regulation of swaps and security-based swaps by CFTC and SEC; and (4) the supervision of insurance groups by state insurance regulators and the Federal Reserve.[3] We chose the specific topics to cover in the discussion groups either because the Dodd-Frank Act altered the regulatory structure in the area or because the issue had been widely identified as a potential cause of the 2007-2009 financial crisis. In each discussion group, we asked participants a series of questions to help identify: (1) areas of fragmentation and overlap in regulators' responsibilities for the specific topic, (2) positive and negative effects of fragmentation and overlap on regulators' oversight activities, and (3) approaches to help mitigate any negative effects fragmentation and overlap might have. Each discussion group consisted of former regulatory officials, industry and advocacy group representatives, and experts. We helped ensure balance in the composition of participants in each discussion group by selecting a mix of participants with different perspectives and limiting the number of participants in each category to help ensure that each type of participant was equally represented. Appendix IV contains a list of the individuals who participated in the discussion groups. Our discussion groups were not designed to achieve agreement or consensus among participants. Rather, we sought participants' help to identify areas of fragmentation and overlap and the effects they have in each of the four topic areas. We had recordings of the discussion groups transcribed and reviewed the transcripts for each group and summarized what participants told us.

After the discussion groups were held, we interviewed relevant officials at the agencies to obtain their perspectives on the fragmentation and overlap identified by discussion group participants and to understand any efforts the regulators were taking to coordinate with other regulators to mitigate negative effects. We also reviewed our previous reports to identify instances in which we have reported on fragmentation and overlap in the financial regulatory structure and its effects. Additionally, we reviewed recent assessments of the U.S. regulatory structure conducted by the Financial Stability Board (FSB), the International Monetary Fund (IMF), and FIO from August 2013 to July 2015.[4] We chose to review assessments conducted by these organizations because they represent international and domestic entities that, respectively, have agreed with their member jurisdictions, or are mandated by their executive board or Congress, to assess parts of the U.S. financial regulatory structure relevant to this review. Finally, we assessed the current regulatory structure and the effects of fragmentation and overlap within it against the characteristics of an effective and efficient regulatory structure that we identified in a January 2009 report in which we developed a framework for evaluating proposals for reforming the regulatory structure.[5] Appendix III contains the nine characteristics we identified in our framework.

Fragmentation in Systemic Risk Oversight

We chose to evaluate agencies' systemic risk oversight activities for the following reasons: (1) the lack of systemic risk responsibilities among regulators was considered by Congress and others to be significant in the 2007-2009 financial crisis; (2) systemic risk is a new area of focus in the financial regulatory structure, resulting from new responsibilities for regulators and agencies contained in the Dodd-Frank Act; and (3) offices with financial stability goals were created within certain regulatory agencies as well as the Financial Stability Oversight Council (FSOC), which has a mandate to monitor and respond to threats to systemic risk. To examine the collaborative efforts and relevant authorities of agencies involved in systemic risk oversight—which includes monitoring the financial system to identify systemic risks and mitigating those risks—we first identified agencies with explicit systemic risk authorities, goals, or activities by reviewing the Dodd-Frank Act, our previous reports, and agencies' strategic plans, websites, and other documents, and by interviewing federal and state financial agencies. We consequently focused our assessment of fragmentation and overlap on the systemic risk monitoring and identification activities of FSOC, OFR, and the Federal Reserve, as those were the three entities that were actively monitoring the broader financial system with the purpose of identifying and analyzing potential systemic risks.

We approached our evaluation of systemic risk monitoring and identification activities of FSOC, OFR, and the Federal Reserve in the following way. First, we evaluated FSOC's systemic risk monitoring efforts. We focused our assessment on the work of FSOC's Systemic Risk Committee, as the FSOC committee where interagency staff meet to identify, monitor, and analyze systemic risks. To conduct this work, we reviewed FSOC's annual reports (2011-2015), bylaws and committee charters, and Systemic Risk Committee agendas and presentations for their monthly meetings held between July 2012 and August 2014. We reviewed previous GAO work evaluating FSOC and the Systemic Risk Committee's efforts.[6] We also interviewed staff from FSOC member agencies who participated in Systemic Risk Committee discussions. We evaluated the committee's actions against federal internal control standards and GAO's key interagency collaboration practices, as well as best practices identified by the International Monetary Fund for systemic risk monitoring.[7]

Second, we compared OFR's and the Federal Reserve's systemic risk monitoring and identification efforts because they are the only two agencies that have established initiatives to create broad-based systemic risk monitoring tools or other outputs. Further, we focused our analysis of OFR's efforts primarily on evaluating its Financial Stability Monitor because it is OFR's only monitor that aims to evaluate risk to the financial system as a whole.[8] To determine similarities and differences in the two agencies' programs we analyzed, among other things, (1) for OFR, OFR's annual reports (2012 through 2015), 2015-2019 Strategic Plan, documents associated with the Financial Stability Monitor, and select research papers; and (2) for the Federal Reserve, the Federal Reserve's 2012-2015 Strategic Framework, Financial Stability Monitoring staff report No. 601, samples of the Federal Reserve's internal quarterly financial stability assessments, and relevant speeches from the Federal Reserve Board Governors.[9] In addition, we interviewed officials from OFR and the Federal Reserve's Office of Financial Stability and Policy Research and academics and industry experts who served on OFR's Financial Research Advisory Council, as well as an expert from the Systemic Risk Council.[10] Finally, we evaluated how OFR and the Federal Reserve collaborate in their systemic risk monitoring efforts and assessed their actions against interagency collaboration best practices identified by GAO.[11]

Finally, to assess FSOC's and FSOC member agencies' authorities to mitigate identified systemic risks, we reviewed the Dodd-Frank Act, FSOC annual report recommendations, and FSOC's proposed Section 120 recommendation. We also interviewed FSOC member agency staff who participated in FSOC's Financial Market Utilities and Payment, Clearing, and Settlement Activities Committee to understand FSOC's authority to designate payment, clearing, and settlement activities as systemically important and actions the committee has taken to implement this authority. We evaluated FSOC's authorities against our January 2009 framework and against IMF's best practices for systemic risk oversight.[12]

We conducted this performance audit from April 2014 to February 2016 in accordance with generally accepted government auditing standards. Those standards require that we plan and perform the audit to obtain sufficient, appropriate evidence to provide a reasonable basis for our findings and conclusions based on our audit objectives. We believe that the evidence obtained provides a reasonable basis for our findings and conclusions based on our audit objectives.

APPENDIX II: HISTORY OF THE U.S. FINANCIAL REGULATORY STRUCTURE

The U.S. financial regulatory structure has evolved in various sectors and the Dodd-Frank Wall Street Reform and Consumer Protection Act (Dodd-Frank Act) made some changes to the financial system.[1] Figure 8 illustrates the history of the U.S. financial regulatory structure over about the last 150 years and shows how it has become complex and fragmented.

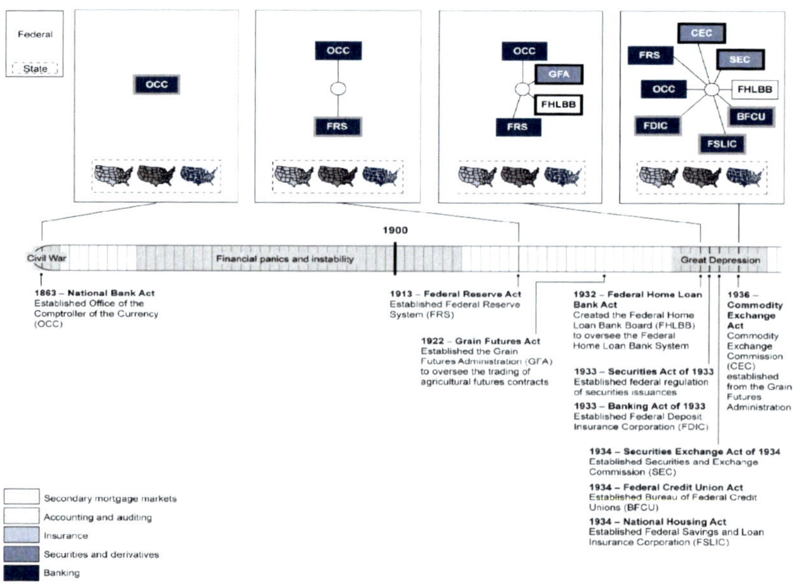

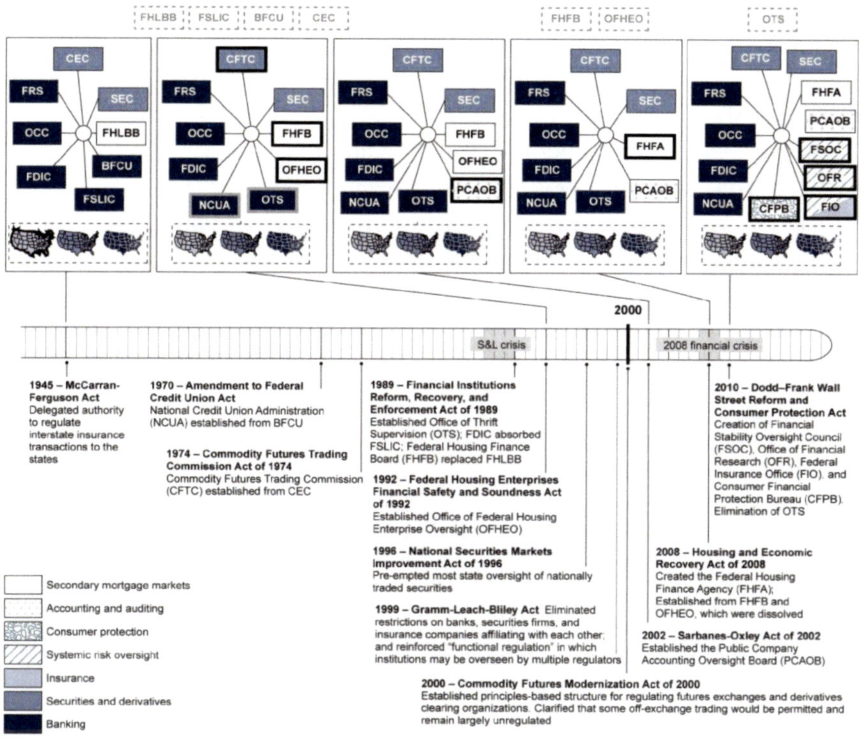

Source: GAO. | GAO-16-175.

Figure 8. Formation of U.S. Financial Regulatory Structure (1863-2015).

Depository Institution Oversight

Banks

Since the early days of our nation, banks have allowed citizens to store their savings and used these funds to make loans to spur business development. Until the middle of the 1800s, banks were chartered by states, and state regulators supervised their activities, which primarily consisted of taking deposits and issuing currency. However, the existence of multiple currencies issued by different banks, some of which were more highly valued than others, created difficulties for the smooth functioning of economic activity. In an effort to finance the nation's Civil War debt and reduce financial uncertainty, Congress passed the National Bank Act of 1863, which provided for issuance of a single national currency. This act also created the

Office of the Comptroller of the Currency (OCC), which was to oversee the national currency and improve banking system efficiency by granting banks national charters to operate and conducting oversight to ensure the sound operations of these banks.

In the years surrounding 1900, the United States experienced troubled economic conditions and several financial panics, including various instances of bank runs as depositors attempted to withdraw their funds from banks whose financial conditions had deteriorated. To improve the liquidity of the U.S. banking sector and reduce the potential for such runs, Congress passed the Federal Reserve Act of 1913. This act created the Federal Reserve System, which consists of the Board of Governors of the Federal Reserve System (Federal Reserve) and 12 Federal Reserve Banks, which are congressionally chartered semiprivate entities that undertake a range of actions on behalf of the Federal Reserve, including supervision of banks and bank holding companies and lending to troubled banks. The Federal Reserve was given responsibility to act as the federal supervisory agency for state-chartered banks—banks authorized to do business under charters issued by states—that are members of the Federal Reserve System.[2] In addition to supervising and regulating member banks including state-chartered banks, the Federal Reserve also develops and implements national monetary policy and provides financial services to depository institutions, the U.S. government, and foreign official institutions, including playing a major role in operating the nation's payments system.

Several significant changes to the U.S. financial regulatory system again were made as a result of the turbulent economic conditions in the late 1920s and 1930s. In response to numerous bank failures that resulted in the severe contraction of economic activity of the Great Depression, the Banking Act of 1933 created the Federal Deposit Insurance Corporation (FDIC), which administers a federal program to insure the deposits of participating banks. Subsequently, FDIC's deposit insurance authority expanded to include thrifts.[3] Additionally, FDIC provides primary federal oversight of any insured state-chartered banks that are not members of the Federal Reserve System. Finally, FDIC has backup examination and enforcement authority over all of the institutions it insures in order to mitigate losses to the deposit insurance funds.

Thrifts and Credit Unions

The economic turmoil of the 1930s prompted the creation of federal regulators for other types of depository institutions, including thrifts and credit unions.[4] These institutions previously had been subject to oversight only by state authorities. However, the Home Owners' Loan Act of 1933 empowered the newly created Federal Home Loan Bank Board to charter and regulate federal thrifts, and the Federal Credit Union Act in 1934 created the Bureau of Federal Credit Unions to charter and supervise credit unions.[5] Congress amended the Federal Credit Union Act in 1970 to establish the National Credit Union Administration (NCUA), which is responsible for chartering and supervising federally-chartered credit unions, as well as insuring deposits in these and state-chartered credit unions.[6] Oversight of these state-chartered credit unions is managed by 47 state regulatory agencies, represented by the National Association of State Credit Union Supervisors.[7]

From 1980 to 1990, over 1,000 thrifts failed at a cost of about $100 billion to the federal deposit insurance funds. In response, the Financial Institutions Reform, Recovery, and Enforcement Act of 1989 replaced the Federal Home Loan Bank Board and, among other things, established the Office of Thrift Supervision (OTS) to improve thrift oversight.[8] The Dodd-Frank Act shuttered OTS and transferred supervision of: (1) thrift holding companies and their nondepository subsidiaries to the Federal Reserve, (2) federal thrifts to OCC, and (3) state thrifts to FDIC.[9]

Securities and Derivatives Markets Oversight

Securities

Prior to the 1930s, securities markets were overseen by various state securities regulatory bodies and the securities exchanges themselves. In the aftermath of the stock market crash of 1929, the Securities Exchange Act of 1934 created a new federal agency, the Securities and Exchange Commission (SEC), and gave it authority to regulate the securities markets and register and oversee securities broker-dealers, as well as securities exchanges, to strengthen securities oversight and address inconsistent state securities rules.[10] In addition to regulation by SEC and state agencies, securities markets and the broker-dealers that accept and execute customer orders in these markets are regulated by industry self-regulatory organizations (SRO), including the securities exchanges and the Financial Industry Regulatory Authority, which are funded by the participants in the industry. Among other things, these SROs establish rules governing their members and conduct examinations related to market integrity and investor protection. SEC also registers and oversees investment companies and advisers, approves rules for the market participants and activities it oversees, and conducts examinations of broker-dealers and mutual funds. State securities regulators— represented by the North American Securities Administrators Association—are generally responsible for registering certain securities products and, along with SEC, investigating securities fraud.[11] SEC is also responsible for overseeing the financial reporting and disclosures that companies issuing securities must make under U.S. securities laws. The Dodd-Frank Act also expanded regulatory oversight to hedge and private equity funds by generally requiring the investment advisers to these funds to register with SEC and become subject to examinations.

SEC is also authorized to issue and oversee U.S. accounting standards for entities subject to its jurisdiction, but it has delegated the creation of accounting standards to a private-sector organization, the Financial Accounting Standards Board, which establishes generally accepted accounting principles. Further, in 2006 Congress passed the Credit Rating Agency Reform Act of 2006, which established limited SEC oversight of credit rating agencies, requiring their registration and certain recordkeeping and reporting requirements.[12]The Dodd-Frank Act imposed further requirements on the credit rating agencies regarding accountability and transparency that SEC must administer.

Derivatives

Oversight of the trading of futures contracts, which allow their purchasers to buy or sell a specific quantity of a commodity for delivery in the future, has also changed over the years in response to changes in the marketplace. Under the Grain Futures Act enacted in 1922, the trading of futures contracts was overseen by the Grain Futures Administration, an office within the Department of Agriculture, reflecting the nature of the products for which futures contracts were traded.[13] However, futures contracts were later created for nonagricultural commodities, including energy products such as oil and natural gas, metals such as gold and silver, and financial products such as Treasury bonds and foreign currencies. In 1974, a new independent federal agency, the Commodity Futures Trading Commission (CFTC), was created to oversee the trading of futures contracts.[14] Like SEC, CFTC relies on SROs, including the futures exchanges and the National Futures Association, to establish and enforce rules governing member behavior. In 2000, the Commodity Futures Modernization Act of 2000 established a principles-based structure for the regulation of futures exchanges and derivatives clearing organizations, and it clarified that some off-exchange derivatives trading—in particular, trading on facilities only accessible to large, sophisticated traders—was permitted and would be largely unregulated or exempt from regulation.[15] In 2010, the Dodd-Frank Act established a new regulatory framework for swaps to reduce risk, increase transparency, and promote market integrity in swaps markets by, among other things, requiring that many trades are to be centrally cleared, and providing for greater public availability of trading information. To implement the act's reforms, SEC has jurisdiction over security-based swaps, SEC and CFTC share joint jurisdiction over mixed swaps, and CFTC has jurisdiction over all other types of swaps.

Insurance Oversight

Unlike most other financial services, insurance activities traditionally have been regulated at the state level. In 1944, a U.S. Supreme Court decision determined that the insurance industry was subject to interstate commerce laws, which could then have allowed for federal regulation, but Congress passed the McCarran-Ferguson Act in 1945 to explicitly return insurance regulation to the states.[16] As a result, 56 state, territorial, or other local jurisdiction authorities oversee insurance activities in the United States, although state regulations and other activities are often coordinated nationally by the National Association of Insurance Commissioners (NAIC).[17] The Dodd-Frank Act created the Federal Insurance Office (FIO), a non-regulatory agency designed to monitor certain aspects of the insurance industry.[18] FIO is not a regulator or supervisor, and its responsibilities include identifying issues or gaps in the regulation of insurers that could contribute to a systemic crisis in the insurance industry or the U.S. financial system. Additionally, the Dodd-Frank Act granted the Federal Reserve oversight over nonbank financial companies that are designated by the Financial Stability Oversight Council (FSOC) (discussed in more detail below) for enhanced prudential standards, including some containing insurance companies.[19]

Secondary Mortgage Markets

The recent financial crisis in the credit and housing markets prompted the creation of a new, unified federal financial regulatory oversight agency, the Federal Housing Finance Agency (FHFA), to oversee the government-sponsored enterprises Fannie Mae, Freddie Mac, and the Federal Home Loan Banks.[20] Fannie Mae and Freddie Mac are private, federally chartered companies created by Congress to, among other things, provide liquidity to home mortgage markets by purchasing mortgage loans, thus enabling lenders to make additional loans. The system of 11 Federal Home Loan Banks provides funding to support housing finance and economic development.[21] Until enactment of the Housing and Economic Recovery Act of 2008, Fannie Mae and Freddie Mac had been overseen since 1992 by the Office of Federal Housing Enterprise Oversight (OFHEO), an agency within the Department of Housing and Urban Development, and the Federal Home Loan Banks were subject to supervision by the Federal Housing Finance Board (FHFB), an independent regulatory agency.[22] OFHEO regulated Fannie Mae and Freddie Mac on matters of safety and soundness, while the Department of Housing and Urban Development regulated their mission-related activities. FHFB served as the safety and soundness and mission regulator of the Federal Home Loan Banks.

With respect to Fannie Mae and Freddie Mac, the Housing and Economic Recovery Act of 2008 gives FHFA such new regulatory authorities as the power to regulate the retained mortgage portfolios, to set more stringent capital standards, and to place a failing entity in receivership. In addition, the law provides FHFA with funding outside the annual appropriations process. In September 2008, Fannie Mae and Freddie Mac were placed in conservatorship, with FHFA serving as the conservator under powers provided in the 2008 act. In November 2008, the Federal Reserve announced plans to purchase mortgage-backed securities guaranteed by Fannie Mae and Freddie Mac on the open market.

Farm Credit System

The farm credit system is a nationwide network generally consisting of cooperatively organized banks and associations that are owned and controlled by their borrowers.[23] The system's entities provide credit and other services to agricultural producers and certain others. The Farm Credit Administration (FCA) is the independent federal agency that charters, regulates, and examines banks, associations, and related entities of the farm credit system, including examining the Federal Agricultural Mortgage Corporation (Farmer Mac), to ensure a dependable source of credit for agriculture and rural America.[24]

The Farm Credit Amendments Act of 1985 amended FCA to give it increased oversight, regulatory, and enforcement powers similar to those of other federal financial regulatory institutions.[25] It required FCA to examine each direct-lending institution under its authority at least annually and to use its new enforcement authority to instill safety and soundness practices on troubled institutions and to take corrective actions against institutions for any regulatory violations. In 1987, Farmer Mac was established to create a secondary market for agricultural real estate and rural home mortgages, and in 1996, it was given further authority to purchase and pool loans and issue mortgage-backed securities with guaranteed payment of principal and interest, rather than guarantee such securities issued by other retail lenders.[26] Today the farm credit system is structured into 3 district farm credit banks, 76 agricultural credit associations, 2 federal land credit associations, and 1 agricultural credit bank.

Gramm-Leach-Bliley Act

Changes in the types of financial activities permitted for depository institutions and their affiliates have also shaped the financial regulatory system over time. Under the Glass-Steagall provisions of the Banking Act of 1933, financial institutions were prohibited from simultaneously offering commercial and investment banking services. However, in the GrammLeach-Bliley Act of 1999 (GLBA), Congress permitted financial institutions to fully engage in both types of activities and, in addition, provided a regulatory process allowing for the approval of new types of financial activity.[27] Under GLBA, qualifying financial institutions are permitted to engage in banking, securities, insurance, and other financial activities. When these activities are conducted within the same bank holding company structure, they remain subject to regulation by "functional regulators," which are the federal authorities having jurisdiction over specific financial products or services, such as SEC or CFTC. As a result, multiple regulators now oversee different business lines within a single institution. For example, broker-dealer activities are generally regulated by SEC even if they are conducted within a large financial conglomerate that is subject to the Bank Holding Company Act, which is administered by the Federal Reserve. The functional regulator approach was intended to provide consistency in regulation, focus regulatory restrictions on the relevant functional area, and avoid the potential need for regulatory agencies to develop expertise in all aspects of financial regulation.

Accounting and Auditing

In addition to the creation of various regulators over time, the accounting and auditing environment for financial institutions and market participants—a key component of financial oversight—has also seen substantial change. In the early 2000s, various companies with publicly traded securities were found to have issued materially misleading financial statements. These companies included Enron and WorldCom, both of which filed for bankruptcy. When the actual financial conditions of these companies became known, their auditors were called into question, and one of the largest, Arthur Andersen, was dissolved after the Department of Justice filed criminal charges related to its audits of Enron. As a result of these and other corporate financial reporting and auditing scandals, the Sarbanes-Oxley Act of 2002 was enacted.[28] Among other things, Sarbanes-Oxley expanded public company reporting and disclosure requirements and established new ethical and corporate responsibility requirements for public company executives, boards of directors, and independent auditors. The act also created the Public Company Accounting Oversight Board, to oversee the audits of public companies by public accounting firms. The activities of this board are, in turn, overseen by SEC.

Dodd-Frank Act

The 2007-2009 financial crisis threatened the stability of the U.S. financial system and the health of the U.S. economy. At the peak of the crisis, the federal government introduced unprecedented support for financial markets, providing hundreds of billions of dollars of capital and over a trillion dollars of emergency loans to financial institutions. Many households suffered as a result of falling asset prices, tightening credit, and increasing unemployment. The causes of the 2007-2009 crisis are complex and remain subject to debate and ongoing research. According to many researchers, around mid-2007, losses in the mortgage market triggered a reassessment of financial risk in other debt instruments and sparked the financial crisis. Uncertainty about the financial condition and solvency of financial entities resulted in a liquidity and credit crunch that made the financing on which many businesses and individuals depend increasingly difficult to obtain. By late summer of 2008, the ramifications of the financial crisis ranged from the failure of financial institutions to increased losses of individual savings and corporate investments.

Congress enacted the Dodd-Frank Act in 2010 with a key goal of the act being to promote the stability of the financial system. The act put forward a number of reforms to achieve this goal, such as provisions related to identifying and addressing systemic risk and enhancing supervision of large, complex financial institutions. Other reforms seek to expand protections for consumers and investors and expand oversight to entities that were previously less regulated. The following are some of the structural changes the act made that altered the U.S. financial regulatory system.

- The act established the Financial Stability Oversight Council (FSOC) to identify risks to the financial stability of the United States, promote market discipline, and respond to emerging threats to the stability of the U.S. financial system.
- The act established the Office of Financial Research (OFR) within the Department of the Treasury (Treasury) to support FSOC and its member agencies by improving the quality, transparency, and accessibility of financial data and information; conducting and sponsoring research related to financial stability and provide advice on the impact of policies related to systemic risk; and developing tools for risk measurement and risk monitoring.[29]
- The act established the Bureau of Consumer Financial Protection, also known as the Consumer Financial Protection Bureau (CFPB), as an independent bureau within the Federal Reserve System and provided it with rulemaking, enforcement, supervisory, and other powers over many consumer financial products and services and many of the entities that sell them.[30] CFPB is also authorized to supervise certain nonbank financial companies and large banks and credit unions with over $10 billion in assets and their affiliates for consumer protection purposes.

APPENDIX III: GAO FRAMEWORK FOR EVALUATING FINANCIAL REGULATORY REFORMS

Characteristic	Description
Clearly defined regulatory goals	Goals should be clearly articulated and relevant.
Appropriately comprehensive	Financial regulations should cover all activities that pose risks or are otherwise important to meeting regulatory goals.
Systemwide focus	Mechanisms should be included for identifying, monitoring, and managing risks to the financial system regardless of the source of the risk.
Flexible and adaptable	A regulatory system that is flexible and forward looking allows regulators to readily adapt to market innovations and changes.
Efficient and effective	Effective and efficient oversight should be developed, including eliminating overlapping federal regulatory missions where appropriate and minimizing regulatory burden without sacrificing effective oversight.
Consistent consumer and investor protection	Consumers and investors should receive consistent, useful information, as well as legal protections for similar financial products and services.
Regulators provided with independence, prominence, authority, and accountability	Regulators should have independence from inappropriate influence, as well as prominence and authority to carry out and enforce statutory missions, and be clearly accountable for meeting regulatory goals.
Consistent financial oversight	Similar institutions, products, risks, and services should be subject to consistent regulation, oversight, and transparency.
Minimal taxpayer exposure	A regulatory system should foster financial markets that are resilient enough to absorb failures and thereby limit the need for federal intervention and limit taxpayers' exposure to financial risk.

Source: GAO. | GAO-16-175

Appendix IV: List of Discussion Group Participants

Bank and Thrift Holding Company Supervision

John Bowman	Former Acting Director Office of Thrift Supervision
Cecelia Calaby	Senior Vice President American Bankers Association
Richard Carnell	Associate Professor of Law Fordham University School of Law
Kieran Fallon	Former Associate General Counsel Federal Reserve Board
Richard Foster	Vice President and Senior Counsel for Regulatory and Legal Affairs Financial Services Roundtable
Aaron Klein	Director of the Financial Regulatory Reform Initiative Bipartisan Policy Center
Margaret Liu	Senior Vice President and Deputy General Counsel Conference of State Bank Supervisors

Consumer Financial Protection Oversight

Sandra Braunstein	Former Director Board of Governors of the Federal Reserve System
Leonard Chanin	Former Assistant Director Consumer Financial Protection Bureau
Lisa Donner	Executive Director Americans for Financial Reform
Ed Mierzwinski	Director of Consumer Programs U.S. PIRG
Benjamin Olson	Former Deputy Assistant Director Consumer Financial Protection Bureau
Richard Riese	Senior Vice President American Bankers Association
Jess Sharp	Managing Director, Center for Capital Markets and Competitiveness U.S. Chamber of Commerce
Heather Slavkin Corzo	Director AFL-CIO

Insurance Group Supervision

Holly Bakke	Principal Strategic Initiatives Management Group, LLC Former Commissioner New Jersey Department of Banking and Insurance
Dan Daveline	Director of Financial Regulatory Services National Association of Insurance Commissioners
Scott Harrington	Alan B. Miller Professor Wharton School of Business, University of Pennsylvania
Robert Hatch	Regulatory Counsel Financial Services Roundtable
Kelly Ireland	Senior Counsel American Council of Life Insurers
Alessandro Iuppa	Senior Vice President and Senior Policy Advisor Zurich Insurance Group Former Superintendent of Insurance Maine Bureau of Insurance
William Marcoux	Partner DLA Piper
Therese Vaughan	Former President and CEO National Association of Insurance Commissioners Former Commissioner State of Iowa Insurance Division
Robert Woody	Vice President Property Casualty Insurers Association of America

Swaps and Security-Based Swaps Regulation

Karen Barr	President and CEO Investment Adviser Association
David Blass	General Counsel Investment Company Institute
Audrey Costabile Blater	Director of Research International Swaps and Derivatives Association
Ronald Filler	Professor of Law New York Law School
Michael Greenberger	Professor of Law University of Maryland School of Law
John Ramsay	Former Acting Director, Division of Trading and Markets Securities Exchange Commission
Chester Spatt	Professor of Finance Carnegie Mellon University

End Notes

[1] Pub. L. No. 111-203, 124 Stat. 1376 (2010).

[2] The Dodd-Frank Act requires FSOC to identify risk to the financial stability of the United States and respond to emerging threats to the stability of the U.S. financial system. Pub. L. No. 111-203, § 112(a), 124 Stat. 1376, 1394 (2010). In this report we use the terms "risks to financial stability," "threats to financial stability," and "systemic risks" interchangeably. Systemic risk refers to the possibility that a single event could broadly affect the entire financial system, causing widespread losses rather than just losses at one or a few institutions.

[3] GAO, *Fragmentation, Overlap, and Duplication: An Evaluation and Management Guide,* GAO-15-49SP (Washington, D.C.: Apr. 14, 2015).

[4] In general, the Dodd-Frank Act defines a swap to include, among other things, an agreement that provides for the exchange of one or more payments based on the value or level of one or more assets, liabilities, or indices or other financial or economic interests or property of any kind that transfers, in whole or in part, the financial risk associated with a future change in the value or level without also conveying a current or future ownership interest in an asset or liability that incorporates the financial risk transferred. Pub. L. No. 111-203, § 721(a)(21), 124 Stat. 1376, 1666 (2010). Financial and nonfinancial firms use swaps and other over-the-counter derivatives to hedge risk, or speculate, or for other purposes. Swaps include interest rate swaps, commodity-based swaps, currency swaps, and broad-based credit default swaps. Security-based swaps include single-name and narrow-based credit default swaps and equity-based swaps.

[5] The Group of Twenty—a forum for international cooperation on global economic and financial issues, whose members include 19 countries and the European Union— established FSB in 2009 as the successor to the Financial Stability Forum to coordinate at the international level the work of national financial authorities and international standard-setting bodies in order to develop and promote the implementation of effective regulatory, supervisory, and other financial sector policies. IMF is an organization of 188 member jurisdictions whose primary purpose is to safeguard the stability of the international monetary system.

[6] GAO, *Financial Regulation: A Framework for Crafting and Assessing Proposals to Modernize the Outdated U.S. Financial Regulatory System,* GAO-09-216 (Washington, D.C.: Jan. 8, 2009).

[7] GAO, *Standards for Internal Control in the Federal Government,* GAO-14-704G (Washington, D.C.: September 2014) and GAO/AIMD-00-21.3.1 (Washington, D.C.: November 1999) and *Results-Oriented Government: Practices That Can Help Enhance and Sustain Collaboration among Federal Agencies,* GAO-06-15 (Washington, D.C.: Oct. 21, 2005). International Monetary Fund, *Staff Guidance Note on Macroprudential Policy* (Washington, D.C.: December 2014) and *Key Aspects of Macroprudential Policy*, IMF Policy Paper (Washington D.C.: June 2013).

[8] Dodd-Frank Act §120 grants FSOC the authority to issue recommendations to a regulator to apply new or heightened standards for a financial activity or practice conducted by a bank holding company or nonbank financial company under the regulator's jurisdiction if FSOC makes certain determinations concerning the risks of the activity.

[9] GAO-09-216. International Monetary Fund, *Staff Guidance Note on Macroprudential Policy* (Washington, D.C.: December 2014); *Key Aspects of Macroprudential Policy*, IMF Policy Paper (Washington D.C.: June 2013); and *Macroprudential Policy: An Organizing Framework*, IMF Policy Paper (Washington D.C.: March 2011).

[10] Pub. L. No. 111-139, § 21, 124 Stat. 8, 29 (2010), 31 U.S.C. § 712 Note.

[11] For more information on GAO's work on fragmentation, overlap, and duplication in the federal government, see GAO, *2015 Annual Report: Additional Opportunities to Reduce Fragmentation, Overlap, and Duplication and Achieve Other Financial Benefits,* GAO-15-404SP (Washington, D.C.: Apr. 14, 2015); *2014 Annual Report: Additional Opportunities to Reduce Fragmentation, Overlap, and Duplication and Achieve Other Financial Benefits,* GAO-14-343SP (Washington, D.C.: Apr. 8, 2014); *2013 Annual Report: Actions Needed to Reduce Fragmentation, Overlap, and Duplication and Achieve Other Financial Benefits,* GAO-13-279SP (Washington, D.C.: Apr. 9, 2013); *2012 Annual Report: Opportunities to Reduce Duplication, Overlap and Fragmentation, Achieve Savings, and Enhance Revenue,* GAO-12-342SP (Washington, D.C.: Feb. 28, 2012); and *Opportunities to Reduce Potential Duplication in Government Programs, Save Tax Dollars, and Enhance Revenue,* GAO-11-318SP (Washington, D.C.: Mar. 1, 2011).

[12] An SRO is a nongovernmental organization that generally has the power to create and enforce industry regulations and standards.

[13] See appendix II for the history of the development of the U.S. financial regulatory structure.

[14] We use the term "thrifts" to refer to federal and state savings associations and the term "thrift holding companies" to refer to savings and loan holding companies that control a thrift or another thrift holding company.

[15] Other areas within the financial regulatory system are housing finance oversight and the farm credit system. This report does not include assessments of fragmentation and overlap in housing finance oversight as they relate to the supervisory duties of the Federal Housing Finance Agency because the agency generally does not share oversight responsibilities over the government-sponsored enterprises—Fannie Mae and Freddie Mac—and the Federal Home Loan Banks. For more information on housing finance market developments and challenges and a framework for assessing reforms, see GAO, *Housing Finance System: A Framework for Assessing Potential Changes,* GAO-15-131 (Washington, D.C.: Oct. 7, 2014). We also did not evaluate fragmentation and overlap in the farm credit system because the Farm Credit Administration is the sole regulator of the system. Appendix II contains additional information on these areas of the financial system.

[16] The Dodd-Frank Act defines Federal consumer financial laws to include the Consumer Financial Protection Act of 2010 (Title X of the Dodd-Frank Act) itself, and a number of other consumer laws and the implementing regulations. 12. U.S.C. § 5481 (14). For example, Federal consumer financial laws include the Equal Credit Opportunity Act, the Truth in Lending Act, the Fair Debt Collection Practices Act, and the Fair Credit Reporting Act.

[17] OTS chartered and supervised federally-chartered thrifts, supervised thrift holding companies, and served as the supervisor for state-chartered thrifts. Rulemaking authority for federal thrifts previously vested in OTS was transferred to OCC. Rulemaking authority for thrift holding companies was transferred to the Federal Reserve. Other authorities were transferred to OCC, FDIC, and the Federal Reserve. 12 U.S.C. § 5412.

[18] The seven agencies were the Federal Reserve, OCC, FDIC, OTS, NCUA, Federal Trade Commission (FTC), and the Department of Housing and Urban Development. The Dodd-Frank Act gave CFPB authority in connection with a number of federal consumer protection laws.

[19] While the primary consumer protection supervisory and enforcement powers over banks, thrifts, and credit unions with $10 billion or less in assets largely remain in those institutions' prudential regulators, on a sampling basis, CFPB may participate in

examinations of these smaller depository institutions that are conducted by the prudential regulator to assess compliance with Federal consumer financial laws. The prudential regulators must involve the CFPB examiner in the entire examination process for any institution included in the sample and consider CFPB's input concerning the scope of the examination, the conduct of the examination, the contents of the examination report, the designation of matters requiring attention, and examination ratings. 12 U.S.C. § 5516(c). In these instances, additional overlap between CFPB and the prudential regulators exists.

[20] *See generally Creating a Consumer Financial Protection Agency: Hearing on H.R. 3126 Before the Senate Committee on Banking, Housing and Urban Affairs*, 111th Cong. 274 (2009) and Congressional Research Service, *The Consumer Financial Protection Bureau (CFPB): A Legal Analysis*, R42572 (Washington, D.C.: Jan. 14, 2014).

[21] 12 U.S.C. § 5552(a)(1).

[22] Because NCUA only supervises federally-chartered credit unions, there is no overlap in the general supervision of credit unions between NCUA and state credit union regulators.

[23] FDIC does not directly supervise other insured depository institutions. Its authority in connection with other depository institutions is different from that of the primary federal regulator in that it has backup examination authority that is concerned with evaluating and mitigating exposure of the deposit insurance fund to insured depository institutions.

[24] NCUA administers the National Credit Union Share Insurance Fund, which insures savings in federal credit unions and most state-chartered credit unions.

[25] For example, the prudential regulators retained responsibility for enforcing depository institutions' compliance with Section 5 of the Federal Trade Commission Act, the Fair Housing Act, and the Servicemembers Civil Relief Act regardless of an institution's size. FDIC and NCUA officials told us that very few of their regulated entities are under CFPB supervision. According to CFPB data, as of September 30, 2015, only 37 state-chartered depository institutions overseen by FDIC and 5 federal credit unions overseen NCUA had more than $10 billion in assets and were under CFPB supervision.

[26] The Bank Holding Company Act of 1956 provides for all bank holding companies, including financial holding companies, to be supervised on a consolidated basis by the Federal Reserve. As amended by the Dodd-Frank Act, the Home Owners Loan Act provides for the consolidated supervision of thrift holding companies by the Federal Reserve. Bank holding companies and thrift holding companies may become or be treated as financial holding companies, respectively, and thereby engage in a range of financial activities broader than those otherwise permitted for bank holding companies.

[27] In general, the Federal Reserve has authority to examine bank holding companies and their subsidiaries in order to inform the Federal Reserve of the nature of the operations and financial condition of the bank holding company and the subsidiary; the financial, operational and other risks within the bank holding company system that may pose a threat to the safety and soundness of the bank holding company or of any depository institution subsidiary or the stability of the financial system of the United States; and the systems of the bank holding company for monitoring and controlling these risks. 12 U.S.C. § 1844(c)(2)(A).

[28] The Federal Reserve also has supervision authorities over nondepository subsidiaries of bank holding companies.

[29] 12 U.S.C § 5514(a)(1)(B). CFPB has issued final rules under this authority, defining nonbank larger participants of the consumer reporting market, the consumer debt collection market, the student loan servicing market, the international money transfer market, and the automobile financing market, which brought those entities under CFPB's supervision

authority. Title X also contains additional authorities and responsibilities for CFPB that are not outlined here.

[30] FTC does not have jurisdiction over depository institutions, except in some instances FTC has enforcement authority over state-chartered credit unions. Under the FTC Act, FTC has investigative and law enforcement authorities to protect consumers from unfair, deceptive, or fraudulent practices in most sectors of the economy. FTC also enforces other consumer protection laws, including financial consumer protection laws such as the Equal Credit Opportunity Act, the Truth in Lending Act, and the Electronic Fund Transfer Act.

[31] In March 2015, the Conference of State Banking Supervisors (CSBS) and the American Association of Residential Mortgage Regulators issued proposed regulatory prudential standards for nonbank mortgage servicers that are licensed and operating in the states. Mortgage servicers are institutions that perform duties, such as sending borrowers monthly account statements, answering customer-service inquiries, collecting monthly mortgage payments, maintaining escrow accounts for property taxes and hazard insurance, and forwarding proper payments to the mortgage owners. The proposal includes a set of baseline standards and enhanced standards, which states can chose whether and how to adopt. The baseline standards would be applied to all nonbank mortgage servicers and the enhanced standards may be appropriate for large, complex nonbank mortgage servicing companies. The public comment period for the proposed prudential standards closed on June 23, 2015. CSBS has reviewed the comments but does not have a timeline for when it expects the proposal to be finalized. We have ongoing work evaluating, among other things, the oversight framework for nonbank mortgage servicers.

[32] Members of the National Futures Association include futures commission merchants, commodity pool operators, commodity trading advisors, introducing brokers, designated contract markets, swap execution facilities, commercial firms, and banks.

[33] An investment adviser is defined, in part, to mean any person who, for compensation, engages in the business of advising others, either directly or through publications or writings, as to the value of securities or as to the advisability of investing in, purchasing, or selling securities. 15 U.S.C. § 80b-2(a)(11).

[34] Municipal securities are debt instruments that state and local governments issue to finance transportation, housing, hospitals, education, and diverse other projects.

[35] The National Securities Markets Improvement Act of 1996, Pub. L. No. 104-290, 110 Stat. 3416 (1996), pre-empted state securities registration requirements for all but a subset of small securities products and limited state supervision of broker-dealers, but left intact the right of states to investigate securities fraud.

[36] Futures commission merchants are individuals or organizations that do both of the following: solicit or accept orders to buy or sell, among other instruments, futures contracts, options on futures, or swaps, and accept money or assets from customers to support such orders. 7 U.S.C. § 1a(28).

[37] In 1944, a U.S. Supreme Court decision determined that insurance was interstate commerce, which could then have allowed for federal regulation, but Congress passed the McCarran-Ferguson Act in 1945 to reaffirm the power of the states to regulate insurance companies. The 56 insurance regulators include the insurance commissioners in the 50 states, the District of Columbia, and five U.S. territories.

[38] 31 U.S.C § 313(c)(1)(A).

[39] 31 U.S.C. § 313(c)(1)(E). The Dodd-Frank Act also provided FIO with a variety of other authorities related to systemic risk.

[40] The Dodd-Frank Act gave the Federal Reserve authority to establish enhanced prudential standards for large bank holding companies and nonbank financial companies supervised by the Federal Reserve. Pub. L. No. 111-203, § 165, 124 Stat. 1376, 1423 (2010) (codified at 12 U.S.C. §5365).

[41] The Federal Reserve has indicated that it does not intend to regulate the manner in which insurance is provided by insurance companies or the types of insurance they provide. Instead, it has said that consolidated supervision and capital requirements that consider the risks across the entire firm will supplement existing legal-entity supervision by the states. See Mark E. Van Der Weide, Deputy Director, Division of Banking Supervision and Regulation, Board of Governors of the Federal Reserve System, *The State of the Insurance Industry and Insurance Regulations*, testimony before the Senate Committee on Banking, Housing, and Urban Affairs, 114th Cong., 1st sess., April 28, 2015.

[42] The council meets at least quarterly to fulfill its systemic risk mandate. Treasury staff provide administrative and analytical support to FSOC, which has created a number of staff committees that meet regularly and help advance the council's various tasks and goals. For additional information on FSOC's structure, see GAO, *Financial Stability: New Council and Research Office Should Strengthen the Accountability and Transparency of Their Decisions,* GAO-12-886 (Washington, D.C.: Sept. 11, 2012).

[43] We have work underway on the processes used to review the resolution plans and plan to issue the report in 2016.

[44] Financial market utilities are multilateral systems that provide the infrastructure for transferring, clearing, or settling payments, securities, or other financial transactions among financial institutions or between financial institutions and the system. Financial market utilities are a subset of financial market infrastructures, which are systems used for the purposes of clearing, settling, or recording payments, securities, derivatives, or other financial transactions.

[45] The Dodd-Frank Act allows the Federal Reserve to object to CFTC or SEC standards if the Federal Reserve concludes that they are insufficient to prevent or mitigate significant risks to the financial markets or financial stability of the United States. CFTC or SEC must explain why the requirements are sufficient or submit an explanation describing actions to be taken in response to the Federal Reserve's determination. If it determines that the response submitted by CFTC or SEC is insufficient, FSOC can require CFTC or SEC to establish stricter standards. 12 U.S.C. § 5464(a)(2)(B)-(E).

[46] The nine characteristics are: clearly defined regulatory goals; appropriately comprehensive; systemwide focus; flexible and adaptable; efficient and effective; consistent consumer and investor protection; regulators provided with independence, prominence, authority, and accountability; consistent financial oversight; and minimal taxpayer exposure. See appendix III for additional information on these characteristics. In addition, see GAO-09-216.

[47] Our framework describes these characteristics as follows (1) efficient and effective oversight includes eliminating overlapping federal regulatory missions where appropriate, and minimizing regulatory burden without sacrificing effective oversight; (2) consistent financial oversight is when similar institutions, products, risks, and services are subject to consistent regulation, oversight, and transparency; and (3) consistent consumer and investor protections are when consumers and investors receive consistent, useful information, as well as legal protections for similar financial products and services. See GAO-09-216.

[48] As mentioned previously, we held four discussion groups to help us identify the current effects of fragmentation and overlap on agencies' oversight activities. The discussion groups consisted of former regulatory officials, industry and advocacy group representatives, and

experts, and they covered (1) the supervision of bank and thrift holding companies and their subsidiaries by FDIC, the Federal Reserve, OCC, and state banking supervisors; (2) consumer protection oversight conducted by CFPB and the federal prudential regulators; (3) the regulation of swaps and security-based swaps by CFTC and SEC; and (4) the supervision of insurance groups by state insurance regulators and the Federal Reserve.

[49] For the purposes of this section, we focused on the division of consumer protection responsibilities between CFPB and the prudential regulators and did not evaluate the effects of overlap between CFPB's and FTC's authorities because FTC does not conduct the same types of oversight activities as those conducted by CFPB and the prudential regulators. FTC is not a regulator under the definition used in this report and does not have supervisory authority over entities, but rather generally has investigative and law enforcement authorities, and rulewriting authority under certain statutes. We also did not evaluate the effects of overlap between CFPB and the state banking regulators. State banking officials told us that the vast majority of states do not examine for compliance with federal financial consumer protection laws.

[50] GAO, *Bank and Thrift Regulation: Improvements Needed in Examination Quality and Regulatory Structure*, GAO/AFMD-93-15 (Washington, D.C.: Feb. 16, 1993).

[51] At the time the report was issued, OTS and OCC generally agreed with our recommendations, while FDIC generally disagreed. The Federal Reserve said it would carefully evaluate the findings and recommendations, but did not specify what action it may take. In December 1993, FDIC, the Federal Reserve, OCC, and OTS issued the *Interagency Policy Statement on the Allowance for Loan and Lease Losses*. The document established uniform interagency guidance for review of overall loan loss reserves and provides guidance to institutions on maintaining an adequate loan loss reserve. We closed these recommendations as implemented because they were, at least partially, responsive to our recommendations. There have been further updates to accounting standards and interagency guidance on this issue since this report was issued in 1993.

[52] GAO, *Bank Secrecy Act: Opportunities Exist for FinCEN and the Banking Regulators to Further Strengthen the Framework for Consistent BSA Oversight,* GAO-06-386 (Washington, D.C.: Apr. 28, 2006). The regulatory system for BSA involves several different federal agencies. Under delegated authority from the Secretary of the Treasury, FinCEN is the administrator of BSA. FinCEN has the authority under 31 U.S.C. § 5318(a)(3) to examine financial institutions for compliance with BSA and regulations promulgated under BSA at 31 C.F.R. Chapter X, as well as to take enforcement actions for violations of BSA and the implementing regulations under 31 U.S.C. §§ 5320-23. The Secretary of the Treasury delegated BSA examination authority to each federal prudential regulator with respect to banking organizations supervised by that regulator. 31 C.F.R. § 1010.810 (b)(1)-(5).The federal prudential regulators have separate authority pursuant to 12 U.S.C. §§ 1786 and 1818 to ensure that banking organizations comply with all laws and regulations, including BSA.

[53] At the time the report was issued, FinCEN and the regulators supported these recommendations and said they were committed to ongoing interagency coordination to address them. In response to our recommendation, FinCEN and the regulators concluded that no additional examiner guidance was needed at that time, but the Federal Financial Institutions Examination Council's BSA working group agreed to discuss these issues on a quarterly basis. We have closed this recommendation as implemented. In addition, in July 2007, the Federal Reserve, FDIC, OCC, OTS, and NCUA issued the *Interagency Statement on Enforcement of Bank Secrecy Act/Anti-Money Laundering Requirements*.

[54] The prudential regulators also had responsibilities for overseeing all of their regulated institutions' compliance with consumer protection laws prior to the passage of the Dodd-Frank Act.

[55] GAO, *Fair Lending: Data Limitations and the Fragmented U.S. Financial Regulatory Structure Challenge Federal Oversight and Enforcement Efforts,* GAO-09-704 (Washington, D.C.: July 15, 2009).

[56] At the time the report was issued, the agencies and regulators generally agreed with the report's analysis. The Dodd-Frank Act included improvements in the supervision of holding company subsidiaries and examination and enforcement of mortgage brokers. This matter for congressional consideration has been closed as implemented.

[57] State regulators have authority to investigate and enforce provisions of the Consumer Financial Protection Act of 2010, including the prohibition against unfair, deceptive, or abusive practices, against any state entity that is state-chartered, incorporated, licensed, or otherwise authorized to do business under state law. Before initiating any action, the state regulator generally must notify CFPB and CFPB may intervene in the action.

[58] The Dodd-Frank Act gave the Federal Reserve the authority to examine depository institution subsidiaries' compliance with federal laws that the Federal Reserve has specific jurisdiction to enforce against the subsidiary. The Federal Reserve is also, to the fullest extent possible, to avoid duplication of examination activities, reporting requirements, and requests for information. The Federal Reserve is required to provide notice to and consult with the appropriate regulatory agency before commencing an examination of a depository institution subsidiary. Similar provisions were added to the Home Owners Loan Act for thrift holding companies.

[59] GAO, *Bank Regulation: Consolidation of the Regulatory Agencies*, GAO/T-GGD-94-106 (Washington: D.C.: Mar. 4, 1994).

[60] GAO, *Financial Market Regulation: Agencies Engaged in Consolidated Supervision Can Strengthen Performance Measurement and Collaboration,* GAO-07-154 (Washington, D.C.: Mar. 15, 2007). In particular, because the holding companies manage some risks on an enterprisewide basis, OCC duplicated the Federal Reserve's assessment of the holding company's consolidated risk management activities or other activities outside of the national bank because it needed to assess the national bank's risk.

[61] In our March 2007 report, we also made this recommendation to OTS and SEC, which also served as consolidated supervisors for thrift holding companies and consolidated supervised entities (CSE), respectively. CSEs were large complex firms that focus primarily on securities and chose to participate in SEC's CSE program. In 2008, SEC terminated its CSE program. In addition, the Dodd-Frank Act eliminated OTS and transferred its holding company supervision responsibilities to the Federal Reserve. The agencies generally agreed with these recommendations. Consistent with our recommendation, in July 2008, the Federal Reserve entered into a memorandum of understanding with SEC regarding collaboration and information sharing in areas of common supervisory interest. In addition, the Federal Reserve and SEC, as well as other functional regulators and international counterparties, also engaged in joint regulatory activities including management of counterparty credit risk exposure to hedge funds and industry-wide operational issues related to credit derivatives. We have closed this recommendation as implemented.

[62] Office of the Inspector General for the Board of Governors of the Federal Reserve System, *2015 List of Major Management Challenges for the Board* (Washington, D.C.: Sept. 30, 2015).

[63] GAO, *Consumer Financial Protection Bureau: Some Privacy and Security Procedures for Data Collections Should Continue Being Enhanced,* GAO-14-758 (Washington, D.C.: Sept. 22, 2014).

[64] The Dodd-Frank Act requires CFPB and prudential regulators to coordinate their supervision of depository institutions with over $10 billion in assets and their affiliates to minimize regulatory burden.

[65] GAO-14-758.

[66] While our review identified duplication, as defined in this report, between CFPB and the prudential regulators' examination activities, in a June 2015 report on the extent to which CFPB and prudential regulators were coordinating their supervisory activities and avoiding duplication of regulatory oversight responsibilities, the Offices of the Inspector General (OIG) for FDIC, the Federal Reserve, CFPB, OCC, and NCUA did not identify duplication of oversight responsibilities. They concluded that the agencies were generally coordinating their regulatory oversight activities, but did identify some opportunities for enhanced coordination. However, the OIGs agreed that the objectives of their review could be addressed with a limited scope review rather than an audit or evaluation. As a result, the review was not conducted under government audit or evaluation standards. See Offices of the Federal Deposit Insurance Corporation, the Federal Reserve, the Consumer Financial Protection Bureau, Office of the Comptroller of the Currency, and the National Credit Union Administration Inspector General, *Coordination of Responsibilities Among the Consumer Financial Protection Bureau and the Prudential Regulators— Limited Scope Review*, Eval-15-004, 2015-SR-X-009, OIG-CA-15-017, and OIG-15-08 (Washington, D.C.: June 2015).

[67] A compliance management system refers to the method by which a supervised entity establishes its compliance responsibilities; communicates those responsibilities to employees; ensures that responsibilities for meeting legal requirements and internal policies are incorporated into business processes; reviews operations to ensure responsibilities are carried out and legal requirements are met; and takes corrective action and updates tools, systems, and materials as necessary.

[68] For example, OCC officials said that their compliance management system reviews are very broad and look across many platforms of an institution to examine for a number of laws, including financial laws (e.g., the Bank Secrecy Act) which remain under the jurisdiction of the prudential regulators. On the other hand, CFPB officials told us that CFPB goes through a prioritization process each year to determine the areas in which it will conduct compliance management system reviews and where follow-up is needed. This may result in CFPB reviewing the compliance management system for compliance with one or two specific consumer protection laws.

[69] GAO/T-GGD-94-106.

[70] GAO-09-216.

[71] 71 *Fed. Reg.* 58609 (Oct. 4, 2006) "Interagency Guidance on Nontraditional Mortgage Product Risks"; 72 *Fed. Reg.* 37569 (July 10, 2007) "Statement on Subprime Mortgage Lending."

[72] The Financial Institutions Regulatory and Interest Rate Control Act of 1978 established FFIEC as a vehicle through which bank regulators could communicate formally. Pub. L. No. 95-630, Title X, 92 Stat. 3641, 3694. While NCUA is a member of FFIEC, it does not possess all the same authorities as the other prudential regulators. For example, NCUA lacks authority to examine the third-party service providers of its regulated credit unions. In July 2015, we suggested that Congress consider granting NCUA authority to examine third-party technology service providers for credit unions. See GAO, *Cybersecurity: Bank and Other*

Depository Regulators Need Better Data Analytics and Depository Institutions Want More Usable Threat Information, GAO-15-509 (Washington, D.C.: July 2, 2015).

[73] The Conference of State Banking Supervisors is a nationwide organization of financial regulators from all 50 states, the District of Columbia, Guam, Puerto Rico, and the U.S. Virgin Islands, which provides state supervisors a national forum to coordinate supervision and develop policy related to their regulated entities. It also provides training to state banking and financial regulators and represents its members before Congress and the federal financial regulatory agencies.

[74] For example, see GAO, *Financial Market Regulation: Benefits and Risks of Merging SEC and* CFTC, GAO/T-GGD-95-153 (Washington, D.C.: May 3, 1995); *Financial Regulation: Industry Changes Prompt Need to Reconsider U.S. Regulatory Structure,* GAO-05-61 (Washington, D.C.: Oct. 6, 2004), and *Financial Regulation: Industry Trends Continue to Challenge the Federal Regulatory Structure,* GAO-08-32 (Washington, D.C.: Oct. 12, 2007).

[75] In this sentence, the term "exchange-traded fund" is not referencing an exchange-traded fund that is registered as an investment company with SEC under the Investment Company Act of 1940.

[76] GAO, *Financial Regulation: Clearer Goals and Reporting Requirements Could Enhance Efforts by CFTC and SEC to Harmonize Their Regulatory Approaches,* GAO-10-410 (Washington, D.C.: Apr. 22, 2010).

[77] The Department of the Treasury, *Financial Regulatory Reform, A New Foundation: Rebuilding Financial Supervision and Regulation* (Washington, D.C.: June 17, 2009).

[78] This agreement was codified in the Securities Acts Amendments of 1982, which amended the federal securities laws, and in the Futures Trading Act of 1982, which amended the Commodity Exchange Act. The accord allowed CFTC to approve a stock index futures contract for trading if CFTC found that the contract was (1) settled in cash; (2) not readily susceptible to manipulation; and (3) based on an index that was a widely published measure of and reflected the market as a whole or a substantial segment of the market, or else was comparable to such a measure. For more information about the Shad-Johnson Jurisdictional Accord, see GAO, *CFTC and SEC: Issues Related to the Shad-Johnson Jurisdictional Accord,* GAO/GGD-00-89 (Washington, D.C.: Apr. 6, 2000).

[79] SEC and CFTC, *Memorandum of Understanding Between the U.S. Securities and Exchange Commission and the U.S. Commodity Futures Trading Commission Regarding Coordination in Areas of Common Regulatory Interest* (Washington, D.C.: Mar. 11, 2008).

[80] The Dodd-Frank Act generally (1) provides for the registration and regulation of swap dealers and major swap participants; (2) imposes mandatory clearing requirements on swaps but exempts certain end users that use swaps to hedge or mitigate commercial risk; (3) requires swaps subject to mandatory clearing to be executed on an organized exchange or swap execution facility (unless no facility makes the swap available for trading); and (4) requires all swaps to be reported to a registered swap data repository or, if no such repository will accept the swap, to CFTC or SEC, and subjects swaps to post-trade transparency requirements (real-time public reporting of swap data).

[81] For the purposes of Title VII, these regulators are the Federal Reserve, OCC, FDIC, Farm Credit Administration, and Federal Housing Finance Agency. Section 712(a)(4) of the Dodd-Frank Act exempts from this requirement orders issued in connection with or arising from a violation of any provision of the Commodity Exchange Act or the securities laws, or in certain administrative hearings.

[82] Pursuant to the Dodd-Frank Act, the regulators issued a joint rulemaking defining swap and security-based swap dealers and major swap and major security-based swap participants in May 2012, and another defining the products that would be regulated under Title VII in August 2012. Further Definition of "Swap Dealer," "Security-Based Swap Dealer," "Major Swap Participant," "Major Security-Based Swap Participant" and "Eligible Contract Participant," 77 Fed. Reg. 30,596 (May 23, 2012); Further Definition of "Swap," "Security-Based Swap," and "Security-Based Swap Agreement"; Mixed Swaps; Security-Based Swap Agreement Recordkeeping, 77 Fed. Reg. 48,208 (Aug. 13, 2012). See GAO, *Dodd-Frank Regulations: Regulators' Analytical and Coordination Efforts [Reissued on December 18, 2014,* GAO-15-81 (Washington, D.C.: Dec. 18, 2014).

[83] GAO-15-81. In July 2015 CFTC issued proposed rules applicable to the cross-border application of margin requirements for uncleared swaps. These proposed rules differ from the existing Cross-Border Guidance and would establish new definitions of U.S. person solely for purposes of the application of margin rules. CFTC noted that the proposed definition of "U.S. person" is similar to the definition of "U.S. person" used by SEC in the context of cross-border security-based swaps. Margin Requirements for Uncleared Swaps for Swap Dealers and Major Swap Participants—Cross-Border Application of the Margin Requirements; Proposed Rule, 80 Fed. Reg. 41,376, 41,382 (July 14, 2015).

[84] CFTC has identified 38 regulatory areas where rules are needed to regulate the swaps marketplace, as mandated under the Dodd-Frank Act. For example, these regulatory areas include registration of swap dealers and major swap participants, clearing requirements, and data recordkeeping and reporting requirements. As of December 2015, CFTC had finalized rules or guidelines in 33 of the 38 self-identified regulatory areas.

[85] SEC has identified 29 regulatory areas where rules are needed to regulate the security-based swaps marketplace, as mandated under the Dodd-Frank Act. For example, these regulatory areas include identification of major security-based swap participants, clearing agencies for security-based swaps, and duties of securities-based swap data repositories. As of December 2015, SEC had finalized rules in 18 of the 29 self-identified regulatory areas.

[86] The Department of the Treasury, *Blueprint for a Modernized Financial Regulatory Structure* (Washington, D.C.: Mar. 31, 2008).

[87] As a result of being both a commodity and securities broker-dealer, MF Global was regulated by both CFTC and SEC, as well as industry SROs. U.S. House of Representatives, *Staff Report Prepared for Rep. Randy Neugebauer, Chairman, Subcommittee on Oversight and Investigations Committee on Financial Services* (Washington, D.C: Nov. 15, 2012).

[88] GAO/T-GGD-95-153.

[89] We use the term "insurance group" to refer to a group of affiliated companies, one or more of which is an insurance company.

[90] Reciprocity is the extent to which state regulators accept other states' regulatory actions, such as granting insurance licenses or approving products for sale in the insurance market, and do not require insurers to meet additional requirements in order to conduct insurance business in their state. Uniformity is the extent to which states have implemented either the same, or substantially similar, regulatory standards and procedures. Generally, a model act or law is meant as a guide for subsequent legislation by states. State legislatures may adopt model acts in whole or in part, they may modify them to fit their needs, or they may opt not to adopt them. Model laws become legally binding only upon enactment as law or regulation by state legislatures, governors, and/or insurance regulators.

[91] During product approval processes, regulators review insurers' products and rates, in some cases, before they enter the market for sale to consumers. Regulators review policy forms,

which are legal contracts that describe the characteristics of the products insurers intend to sell and the rates or prices they intend to charge, and then grant or deny product approval. GAO, *Insurance Reciprocity and Uniformity: NAIC and State Regulators Have Made Progress in Producer Licensing, Product Approval, and Market Conduct Regulation, but Challenges Remain,* GAO-09-372 (Washington, D.C.: Apr. 6, 2009).

[92] At the time the report issued, NAIC agreed with our recommendation. Consistent with our recommendation, in 2013, NAIC worked with regulators and industry through a task force to identify ways to improve the efficiency of product filing submission, review, and approval.

[93] State-based insurance regulation in the United States is comprised of 56 jurisdictions including the 50 states, the District of Columbia, and five U.S. territories.

[94] GAO, *State Insurance Regulation: Efforts to Streamline Key Licensing and Approval Processes Face Challenges,* GAO-02-842T (Washington, D.C.: June 18, 2002).

[95] In 1999, Congress passed the Gramm-Leach-Bliley Act, which encouraged at least 29 states to meet reciprocity or uniformity conditions within 3 years of the act's passage in order to avoid preemption of certain state producer licensing laws and the potential formation of a federal regulatory body for insurers. To help meet the requirements of the act, NAIC developed the Producer Licensing Model Act to promote a framework for reciprocal producer licensing relationships among states.

[96] GAO-09-372.

[97] NAIC generally agreed with this matter for congressional consideration. The enactment of the National Association of Registered Agents and Brokers Reform Act of 2015 established the National Association of Registered Agents and Brokers which, among other things, requires insurance producers to successfully pass a criminal background check in order to become members. This matter for congressional consideration has been closed as implemented.

[98] GAO, *Insurance Markets: Impacts of and Regulatory Response to the 2007-2009 Financial Crisis,* GAO-13-583 (Washington, D.C.: June 27, 2013).

[99] The key sources of financial trouble for AIG were primarily held in two noninsurance subsidiaries. First, the company conducted its credit default swap business through the AIG Financial Products subsidiary, whereby AIG Financial Products would enter into bilateral contracts that were sold over the counter and transfer credit risks from one party to another. Second, the AIG Securities Lending Corporation conducted securities lending activity, through which AIG's insurance subsidiaries authorized AIG Securities Lending Corporation to act on their behalf to loan securities to other financial institutions in exchange for cash collateral. Both of these programs strained AIG's liquidity and ultimately required federal financial assistance from the Federal Reserve and Treasury to avoid bankruptcy. Prior to the Dodd-Frank Act, OTS was AIG's consolidated supervisor. For additional information on federal financial assistance provided to AIG during the 2007- 2009 financial crisis, see GAO, *Financial Crisis: Review of Federal Reserve System Financial Assistance to American International Group, Inc.,* GAO-11-616 (Washington, D.C.: Sept. 30, 2011); *Troubled Asset Relief Program: Third Quarter 2010 Update of Government Assistance Provided to AIG and Description of Recent Execution of Recapitalization Plan,* GAO-11-46 (Washington, D.C.: Jan. 20, 2011); and *Troubled Asset Relief Program: Government's Exposure to AIG Lessens as Equity Investments Are Sold,* GAO-12-574 (Washington, D.C.: May 7, 2012).

[100] Federal Insurance Office, *How To Modernize and Improve the System of Insurance Regulation in the United States* (Washington, D.C.: December 2013).

[101] As of January 2016, four nonbank financial companies, AIG, General Electric Capital, Prudential Financial, and MetLife, had received this designation. Of these, three (AIG, Prudential Financial, and MetLife) are insurance groups. As mentioned previously, the Federal Reserve also serves as the holding company supervisor for thrift holding companies previously overseen OTS—some of which have insurance subsidiaries. In this capacity, the Federal Reserve has authority to review the activities of any subsidiary in the thrift holding company structure. According to IMF, as of April 2015, the Federal Reserve supervised 15 insurance groups—4 of the largest in the United States—with its authorities to oversee thrift holding companies.

[102] The International Association of Insurance Supervisors defines a supervisory college as a forum for cooperation and communication between the involved supervisors established for the fundamental purpose of facilitating the effectiveness of supervision of entities which belong to an insurance group; facilitating both the supervision of the group as a whole on a group-wide basis and improving the legal entity supervision of the entities within the insurance group.

[103] The NAIC Accreditation Program was established to develop and maintain standards to promote effective insurance company financial solvency regulation, particularly with respect to regulation of multistate insurers. Accreditation is a certification given to a state insurance department once it has demonstrated that it has met and continues to meet an assortment of legal, financial, and organizational standards as determined by a committee of its peers.

[104] ederal Insurance Office, *How To Modernize and Improve the System of Insurance Regulation in the United States* (Washington, D.C.: December 2013).

[105] Financial Stability Board, *Peer Review of the United States* (Basel, Switzerland: August 2013).

[106] Federal Insurance Office, *How To Modernize and Improve the System of Insurance Regulation in the United States* (Washington, D.C.: December 2013) and International Monetary Fund, *Financial Sector Assessment Program: Detailed Assessment of Observance of Insurance Core Principles,* IMF Country Report No. 15/90 (Washington, D.C.: April 2015).

[107] The Department of the Treasury, *Blueprint for a Modernized Financial Regulatory Structure* (Washington, D.C.: Mar. 31, 2008) and *Financial Regulatory Reform, A New Foundation: Rebuilding Financial Supervision and Regulation* (Washington, D.C.: June 17, 2009).

[108] Federal Insurance Office, *How To Modernize and Improve the System of Insurance Regulation in the United States* (Washington, D.C.: December 2013).

[109] GAO-05-61.

[110] In general, many of these bodies operate on a consensus basis and have no legally binding authority. Thus, financial reform agreements reached by these bodies must be adopted voluntarily by their member jurisdictions, such as through legislative or regulatory changes (or both), to take effect.

[111] NAIC was a founding member of IAIS in 1994. FIO became a member of IAIS in 2011, after the Dodd-Frank Act created the office and gave it a range of authorities, including coordinating on international insurance matters and representing the United States in IAIS, as appropriate. Pub. L. No. 111-203, § 502, 124 Stat. 1376, 1580 (codified at 31 U.S.C. § 313). The Federal Reserve became a member in 2013, after FSOC designated some insurers for enhanced supervision by the Federal Reserve. According to the Federal Reserve, some of the insurance holding companies subject to Federal Reserve supervision are internationally active firms that compete with other global insurers to provide insurance products to businesses and consumers around the world. As part of its supervisory activities

for these firms, the Federal Reserve collaborates with its regulatory counterparts internationally and, as part of this role, the Federal Reserve joined IAIS.

[112] GAO-05-61. Basel II refers to the risk-based capital framework issued in June 2004 by the Basel Committee.

[113] According to IAIS, insurance groups qualify as internationally active insurance groups if they (1) write premiums in not fewer than three international jurisdictions and have at least 10 percent of gross premiums written outside of their home jurisdiction and (2) have at least $50 billion in total assets, or have at least $10 billion in gross written premiums.

[114] GAO, *International Insurance Capital Standards: Collaboration among U.S. Stakeholders Has Improved but Could Be Enhanced,* GAO-15-534 (Washington, D.C.: June 25, 2015).

[115] International Monetary Fund, *United States: Financial Sector Assessment Program: Detailed Assessment of Observance of Insurance Industry Core Principles*, IMF Country Report No. 15/90 (Washington, D.C.: April 2015).

[116] FIO concurred with the recommendation, stating that it would build on existing collaboration efforts. The Federal Reserve and NAIC did not indicate if they concurred or disagreed with the recommendation. As of January 2016, the recommendation remains open.

[117] For example, see Bipartisan Policy Center, *Dodd-Frank's Missed Opportunity: A Road Map for a More Effective Regulatory Structure* (Washington, D.C.: April 2014); International Monetary Fund, *Financial Sector Assessment Program: Detailed Assessment of Observance of the Basel Core Principles for Effective Banking* Supervision, IMF Country Report No. 15/89 (Washington, D.C.: April 2015); International Monetary Fund, *United States: Financial Sector Assessment Program: Detailed Assessment of Observance of Insurance Industry Core Principles*, IMF Country Report No. 15/90 (Washington, D.C.: April 2015); and The Volcker Alliance, *Reshaping the Financial Regulatory System: Long Delayed, Now Crucial* (New York: NY: April 2015).

[118] The Department of the Treasury, *Financial Regulatory Reform, A New Foundation: Rebuilding Financial Supervision and Regulation* (Washington, D.C.: June 17, 2009).

[119] AIG was a thrift holding company by virtue of its ownership of a federal savings bank and was under consolidated supervision of OTS. In a March 2007 report, we found differences in policies and approaches used by the Federal Reserve and OTS for consolidated supervision. We concluded that these agencies could perform consolidated supervision more efficiently and effectively by adopting management practices in the areas of performance management and collaboration. We recommended that the agencies foster more systematic collaboration to promote supervisory consistency, particularly for firms that provide similar services. As indicated previously, at the time of this report SEC also served as a consolidated supervisor for consolidated supervised entities, but SEC terminated this program in 2008. This recommendation was also made to SEC. Each of the three agencies addressed this recommendation, and the recommendation is closed as implemented. For more information, see GAO-07-154.

[120] The Department of the Treasury, *Financial Regulatory Reform, A New Foundation: Rebuilding Financial Supervision and Regulation* (Washington, D.C.: June 17, 2009).

[121] Pub. L. No. 111-203, § 612, 124 Stat. 1376, 1612 (2010).

[122] Federal Financial Institutions Examination Council, *Statement on Regulatory Conversion* (Washington, D.C.: July 1, 2009).

[123] International Monetary Fund, *Financial Sector Assessment Program: Detailed Assessment of Observance of the Basel Core Principles for Effective Banking* Supervision, IMF Country Report No. 15/89 (Washington, D.C.: April 2015).

[124] This number does not reflect charter conversions resulting from mergers and acquisitions or credit union charter conversions; nor does it reflect institutions that choose to end their status as a depository institution. The Consolidated Reports of Condition and Income (Call Reports) are a primary source of financial data used for the supervision and regulation of banks and thrifts. They consist of a balance sheet, an income statement, and supporting schedules. The Report of Condition schedules provide details on assets, liabilities, and capital accounts. The Report of Income schedules provide details on income and expenses.

[125] GAO-09-216.

[126] GAO, *Bank Oversight Structure: U.S. and Foreign Experience May Offer Lessons for Modernizing U.S. Structure,* GAO/GGD-97-23 (Washington, D.C.: Nov. 20, 1996).

[127] GAO-05-61.

[128] "Functional" regulation is when financial products or activities are generally regulated according to their function, no matter who offers the product or participates in the activity. The functional regulator approach is intended to provide consistency in regulation and avoid the potential need for regulatory agencies to develop expertise in all aspects of financial regulation.

[129] A federal charter option for insurance could allow insurance companies to decide whether to be subject to state or federal regulation, similar to the chartering system for depository institutions.

[130] As of January 2016, federal financial regulators other than the Federal Reserve did not conduct broad-based assessments of systemic risks. However, they did conduct their own assessments of risk within their regulatory jurisdictions and participated in FSOC.

[131] As of January 2016, FSOC's functional committees were the Data Committee; Financial Market Utilities and Payment, Clearing, and Settlement Activities Committee; Nonbank Financial Companies Designations Committee; Regulation and Resolution Committee; and the Systemic Risk Committee.

[132] Other FSOC committees also perform analysis of systemic risks related to their own missions. For example, FSOC's Nonbank Financial Companies Designations Committee and Financial Market Utilities and Payment, Clearing, and Settlement Activities Committee both are tasked with analyzing potential risks and providing recommendations to FSOC related to potential designations under titles I and VIII of the Dodd-Frank Act, respectively.

[133] GAO-12-886.

[134] Systemic Risk Committee agendas show that sometimes there is time allotted for discussion of new potential threats during committee meetings.

[135] Other monitors in development include some that examine particular market segments or asset classes, such as hedge funds, money market funds, and credit default swaps. According to OFR and Treasury staff, as of January 2016, OFR shared its Financial Markets Monitor monthly with the Systemic Risk Committee. However, this monitor is a review of themes and developments in financial markets and is not intended to measure or identify systemic risks. As is the case with the Financial Stability Monitor, the monitor uses only publicly and commercially available data. OFR also began making the Financial Markets Monitor available for the public on its website in February 2015.

[136] Federal Reserve staff stated that the agency has met with FDIC and OCC staff to discuss their assessments as part of the agencies' coordination efforts regarding the implementation of countercyclical capital buffer requirements on certain regulated entities.

[137] See GAO/AIMD-00-21.3.1 and GAO-14-704G. We updated the standards in 2014. The new standards, which became effective on October 1, 2015, call for the use of quality information to achieve an entity's objectives.

[138] International Monetary Fund, *Staff Guidance Note on Macroprudential Policy* (Washington, D.C.: December 2014) and *Key Aspects of Macroprudential Policy*, IMF Policy Paper (Washington D.C.: June 2013).

[139] GAO-06-15.

[140] We have ongoing work that provides a more comprehensive examination of OFR's major activities and challenges it faces in carrying out its mission, which we anticipate issuing in 2016.

[141] Section 165(i)(1) of the Dodd-Frank Act requires the Federal Reserve to conduct stress tests of nonbank financial companies designated by FSOC and bank holding companies with $50 billion or more in assets to assess whether they have sufficient capital necessary to absorb losses as a result of adverse financial conditions. The act also specifies that the Federal Reserve may develop and apply such other analytic techniques as are necessary to identify, measure, and monitor risks to the financial stability of the United States.

[142] While OFR has other monitors, we chose to compare OFR's Financial Stability Monitor to the Federal Reserve's monitoring program because it is OFR's only monitor that aims to evaluate risks to the financial system as a whole. OFR's other tools focus on assessing risks in specific areas of the financial system and can complement the aggregate perspective of the Financial Stability Monitor.

[143] Vulnerabilities are weaknesses that transmit and amplify shocks. Vulnerabilities include credit or asset price bubbles, lax loan underwriting standards, insufficient bank capital or liquidity buffers to absorb losses or withdrawals, and risk exposure through a maturity mismatch between assets and liabilities. A triggering event, or shock, could be political or economic, such as turmoil in a region or the collapse of a market, or even a natural disaster.

[144] A description of the conceptual framework for the Federal Reserve monitoring program was made public in a report. See Tobias Adrian, Daniel Covitz, and Nellie Liang, *Financial Stability Monitoring,* Federal Reserve Bank of New York Staff Report No. 601 (February 2013, revised June 2014). According to that paper, shadow banking involves financial intermediation activities without an explicit government backstop. Some examples include securitized credits, mortgages, and loans facilitated by securities broker-dealers in markets outside of the traditional banking system.

[145] To assess the quality of the underlying indicators in the monitor, OFR tested each indicator for its ability to capture extreme events such as market peaks and troughs, identify turning points, and give early warning signals of stress at a reasonable horizon during prior crises.

[146] We have ongoing work evaluating the Federal Reserve's stress testing activities, which we anticipate issuing in 2016.

[147] OFR research generally presents stress test methodologies that aim at analyzing the stability of the financial system as a whole. See, for example, Office of Financial Research, *Dynamical Macroprudential Stress Testing Using Network Theory*, OFR Working Paper #15-12 (June 18, 2015); *Process Systems Engineering as a Modeling Paradigm for Analyzing Systemic Risk in Financial Networks*, OFR Working Paper #15-01 (Feb. 11, 2015); and *Stress Tests to Promote Financial Stability: Assessing Progress and Looking to the Future,* OFR Working Paper #0010 (July 18, 2013).

[148] OFR's Financial Research Advisory Committee, whose membership includes academics, financial market experts, and former regulators, recommended that OFR explore the Federal Reserve's stress test data to, among other things, identify the build-up of systemic risk in asset classes and/or sectors, and highlight systemwide vulnerabilities and pressure points in response to prescribed market shocks. OFR has requested stress-test data from the Federal

Reserve to fulfill its stress-tests evaluation mandate. As of January 2016, OFR had not yet received access to the data, but the Federal Reserve announced in September 2015 that it plans to share the data with OFR in light of the assurances of confidentiality from OFR. See Proposed Agency Information Collective Activities; Comment Request, 80 Fed. Reg. 55621 (Sept. 16, 2015).

[149] See Tobias Adrian, Daniel Covitz, and Nellie Liang, *Financial Stability Monitoring,* Federal Reserve Bank of New York Staff Report No. 601 (February 2013, revised June 2014).

[150] Collaboration can be broadly defined as any joint activity that is intended to produce more public value than could be produced when the organizations act alone. See GAO-06-15.

[151] In 2012 we found that the systemic risk monitoring activities of FSOC's Systemic Risk Committee were not sufficiently systematic or comprehensive, and we recommended that FSOC and OFR clarify responsibility for implementing requirements to monitor threats to financial stability across FSOC and OFR, including member agencies, to better ensure that the monitoring and analysis of the financial system are comprehensive and not unnecessarily duplicative (see GAO-12-886). FSOC Secretariat staff disagreed with our recommendation and stated that agencies have defined specific roles and responsibilities for themselves when developing analyses of identified threats on a voluntary basis. As of January 2016, this recommendation remained open.

[152] FSOC's own authorities do not divest its members of their existing authorities.

[153] FSOC has other authorities that could mitigate systemic risk such as upon a determination by the Federal Reserve that a designated nonbank financial company or a bank holding company with $50 billion or more in assets supervised by the Federal Reserve poses a grave threat to U.S. financial stability, a two-thirds vote by FSOC triggers the Federal Reserve to undertake multiple actions including limiting the company's ability to merge, acquire or consolidate with another company and restricting the company's ability to offer financial products. Pub. L. No. 111-203, § 121(a), 124 Stat. 1376, 1410 (2010).

[154] FSOC issued this proposed Section 120 recommendation in November 2012, offering specific alternatives that SEC could adopt to reform money market mutual funds. In summer 2014, SEC adopted final rulemakings to address risks of investor runs in money market mutual funds. FSOC intends to review and consider the effects of these reforms and their broader implications for financial stability once they are implemented.

[155] A final Section 120 recommendation to an agency requires that the agency impose the recommended reforms, or within 90 days, explain in writing why the agency determined not to follow the recommendation.

[156] A PCS activity is an activity carried out by one or more financial institutions to facilitate the completion of financial transactions. The Dodd-Frank Act defines a financial transaction to include funds transfers, securities contracts, contracts of sale of a commodity for future delivery, forward contracts, repurchase agreements, swaps, security-based swaps, swap agreements, security-based swap agreements, foreign exchange contracts, financial derivatives contracts, and any similar transaction that FSOC determines to be a financial transaction. When conducted with respect to a financial transaction, PCS activities may include (1) the calculation and communication of unsettled financial transactions between counterparties; (2) the netting of transactions; (3) provision and maintenance of trade, contract, or instrument information; (4) the management of risks and activities associated with continuing financial transactions; (5) transmittal and storage of payment instructions; (6) the movement of funds; (7) the final settlement of financial transactions; and (8) other similar functions that FSOC may determine applicable.

[157] For more information on FSOC's nonbank designation authorities and the processes it uses in making designations, see GAO, *Financial Stability Oversight Council: Further Actions Could Improve the Nonbank Designation Process,* GAO-15-51 (Washington, D.C.: Nov. 20, 2014).

[158] The Dodd-Frank Act excludes any offer or sale of a security or any quotation, order entry, negotiation or other pre-trade activity or execution activity, as well as public reporting of swap transactions from the definition of a PCS activity.

[159] GAO-09-216.

[160] International Monetary Fund, *Staff Guidance Note on Macroprudential Policy* (Washington, D.C.: December 2014); *Key Aspects of Macroprudential Policy*, IMF Policy Paper (Washington D.C.: June 2013); and *Macroprudential Policy: An Organizing Framework*, IMF Policy Paper (Washington D.C.: March 2011).

End Notes for Appendix I

[1] For example, The Department of the Treasury, *Blueprint for a Modernized Financial Regulatory Structure* (Washington, D.C.: Mar. 31, 2008); The Department of the Treasury, *Financial Regulatory Reform, A New Foundation: Rebuilding Financial Supervision and Regulation* (Washington, D.C.: June 17, 2009); International Monetary Fund, *United States: Publication of Financial Sector Assessment Program Documentation—Financial System Stability Assessment* (Washington: D.C.: July 2010); International Monetary Fund, *United States: Publication of Financial Sector Assessment Program Documentation—Reports on Observance and Codes* (Washington: D.C., July 2010); Financial Stability Board, *Peer Review of the United States* (Basel, Switzerland: August 2013); GAO, *Financial Regulation: Industry Changes Prompt Need to Reconsider U.S. Regulatory Structure,* GAO-05-61 (Washington, D.C.: Oct. 6, 2004); *Financial Regulation: Industry Trends Continue to Challenge the Federal Regulatory Structure,* GAO-08-32 (Washington, D.C.: Oct. 12, 2007); *Financial Regulation: A Framework for Crafting and Assessing Proposals to Modernize the Outdated U.S. Financial Regulatory System,* GAO-09-216 (Washington, D.C.: Jan. 8, 2009); and *Financial Regulatory Reform: Financial Crisis Losses and Potential Impacts of the Dodd-Frank Act,* GAO-13-180 (Washington, D.C.: Jan. 16, 2013).

[2] GAO, *Fragmentation, Overlap, and Duplication: An Evaluation and Management Guide,* GAO-15-49SP (Washington, D.C.: Apr. 14, 2015).

[3] In general, the Dodd-Frank Act defines a swap to include, among other things, an agreement that provides for the exchange of one or more payments based on the value or level of one or more assets, liabilities, or indices or other financial or economic interests or property of any kind that transfers, in whole or in part, the financial risk associated with a future change in the value or level without also conveying a current or future ownership interest in an asset or liability that incorporates the financial risk transferred. Pub. L. No. 111-203, § 721(a)(21), 124 Stat. 1376, 1666 (2010). Financial and nonfinancial firms use swaps and other over-the-counter derivatives to hedge risk, or speculate, or for other purposes. Swaps include interest rate swaps, commodity-based swaps, currency swaps, and broad-based credit default swaps. Security-based swaps include single-name and narrow-based credit default swaps and equity-based swaps. We use the term "insurance group" to refer to a group of affiliated companies, one or more of which is an insurance company.

[4] The Group of Twenty—a forum for international cooperation on global economic and financial issues, whose members include 19 countries and the European Union— established FSB in 2009 as the successor to the Financial Stability Forum to coordinate at the international level the work of national financial authorities and international standard-setting bodies in order to develop and promote the implementation of effective regulatory, supervisory, and other financial sector policies. IMF is an organization of 188 member jurisdictions whose primary purpose is to safeguard the stability of the international monetary system.

[5] GAO-09-216.

[6] GAO, *Financial Stability: New Council and Research Office Should Strengthen the Accountability and Transparency of Their Decisions,* GAO-12-886 (Washington, D.C.: Sept. 11, 2012).

[7] GAO, *Standards for Internal Control in the Federal Government,* GAO-14-704G (Washington, D.C.: September 2014) and GAO/AIMD-00-21.3.1 (Washington, D.C.: November 1999); *Results-Oriented Government: Practices That Can Help Enhance and Sustain Collaboration among Federal Agencies,* GAO-06-15 (Washington, D.C.: Oct. 21, 2005). International Monetary Fund, *Staff Guidance Note on Macroprudential Policy* (Washington, D.C.: December 2014) and *Key Aspects of Macroprudential Policy*, IMF Policy Paper (Washington D.C.: June 2013).

[8] OFR's other tools focus on assessing risks in specific areas of the financial system and can complement the aggregate perspective of the Financial Stability Monitor.

[9] Federal Reserve, *2012-2015 Strategic Framework, and* Tobias Adrian, Daniel Covitz, and Nellie Liang; *Financial Stability Monitoring,* Federal Reserve Bank of New York Staff Report No. 601 (February 2013, revised June 2014).

[10] OFR's Financial Research Advisory Committee—whose membership includes academics, financial market experts, and former regulators—provides advice to OFR, bringing diverse perspectives to inform OFR's research and data agendas and helping OFR to fulfill its mission. The Systemic Risk Council is a private sector, nonpartisan body of former government officials and financial and legal experts committed to addressing regulatory and structural issues relating to systemic risk in the United States. According to its website, it has been formed to provide a strong, independent voice for reforms that are necessary to protect the public from financial instability.

[11] GAO-06-15.

[12] GAO-09-216. International Monetary Fund, *Staff Guidance Note on Macroprudential Policy* (Washington, D.C.: December 2014); *Key Aspects of Macroprudential Policy*, IMF Policy Paper (Washington D.C.: June 2013); and *Macroprudential Policy: An Organizing Framework*, IMF Policy Paper (Washington D.C.: March 2011).

End Notes for Appendix II

[1] Pub. L. No. 111-203, 124 Stat. 1376 (2010).

[2] Staff at the Federal Reserve Banks act as supervisors in conjunction with the Board.

[3] Thrifts, also known as savings and loans, are financial institutions that accept deposits and make loans, particularly for home mortgages. Until 1989, thrift deposits were federally insured by the Federal Savings and Loan Insurance Corporation, which was created by the National Housing Act of 1934. After experiencing solvency problems in connection with the savings

and loan crisis of the 1980s, FSLIC was abolished and its insurance function was transferred to FDIC.

[4] Credit unions are member-owned financial institutions that generally offer their members services similar to those provided by banks.

[5] Home Owners' Loan Act of 1933, 48 Stat. 128 (1933). The administration of the Federal Credit Union Act was originally vested in the Farm Credit Administration (48 Stat. 1216 (1934)) Executive Order No. 9148, dated April 27, 1942 (7 F.R. 3145), transferred the functions, powers, and duties of the Farm Credit Administration to FDIC. Effective July 29, 1948, the powers, duties, and functions transferred to FDIC were transferred to the Federal Security Agency. (Pub. L. No. 80-813, 62 Stat. 1091 (1948)) Reorganization Plan No. 1 of 1953, effective April 11, 1953, abolished the Federal Security Agency and transferred the Bureau of Federal Credit Unions, together with other agencies of the Federal Security Agency, to the Department of Health, Education, and Welfare. (18 Fed. Reg. 2053 (April 11, 1953)).

[6] Pub. L. No. 91–206, 80 Stat. 49 (1970) created NCUA as an independent agency and transferred all of the functions of the Bureau of Federal Credit Unions to the new administration.

[7] Federally insured state credit unions also are subject to supervision by NCUA.

[8] Pub. L. No. 101-73, 103 Stat. 183 (1989).

[9] Pub. L. No. 111-203, § 312(b), 124 Stat. 1376, 1521 (2010).

[10] The Securities Act of 1933 (1933 Act), 48 Stat. 74, 15 U.S.C. § 78a, had assigned federal supervision of securities to the Federal Trade Commission (FTC) by, among other things, requiring that securities offerings subject to the act's registration requirements be registered with FTC. See 1933 Act, §§ 2, 5, 6 (1933). In the Securities Exchange Act of 1934, Congress replaced FTC's jurisdiction by transferring its powers, duties, and functions under the 1933 Act to SEC. See Securities Exchange Act of 1934, 48 Stat. 881, §§ 3(a), 210 (1934). SEC has the responsibility of administering all the securities laws, including the Investment Company Act of 1940, the Investment Advisers Act of 1940, and the Sarbanes-Oxley Act of 2002.

[11] The National Securities Markets Improvement Act of 1996, Pub. L. No. 104-290, 110 Stat. 316 (1996) pre-empted state securities registration requirements for all but a subset of small securities products and limited state supervision of broker-dealers, but it left intact the right of states to investigate securities fraud.

[12] Credit Rating Agency Reform Act of 2006, Pub. L. No. 109-291, 120 Stat. 1327 (2006). Under the act, a credit rating agency seeking to be treated as a nationally recognized statistical rating organization (NRSRO) must apply for, and be granted, registration with SEC, make public in its application certain information to help persons assess its credibility, and implement procedures to manage the handling of material nonpublic information and conflicts of interest. In addition, the act provides SEC with rulemaking authority to prescribe the form of the application (including requiring the furnishing of additional information); the records an NRSRO must make and retain; the financial reports an NRSRO must furnish to SEC on a periodic basis; the specific procedures an NRSRO must implement to manage the handling of material nonpublic information; the conflicts of interest an NRSRO must manage or avoid altogether; and the practices that an NRSRO must not engage in if SEC determines they are unfair, coercive, or abusive. The act expressly prohibits SEC from regulating the rating agencies' methodologies or the substance of their ratings. Pub. L. No. 109-291 § 4(a).

[13] The Grain Futures Act, Pub. L. No. 42-331, 42 Stat. 998 (1922). In 1936 the act was substituted with the "Commodity Exchange Act (CEA)," which, among other things,

created the Commodity Exchange Commission, a predecessor agency to the Commodity Futures Trading Commission. Pub. L. No. 49-675, 49 Stat. 1491 (1936).

[14] Commodity Futures Trading Commission Act of 1974, Pub. L. No. 93-463, 88 Stat. 1389 (1974).

[15] A derivative is a financial instrument representing a right or obligation based on the value at a particular time of an underlying asset, reference rate, or index, such as a stock, bond, agricultural or other physical commodity, interest rate, currency exchange rate, or stock index. Derivatives contracts are used by firms around the world to manage market risk—the exposure to the possibility of financial loss caused by adverse changes in the values of assets or liabilities—by transferring it from entities less willing or able to manage it to those more willing and able to do so. Common types of derivatives include futures, options, forwards, and swaps and can be traded through an exchange, known as exchange-traded, or privately, known as over-the-counter.

[16] Up until 1944, insurance was not considered interstate commerce and, therefore, was not subject to federal regulation. In *United States v. South-Eastern Underwriters Ass'n*, 322 U.S. 533 (1944) the Supreme Court held that Congress could regulate insurance transactions that truly are interstate. Congress subsequently enacted the McCarranFerguson Act, 59 Stat. 33 (1945), which provides that state laws apply to insurance unless they are specifically pre-empted by Congress. See 15 U.S.C. § 1011.

[17] NAIC is made up of the heads of the insurance departments of 50 states, the District of Columbia, and U.S. territories to provide a forum for the development of uniform policy when uniformity is appropriate.

[18] Pub. L. No. 111-203, § 502, 124 Stat. 1376, 1580 (2010).

[19] Pub. L. No. 111-203, § 113, 124 Stat. 1376, 1398 (2010). According to the Dodd-Frank Act, nonbank financial companies are domestic companies or foreign companies that predominantly are engaged in financial activities (such as insurance companies, consumer finance providers, commercial lenders, asset managers, and investment funds) but that are not bank holding companies or certain other types of firms (such as registered securities exchanges, clearing agencies, and swap execution facilities).

[20] Housing and Economic Recovery Act of 2008, Pub. L. No. 110-289, title I, subtitle A, 122 Stat. 2654, 2661 (2008).

[21] The Federal Home Loan Banks form a system of regional cooperatives, each with its own president and board of directors, located in different regions of the country. Their statutory mission is to provide cost-effective funding to members for use in housing, community, and economic development; to provide regional affordable housing programs, which create housing opportunities for low- and moderate-income families; to support housing finance through advances and mortgage programs; and to serve as a reliable source of liquidity for their membership. The Federal Home Loan Bank of Seattle merged with the Federal Home Loan Bank of Des Moines in 2015 reducing the system to 11 Federal Home Loan Banks.

[22] OFHEO was created in title XIII of the Housing and Community Development Act of 1992, Pub. L. No. 102-550, 106 Stat. 3672, 3941 (1992). In 1932, the Federal Home Loan Bank Act created the Federal Home Loan Bank System to provide liquidity to member entities to make home mortgages. Oversight of these responsibilities was later transferred to the Federal Housing Finance Board.

[23] The Farm Credit System started with the Federal Farm Loan Act of 1916 which established the Federal Land Banks. Pub. L. No. 64-158, 39 Stat. 360 (1916). The Federal Land Banks was the first component of what became the Farm Credit System. The Farm Credit Act of 1933

completed the establishment of the Farm Credit System. Pub. L. No. 73-75, 48 Stat. 257 (1933). The Farm Credit Act of 1971 gave banks and other entities more flexibility in lending to agriculture and authorized lending to, among others, rural homeowners. Pub. L. No. 92-181, 85 Stat. 583 (1971).

[24] Farmer Mac is a government-sponsored enterprise with the mission of providing a secondary market for a variety of loans made to borrowers in rural America.

[25] Pub. L. No. 99-205, 99 Stat. 1678 (1985).

[26] Agricultural Credit Act of 1987, Pub. L. No. 100-233, 101 Stat. 1568 (1987); Farm Credit System Reform Act of 1996, Pub. L. No. 104-105, 110 Stat. 162 (1996).

[27] Gramm-Leach-Bliley Act, Pub. L. No. 106-102 (1999). Although originally precluded from conducting significant securities underwriting activities, bank holding companies were permitted to conduct more of such activities over the years. For example, in 1987, the Federal Reserve allowed the subsidiaries of bank holding companies to engage in securities underwriting activities up to 5 percent of their revenue. Over time, the Federal Reserve also expanded the types of securities that banks could conduct business in and raised the revenue limit to 10 percent in 1989 and to not exceed 25 percent in 1996 (effective in March 1997).

[28] Pub. L. No. 107-204, 116 Stat. 745 (2002).

[29] For additional information on FSOC and OFR, see GAO, *Financial Stability: New Council and Research Office Should Strengthen the Accountability and Transparency of Their Decisions,* GAO-12-886 (Washington, D.C.: Sept. 11, 2012).

[30] 12 U.S.C. §§ 5481–5603.

INDEX

A

B

D

E

F

G

H

I

J

L

S

T

U

V

W